IT WAS
MY WAR

I'll remember it
the way I want to!

IT WAS MY WAR

I'll remember it the way I want to!

George William Sefton
501st Parachute Infantry Regiment Officer

Sunflower University Press®
1531 Yuma (Box 1009), Manhattan, Kansas 66502-4228 USA

ISBN 0-89745-177-5

Cover: On the way to Normandy — loading into troop aircraft, 5 June 1944. (National Archives, 111-SC-190367)

Edited by Sandra J. Rose

Layout by Lori L. Daniel

Contents

Prologue

It was H-hour minus 4½ on D-Day, June 6, 1944, 1:30 a.m. in civilian parlance. We had been flying over Normandy for five uneventful minutes, dropping from 2,000 feet as we crossed the east coast to 300 feet as we came down the Douve River. Our Drop Zone was three minutes ahead; the seaborne invasion beaches were four minutes beyond the DZ in flight time.

I was jumpmastering a stick of 17 Dog Company men, which meant I was standing beside the open door of the C-47 and would give the command to jump, then follow them out. A heavy equipment bundle lay at my feet, to be shoved out the door ahead of the men who were hooked up and crouching in the aisle. The moment for which we had trained so long and so hard was at hand.

Looking ahead from my doorside vantage point, I could see fires on the ground, which I took to be burning buildings. "We're in great shape," I shouted above the noise in the plane. "The Air Corps has bombed hell out of things!" I didn't realize the fires were planes shot down from the serial we were following.

The plane crew chief was helping me nudge the equipment bundle closer to the door when I sensed something different was happening outside. I stood up to see what it was and found the night sky was lacerated with streams of tracers from ground fire, groping for our C-47 lumbering 300 feet overhead. Instinctively, I ducked aside from the door.

That was a bad move from the troop morale angle. The men nearest me started cringing toward the floor, pulling lengths of static line from their chutes in the process. I hadn't stopped to think. But OCS leadership principles prevailed, and, standing fully in the door with a bravado feigned but unfelt, I shouted again, "It's okay. They can't hit us!" In the same moment, a burst of automatic fire went through the plane somewhere near the front, sounding like blows of a sledgehammer and severely damaging my pose as a prophet.

By then I could see our Drop Zone just ahead, visible even in the intermittent light of the partial moon peeking between cloud banks. I looked at the two-light panel beside the door, which was controlled by the pilot. The red one had come on 5,000 yards offshore, telling us to stand up and hook up so that we could abandon ship if hit by coastal battery fire. But there had been no such danger lurking as we made landfall.

The red light was still glowing. When it went out and the green one came on, we would jump. I could see the dirt crossroads just outside the village of Angoville Au Plain, the near boundary of our DZ. It was sliding away under the wing. The red light glowed balefully.

It posed one hell of a quandary. Had the pilot been hit by the ground fire? Had he just forgotten to turn on the green? Or did he know there was another plane right below us, ready to grind us up in its propellers? Meanwhile, we were flying briskly toward the invasion beaches, less than four minutes away.

Then I saw dark puffs in the sky in the near distance. They were the camouflaged chutes from planes to our left. Everyone else was jumping! I took one last look at the red light and yelled, "Let's Go!" The lead man and the crew chief helped me slide the six-foot-long equipment bundle through the door. It got halfway out before the slipstream caught the front end and twisted it to jam in the doorway. We cursed, clawed, and kicked until it finally departed. The first five men followed in rapid-fire order.

As the number six man reached the exit, the plane yawed wildly, throwing him against the side of the aperture. The barrel of his carbine, protruding from under his webbing, broke through the paper tape covering the two thicknesses of the aluminum door jamb, holding him firmly in place. The men behind simply kept coming until the pressure popped him out like the insides of a squeezed grape.

The exit of "Geronimo" number 12 was expedited by the plane, which chose that moment to turn up on its left wing, expelling him without need to jump and causing me to look directly down at moonlight reflecting in water. The C-47 righted itself immediately, but not before my fleeting glimpse recorded whitecaps on the surface. While I had not been timing all events since passing the DZ, it seems highly probable we had exhausted the four minutes of flying time from there to the English Channel.

The remaining five men had regained their feet and were storming down the aisle toward me. I crouched in front of the door and yelled, "Stop! We're over the ocean!" The first man hit me like a Notre Dame fullback going through a PeeWee football team line and went right on out the door. I bounced off the door to the toilet behind me and landed on my knees in time to try stopping the next man. Same impact, same result, with him and the three behind him. None had the slightest intention of remaining in that plane.

Suddenly I was all alone in the empty C-47 passenger compartment. Even the crew chief was gone! I had a momentary impulse to go up to the cockpit, tap the pilot on the shoulder, providing he was alive, and say, "I didn't have a chance to get out, Mac. Do you mind making another pass over the DZ?" I decided against it.

They had made it perfectly clear in England that to return to base with the plane would constitute desertion in the face of the enemy. A capital offense by military justice standards. Then there was the prospect of disgracing the family name, what with my father back in service and all. Obviously, I had to jump, then and there, regardless of consequences.

I was, of course, wearing a Mae West inflatable life preserver under all other equipment. And we'd been told that one could live four hours in the Channel before succumbing to hypothermia. Surely the seaborne invasion forces would pluck me from the water before then.

We had been trained with repetitive monotony as to how to exit a plane. You crouched with your left foot on the door sill, hands with fingers and thumbs gripping the outer skin of the plane. Then you kicked out with the right leg extended to catch the slipstream, theoretically turning your plummeting body one-quarter way to the left, thus lessening the opening shock.

Our battle cry going into Normandy was supposed to be "Bill Lee," in respect for the major general who had pioneered the American Army Airborne program. He had come to England in command of the 101st Airborne Division, welcomed our 501st Regiment on its arrival, then was invalided home with a heart attack.

Having decided to jump, regardless, I stood bolt upright in the door and toppled out as stiff and straight as a pine log. I did utter a battle cry: "Oh, shit!"

It took 83 feet for a chute to open after hitting the end of the static line; then you looked upward immediately to make sure the canopy was fully deployed. The opening shock rattled my molars, but I did look up in an instant and simultaneously plowed into solid earth! The plane could not have been flying at more than 90 feet of altitude.

Had I landed on an island in the Channel? Before I could even grapple with that question, I heard hobnail boots pounding the ground in my direction and caught the glint of moonlight on bayonets.

My folding stock carbine was wedged under my webbing, but my father's World War I .45 pistol was holstered on my hip. Unfortunately, I had secured it with baling wire to prevent separation on the jump. I clawed at it to no avail. I would not take a single Nazi with me to that Last Roll Call in the sky!

* * * * *

This is the story of how I arrived at that moment, and of how I survived the following eleven months with the 501st Parachute Infantry Regiment.

All incidents related are as factual as my memory permits. My wife assures me I have been telling all of the stories without change of word or inflection since we met in France as the war with Germany was ending. It should be noted, however, that no two veterans of a particular infantry action are apt to agree as to precisely what happened from their respective points of view.

One other thought: Although I am fully as fluent in barracks-room language as any other ex-paratrooper, this is written primarily for the descendants of our ten offspring. And for their descendants, *ad infinitum*. For that reason I have restricted the use of vulgarities, except where their lack would detract too much from the nature of the incident being described.

Plod on if you're so inclined.

Introduction

Looking back over more than five decades, I was eminently pre-conditioned to volunteer for military service in the emotional aftermath of Pearl Harbor. A product of small-town mid-America, I had graduated from a Catholic high school in 1940 at the tail end of the Great Depression during which my father's retail furniture business had gone belly up in Anderson, Indiana, prompting his three-year sojourn 30 miles south to Rushville to try again with the same results.

The family returned to Anderson when I was entering the sixth grade and moved into an elderly brick home in Mounds State Park. The park was managed by my mother's brother, who resided with his wife and four children in the manager's cottage. The brick house we inhabited had no plumbing or central heating, but was large enough for our family of eight, counting my parents, maternal grandparents, a brother, two sisters, and me, the senior sibling.

The park, which featured three pre-historic mounds constructed by natives of origin and fate unknown, was situated on the White River three miles upstream of Anderson. There was a pavilion with snack bar and dance floor, a boathouse with rowboats and canoes for rent on the river, plus a livery stable for riders. Admission fee at the gatehouse was ten cents per adult during those Depression years. Even so, attendance was very light by today's state park standards.

The terrain was heavily wooded and laced with trails and springs. For outdoor-minded youngsters, adventure beckoned at any turn. My brother was four years younger than I, but my oldest cousin was only two years my junior and just as eager to try anything at least once. So Charlie Norton and

I became inseparable during most out-of-school hours for the next three years. It was a great place and era in which to be a kid.

No other companions were locally available for team sports, so Charlie and I became exceptionally accomplished with slingshots and .22-caliber rifles, breaking bottles tossed in the air with either weapon. We also became adept at fishing, trapping, camping, and identifying anything edible that grew in the woods, swamps, or fields.

In the interim, my father had re-established his furniture store; and by the time I finished the eighth grade, the family moved back into Anderson. By then I had reached the enviable status of apprentice quail hunter. Father was a rock-ribbed Episcopalian Republican. Grandfather Norton was an Irish Roman Catholic and straight-ticket Democrat. Both were avid bird hunters and thus would readily agree to go quail hunting together on election day on the grounds that their respective votes would merely cancel each other. Why waste a day at the polling booth when they could be following their beloved dogs from covey to covey? I was provided with a single-shot .20 gauge and was privileged to go along.

The opening day of quail season soon became a bigger event than Christmas on my personal calendar. Wake-up call at 3:00 a.m. would pre-cede a two-hour drive downstate, with breakfast of buckwheat cakes and sausage at some roadside diner en route. The objective was always to be in the field at first light as the coveys were starting their morning feed cycle. At noon we'd break for sandwiches eaten as we sat on the running boards of the car, then we kept going hard until dusk. This routine applied on nearly every Saturday of the season.

The thought that there might be a less arduous way to hunt never seemed to occur. Certainly not to me.

Throughout my early childhood years, my father had been a relatively distant authoritarian figure. His mother had named him Earle Mohler Sefton after tracing family genealogy back to the Earl of Sefton in England. On his first day of school — as the story goes — he got into a fight. A bystander who liked his spirit yelled, "Hit him again, Pete!" and he was "E. M. 'Pete' Sefton" thenceforth. At six feet two inches and 225+ pounds, he didn't look at all like anyone you might call Earle.

Pete had commanded a rifle company in the famed Rainbow Division during World War I, and, in my young perspective, his collection of battle-field souvenirs was a major factor in the mystique surrounding him. He would display them in the window of his furniture store each Armistice Day. A sepia-tone photo cutout of him in captain's uniform, complete with put-tees, always stood on mother's dresser. Throughout my childhood, he was a heroic figure of epic proportions.

My first glimpse of his more temporal side occurred the first time he took me hunting, well before I was old enough to carry a gun. He removed a pack of chewing tobacco from his pocket and tucked a wad into his mouth with obvious relish. Then said, "Kid, it isn't necessary to mention this to your mother." I was to learn she abhorred the filthy habit. But then my wife doesn't exactly favor my practice of it, either. As I also learned later, he had taken up chewing in the stress of combat. So did I.

When the National Guard was mobilized in 1940, Indiana formed a State Guard. Pete Sefton was appointed commander of the rifle company stationed in Anderson, based on his World War I experience. I enlisted immediately, of course, despite his admonition that he could never promote me "for obvious reasons." The unit was composed of World War I veterans attempting to recapture their lost youth, and 18-year-olds, such as I.

Within the first year, the company executive officer was saying, "Pete, you've gotta promote him — he's the best close-order drill and bayonet instructor we have." So I became a platoon sergeant, and no one seemed to resent the advancement.

By then I had a job with the Delco Remy division of General Motors, Anderson's pre-eminent employer. I was working the ll:00 p.m. to 7:00 a.m. shift, seven nights per week, machining aluminum parts for Allison aircraft engines and making more money in one week than Pete had generated in any one month with the furniture stores. I also was driving 30-some miles to Muncie four mornings each week to take English, Chemistry, and Typing courses at what was then Ball State Teachers College, then going to bed at 2:00 p.m. and arising at 10:00 p.m. for work.

When the Japanese attacked Pearl Harbor, I knew I was not long for General Motors. My parents were urging that I remain at Ball State for the rest of the school year. Pete was a World War I friend of Illinois Senator Sherman Minton, and he was saying, "Kid, stick it out until June and I'll wangle you a commission through him." My teen-age reaction was, "If I need a commission for this war, I'll damned well earn it myself."

At that time, you had to be 21 to enlist without parental permission. And I was only 19. A high school friend was working for Consolidated Aircraft in San Diego, and my parents finally agreed I could visit him there during Christmas break, providing I would seriously consider returning to complete my full year at Ball State. But no one was really kidding anyone. They signed the parental consent papers before I left.

Meanwhile, I had been reading news releases about a new wrinkle of Army service — the paratroops. I knew what I wanted to do.

Chapter 1

Joining the Army

The recruiting sergeant sent me out to Fort Rosecrans, a coast artillery post near San Diego, for the physical exams. I flunked them. It seems I had a "low threshold" — meaning any significant intake of sugar showed up promptly in the urine specimen. And I had been indulging hell out of my sweet tooth for weeks. The first sample rated a sterling +2. "Totally unacceptable, son, but we'll give you four more shots at it. One day at a time."

I quit eating or drinking anything remotely sweet, of course, and by the third day was showing less than +1. Obviously, the thing to do was drink lots 'n lots of water, thereby flushing the remainder out of my system. Worked like a charm! The fourth specimen was totally devoid of sugar. Unfortunately, all that water had made the specific gravity too low. And on the fifth day a trace of sugar returned. The picky bastards rejected me.

Noting that they were "losing a damned good man to Arizona," I started hitchhiking for Tucson, arriving at frosty dawn two days later and waited for the recruiting office to open. There the physical consisted primarily of counting my eyes and listening to me breathe. Because they never asked about any previous attempt to enlist I did not feel compelled to mention Fort Rosecrans. Within the hour I was raising my right hand and swearing to defend the country, come hell or high water.

The next stop was the induction center at Fort Bliss near El Paso, Texas — land of the red sand dust and plenty of wind to blow it into every pyramidal tent occupied by recruits. Lift your head at reveille and the only white spot on the pillowcase is where your head had been. The dust that would have eliminated it was on your face and in your hair and ears. Fort Bliss confirmed the opinions of many experienced observers: If there is a truly miserable tract of land anywhere in the country, the Army probably owns it.

After drawing uniforms full of creases and reeking of mothballs, we were ushered through a battery of IQ and aptitude tests. Later, each of us sat down at a small table across from some corporal who interpreted results of the tests and assigned us to an appropriate branch of service.

One of my tentmates was of Hispanic descent with a limited command of English. He returned from his interview with one of the corporals somewhat bemused. "He ask do I like to go for walks in zee woods. I say, Si! He say, good, you in the infantry." So much for the science of military assignment.

Apparently my own test scores were sufficiently high to arouse the interest of my corporal interviewer who started suggesting a range of — to him — the more acceptable career roles. And I kept insisting, "Parachute infantry." In the end, he wrote that down, along with some footnote, which I've always suspected read "Mentally retarded."

From Fort Bliss it was back to California for three months of basic infantry training at Camp Roberts. The vast parade ground was still studded with military vehicles parked at random to foil the possible landing of Japanese troop-carrying planes. And the training cadres were organized into task forces to help repel such attack.

Members of the platoon to which I was assigned were all from the Southwest, and most had volunteered for Airborne. Being the only one from north of the Mason-Dixon line, I promptly became "Indiana," no surname necessary.

The two other platoons in the company were comprised almost entirely of draftees from the Pittsburgh area with social manners somewhat less gracious than those of the Dead End kids, as featured in the movie by that title showing at the time. There were a number of brief but decisive confrontations before they learned to steer clear of our area, including our tables in the mess hall.

The cadre first sergeant was white-haired, potbellied, and reportedly inflicted with ulcers and six kids. A World War I veteran, he seemed to disdain draftees in general, and his consistent demeanor generated a mixture of fear and awe among the troops.

Oddly, Tucson had issued me a prewar serial number, much lower than those on records of draftees. This happenstance seemed to mellow the top kick's regard to the extent of remarking, "Well, Sefton, I see you're Regular Army" — with facial expression somewhat softer than his habitual glare.

The pay for a private that early in 1942 was $21 per month. By the time the post finance section deducted for laundry and the war bond I had been convinced to buy, I drew $6.25 every payday, whether I needed it or not.

The author clowning with Donald "Red" Townsend during basic training at Camp Roberts, CA.

We trained with Springfield .03 rifles, wearing the World War I flat helmets and accouterments of similar vintage. The Army seemed fully prepared to fight the last war again. Fortunately, the drill had been streamlined to eliminate such cumbersome maneuvers as "right by squads, squads right" that had been the bane of recruits a generation before.

Some vignettes of memory regarding barracksmates remain undimmed. There was the farmer, well into his thirties, who was always sitting on his footlocker, fully dressed except for his shoes, when the reveille bugle awoke the rest of us. His bunk would already be made up and the surrounding floor swept. He had remained stocking-footed rather than disturb the city boys who could stay asleep that long after time to milk the cows.

Another 30-plusser was prematurely white-haired and obviously had a business background. He smoked in bed after lights-out a lot, but I remember him best for his remark regarding his ex-wife. "When she heard I was volunteering for this war she sent me a telegram: 'God bless you, God damn you.' "

Then there was the odd little intellectual who wrote poetry and walked with a waddle that immediately inspired the nickname, "Duck." When I once asked if that bothered him, he replied, "Not at all — the last place I worked they called me 'Shithead.' "

My closest buddy through basic training was a big, rawboned, redheaded Texan by the name of Donald Townsend, also an Airborne volunteer. A former oil field roustabout, he was enough older than I to adopt a big-brother interest in my personal welfare. He went directly from basic training to jump school and the 82nd Airborne Division. I never saw or heard from him again, despite trying to locate him at the 82nd's training area in England. Should this thing ever get published, and anyone chancing to read it know if and where he might be found, I would depart for such site in a heartbeat.

One observation regarding Texans. They can be a touchy bunch. We were resting on our bunks following noon mess one day, waiting for drill call, when someone down the line drawled, "Tell ya somethin' about Texas — it's the only state in the union could build a wall all around its borders and still support itself."

Being the only Yankee in the platoon, I felt compelled to offer an entertaining repartee. "That may be true," I observed innocently, "but why is it that every time a Texan strikes oil and gets rich, he sends his daughters East to learn how to wear shoes?"

I had hardly started chuckling at my wit when three of the brawnier Texans — including best buddy Townsend — held me by the ankles and tried earnestly to pound a hole through the floor with my head. If drill call hadn't blown at that instant, you might not be reading this.

Chapter 2

Getting to OCS

Sometime during the basic training cycle, the Army announced a major policy change regarding selection of enlisted men to be trained for commissioned officer status. Until then, only experienced non-coms were accepted for admission to Officer Candidate School. And they had to be 21 or older.

The new policy was established in view of the impending need for rapid expansion of the officer corps, particularly in the combat arms. The policy mandated consideration of selected infantry basic-training graduates for assignment to OCS at Fort Benning, Georgia. Boards of officers were appointed at infantry training centers to screen applicants recommended by their unit commanders. The 21-year age stipulation no longer applied. When notice of application for OCS went up on our company bulletin board, some 35 of us lined up in front of the orderly room. Most by far were from the Pittsburgh platoons. This generated some derisive taunts from one of their number who had not joined the parade.

"Whata buncha idiots! The only one here who's gonna make it is Sefton!" I didn't know his name and never did learn how he had formed that opinion, but he was wrong. The captain chose three of us, all from my platoon. I've often wondered how much the first sergeant's regard for my "Regular Army" serial number had influenced his decision in my favor, especially since I was the youngest of the three by several years.

The company commander was a major hurdle. Subsequent interviews with the battalion and regimental commanders were "rubber-stamp" procedures consisting primarily of congratulations and best wishes. But the trauma of facing the post Selection Board loomed ahead.

The Board was chaired by a major flanked by two captains and four lieutenants. Each prospective OCS candidate arrived at the appointed moment, saluted, and identified himself to the chairman.

"Private Sefton reporting to the Board as ordered, Sir." (I wondered just how tough this grilling was gonna be.)

"Sefton, what makes you think you want to be an infantry officer?"

(Who says there is no God!)

"Sir, my father commanded a Rainbow Division rifle company in France during the last war. I grew up convinced there is no more important way to serve our country at a time such as this." (Some of them almost smiled!)

I don't recall what all of the following questions were, but there were no real "stumpers" among them. I do recall the final one.

"Sefton, what immediate action do you take for a stoppage in the third position of the BAR?"

Having reviewed the Browning Automatic Rifle field manual just the night before, I rattled off each paragraph of the instructions with virtually every comma in place. The Board members glanced at each other with looks that could be interpreted only as, "Wow! What fine soldiers we're turning out here at Camp Roberts!"

"That will be all, Sefton. Your company commander will let you know our decision in a day or so." On my way back to the barracks, I realized I had given them the immediate action for a stoppage in the second position instead of the third. And no one had caught the very considerable difference. There is, indeed, a compassionate, loving God!

Within a few days, the word came down. Two of us had cleared the Selection Board hurdle. The other survivor was Don Rickard, a New Mexican in his mid-twenties. He was of medium height, trim build, and natural military bearing. He also was uncommonly astute. Don had been a member of the Civilian Military Training Corps, if I recall that nomenclature correctly. It seems they spent part of each summer in the Southwest practicing cavalry tactics, primarily because they liked riding horses, according to Don.

It may have been that his smattering of CMTC experience, like my year in the Indiana State Guard, was a significant factor in the Board approvals. The third applicant from our platoon, who seemed otherwise as qualified as we, was rejected. We were never to learn why we passed and he didn't.

The only obstacle left on the road to Fort Benning was the physical exam. Twenty or so successful applicants from all over the post were assembled to fill out their medical history forms prior to being poked, prodded, and otherwise abused by assembly-line doctors. The form with which each of us was supplied featured several columns listing almost all diseases, afflictions, and abnormalities known to affect mankind.

An officer stood in front of the group and troop-led us through the lists, reading each ailment aloud and asking each time if anyone present had experienced the one in question. Recalling my boyhood days when I would awaken each morning during ragweed season with my eyes glued shut from allergic secretions, I raised my hand at the mention of hay fever. The officer skidded to a dead halt in his reading and gave me a look that set alarm bells ringing in my head.

"What does that mean?" I asked as casually as I could manage.

"It means you're disqualified."

"Just a minute! Just a minute! I haven't had it since I was two years old and only sneezed twice then!" (The Army teaches you to lie creatively when faced with imminent disaster.)

The upshot was that I was "placed on waivers" and waited another month for final approval for assignment to OCS. Only one other applicant in the group encountered a similar delay. Oddly, it was Don Rickard, for some reason other than hay fever, which I can no longer recall.

During that month we helped the cadre staff in training the new batch of recruits and received our *pro forma* promotions to corporal. No one went to OCS as a lowly private.

I will always remember the day we departed Camp Roberts. We reported to the orderly room with our duffle bags to await transportation to the railroad station. As time for it to arrive approached, our venerable first sergeant came out and picked up the bags. With impregnable dignity he carried them across the road to the bus stop, then gave us his final words of counsel.

"You are going to become officers and gentlemen. I have only this advice. Don't ever forget the enlisted man's point of view."

And I never did, throughout the following 30 years of Active Duty and Army Reserve service.

Chapter 3

Sweating That Little Gold Bar

The train to Fort Benning was routed over land-grant railroads, which meant going through Utah, among other things. It is not true that the passenger cars featured signs reading, "Please do not shoot buffalo from the windows," but they seemed to be of that vintage. There being no air conditioning, soot from the engine entered freely through the windows we opened for relief from the heat. It was a miserable trip.

Because the war was already seven months old, the civilian populace at the stops we made were somewhat less than enthusiastic in their receptions. But I kept insisting things would change should we chance to stop in Indiana. We did, indeed, pull in somewhere near midnight in Evansville.

To my delight, the Red Cross Gray Ladies were out in force on the station platform with long tables laden with homemade goodies. It was, far and away, the most impressive hospitality offered on the entire trip.

OCS companies were formed every week for the "90-day wonder" course. Our group had been scheduled for Class 74, but delays on the trip had caused us to miss the starting date. We ended up in Class 74-A, which was wedged into the Infantry School schedule with a normal complement of 200+ candidates.

Our classmates were an interesting mixture. Approximately one-third were seasoned non-coms, mostly high-ranking sergeants. Another third, such as Don Rickard and I, were Selection Board survivors from basic infantry training centers. The remainder were VOCs — Volunteer Officer Candidates — men mostly in their thirties who had attained some academic or occupational status in civilian life. The VOC program had permitted them to volunteer for service with the understanding that they would be sent to

OCS after completing basic training. But if they flunked that course, they would return to civilian life to face the possibility of being drafted as privates.

We were quartered in two-story barracks, 20 men per floor. The emotional pressure of striving for an OCS commission can be appreciated only by someone who has experienced it. This point is well illustrated by the Fort Benning instructor who was comparing OCS classes with Basic Officer classes. Those were composed primarily of ROTC or military school graduates who already had their commissions, but were taking the same courses as were OCS students.

"When I say 'Good morning' to a Basic Officer class," he explained, "they all reply, 'Good morning.' When it's an OCS class, they write it down!"

The intensity of the pressure was generated in part by the continuous presence of the tactical officers on the cadre staff who accompanied us to every class or other scheduled activity. They reported their observations of individual performance and progress throughout the three-month course. But the greatest pressure by far was the requirement of submitting a personal rating of each classmate on our floor of the barracks.

We had to rate each in numerical order as to troop-leading potential. In doing so, we had to give our reasons for ranking the top five of the twenty in terms of strengths perceived. In the case of the lowest five, we had to specify the weaknesses that warranted such a rating.

The real joker in the deck was the fact that our list was compared with those prepared by every other barracksmate. If it was significantly out of step with the majority opinions, our competence as a judge of men was in serious question. And if you were caught comparing your list with anyone else before submitting it, you were shortly gone from Fort Benning.

As I recall, we had to go through that exercise at the end of each month. After the first month, one candidate suddenly and quietly disappeared from the ranks. He had been rated at the bottom of several lists on the grounds that he had cheated at cards — which, of course, he had.

In another instance there was a staff sergeant who was highly educated, well-bred, and always well-groomed. In fact, he carried a long nail file at all times and used it often daily. He was dropped at the end of the third month because several raters felt anyone that concerned with personal pampering would have too little concern left over for his troops.

Due to the age mix on the floor of our barracks, the older VOC candidates often felt that the 20-year-olds were too young to lead troops in combat, while those of us in the junior age group sometimes wondered if they, in fact, were too old for the physical demands of the job. In short, the trauma of having to rate each other, and the obvious impact of those ratings, was certainly the most horrendous tension generator, as far as I was concerned.

Whatever the combination of factors, the compulsion to win that commission was ever-present. As a child I had been afflicted with eczema, a rash on the back side of my knees and in the bends of my arms. It was finally diagnosed as a sun-vitamin deficiency. In OCS we wore our fatigues buttoned down to the wrists, so when the rash started recurring, I put on my swimming trunks one August Sunday afternoon, spread a blanket outside the barracks, and stretched out on my stomach to read a magazine while old Sol solved the problem.

The articles I was reading must have been engrossing, because when I went back inside there were several comments regarding the bright pink shade of my back and legs, except for the area protected by the trunks. I might have overdone it just a tad.

When I awoke the next morning, I couldn't get off my cot. Every inch of skin from the back of my neck to my ankles, except for the trunks-protected area, was covered with water blisters the size of dimes and quarters. I lay there face down throughout the day, including during the visit of an inspecting cadre officer who observed my plight without comment and left.

If a candidate missed two consecutive days of the course, he would be transferred to the following class. So that evening compassionate buddies helped me over to the dispensary to be smeared with ointment. The next morning I put on my fatigues and was present for duty. The schedule that day included bayonet training and firing positions with the BAR. Every time I executed the long thrust with the bayonet or dropped into the kneeling position with the BAR, I could feel those blisters popping under the fatigues.

By the end of the week, the skin was peeling off my back and legs in strips, but I hadn't missed another hour of instruction. I still suspect that demonstration of my idiotic desire to win a gold bar probably elevated the ratings of some of my fellow candidates. On the other hand, it may have lowered others. Whichever the case, I'll never know.

During those three months, we had to study the operation and employment of every infantry weapon and master the theory and practice of platoon tactics in the attack and on the defensive — plus the intricacies of morning reports, company funds, equipment salvage procedures, etc., etc., not to mention the Code of Military Justice and the etiquette expected of officers and gentlemen. I, for one, never found time to leave the post for recreational purposes.

Throughout the course, Don Rickard's bunk was next to mine, and the friendship that had started at Camp Roberts flourished. Don had been a successful business administrator in civilian life, as well as married and divorced. He was very much a man of the world from my callow youthful perspective, and he tended to adopt the same "big brother" protective stance as had "Red" Townsend during basic training.

When our company of cadets was introduced to the obstacle course, we tackled each obstacle "by the numbers" with an instructor supervising our negotiation of each in turn. As we re-formed ranks for return to barracks, one member of rather simian build approached the tactical officer in charge. The officer announced that "Candidate so-and-so will now demonstrate how to run the obstacle course for time."

Don, among many others, considered this a "showboat" gesture inappropriate to the occasion, so he turned to me and said, "Let's run it with him." Why th'hell not? We stepped out of ranks and advised the officer of our intention. Interest within the class perked up promptly.

The first obstacle was a landing net, a rope construction used by infantry in leaving a troopship to enter a landing craft alongside. It was stretched over a steep A-frame some 30 feet wide and 25 feet high. When the officer yelled "Go!" the three of us hit it full stride to scramble up the rungs of rope.

As I cleared the top of the A-frame, I failed to grab the next rung and fell halfway to the ground before catching another, thereby gaining several feet, however inadvertently. The next obstacle was comprised of parallel tunnels to be negotiated on hands and knees. I went into mine still in the lead and emerged looking at the seat of Don's pants as he exited the one to my left. That sucker could crawl!

I stayed on his heels through the nine-foot-high board wall, which you had to hit with one foot hard enough to propel you within reach of the top and then flop over without losing momentum. And I was right behind him through most of the remaining obstacles, which I can no longer recall precisely.

At or near the end of the course was a broad pit, some 4 feet deep and maybe 30 feet wide, spanned by logs about 8 inches in diameter. Don fell off of his and had to scramble out of the pit. I crossed mine successfully, beating him to the finish line by a matter of feet. The candidate who was going to "show us how to run it for time" was still two obstacles back.

Don and I were the toast of our barracks for having shown up the showboater, which may have had something to do with our respective rankings on the rate-your-buddies lists.

When we weren't using the M-1 rifles assigned to each of us for training, they were locked in A-frame racks down the middle aisle of the barracks. The more experienced and/or confident candidates would remove the guts of the piece between scheduled uses of the weapons, wrap them in cloth, and stow them in their footlockers. This saved valuable minutes preparing for

The brand-new "shave-tail," with his World War I veteran father.

Saturday inspections, since no dust could collect on these components. Don Rickard was among those who practiced this unauthorized shortcut.

One afternoon in the final week of the course, we were enjoying "Commander's Time," a period during which no training was scheduled, leaving us free to our own pursuits. Don had left the post for Columbus; I was reclining on my bunk. Someone shouted, "Attention!" as an unfamiliar captain entered carrying a sawed-off broomstick and followed by a sergeant. The officer went down the row of rifle racks, using the broomstick to depress the operating rod handle of each in turn. The sergeant stuck his thumb in the opened chamber to release the compressed operating spring, proving each weapon was functional and ready to be accepted by the captain for his new OCS class starting the following week.

I was only mildly interested in the procedure until they arrived at the rack across from my bunk in which the rifles assigned to both Don and me were locked, among others. One of them did not respond to the sergeant's thumb, meaning the internal parts were elsewhere. I knew instinctively it was Don's.

"Here's one that doesn't work," the sergeant announced.

"We'll see about that!" the captain replied, and both headed for our company orderly room, only a wedge shot away.

Don's footlocker was locked, but I ripped the lid from the back hinges without benefit of tools, losing parts of several fingernails in the process. The guts of his rifle were there, wrapped neatly in cloth. It was an accepted premise that one could not possibly reassemble an M-1 while locked in a rack. But I did.

I barely had time to flop back on my bunk with hands clenched to hide the bleeding nails when the captain and sergeant returned with our concerned company commander in tow. They proceeded directly to our rifle rack and repeated the broomstick-sergeant's-thumb procedure. Every weapon responded as prescribed. "Which one was it?" our CO asked in obvious relief.

"It was one of these right here!" the other captain insisted.

"Well, they all seem perfectly okay to me," the CO noted, concluding the conversation and heading back to the sanctuary of his orderly room.

The other captain, knowing damned well something undetectable had happened, glared suspiciously at everyone present, to no avail, and also departed. I have no idea how serious the potential trouble for Don might have been, but I figured I had repaid his consideration for my welfare to some extent.

That last week of the course also featured the Victory March a few days before our scheduled graduation. When the company had formed for the march, a dozen or so names were called and those candidates instructed to report to the orderly room. The rest of us moved out on a two-hour hike without equipment, care, or concern. We had made it! We would become commissioned infantry officers!

When we returned, those called to the orderly room were gone, along with all vestiges of their former presence. Even their bunks had been removed, and those remaining were more spaciously arranged. They had not made it, for whatever unrevealed combination of reasons.

All that was left was to receive the officers' uniforms we had ordered and learn how to affix the insignia properly, then march to the assembly hall on graduation day and be sworn in as infantry officers, thereafter honoring the tradition of handing a dollar bill to the first enlisted man to render a salute.

I don't remember why I almost missed my train in going on leave, but I did have to chase it as it pulled out of the Columbus station. A Pullman porter stood on the little platform of the last car calling "C'mon, Cap'n, you can make it!" I had no doubt he knew a brand new shavetail from a captain when he saw one, but he sure knew how to generate a healthy tip.

Chapter 4

Finally Getting to Airborne

Don Rickard and I had both applied for parachute infantry assignments on arrival at OCS. No problem, plenty of openings! Unfortunately, however, our cadre company commander had gone on leave without submitting the applications. So upon graduating on September 22, I was assigned to the 131st Infantry Regiment guarding the Soo Locks at Sault St. Marie on the Canadian border of Michigan's upper peninsula. Don was sent to an infantry division elsewhere. We haven't seen each other since.

Arriving at Fort Brady in early October, I was assigned as machine-gun platoon leader in M Company. My first move was to re-apply for parachute infantry duty.

The 131st Infantry was an anti-aircraft artillery battalion and a barrage balloon unit. I was impressed. Security of the Soo Locks was deemed critical to the war effort because iron ore from the Mesabi Range in Minnesota was shipped through them to plants manufacturing war matériel in Detroit and points east.

The barrage balloons were always aloft and the artillery pieces manned. The infantry maintained 24-hour defensive positions on both sides of the river. The ones on the Canadian side included elements of my machine-gun platoon, which I would visit occasionally, primarily on payday. This feat of derring-do qualified me for the new American Theater Ribbon, automatically awarded to anyone serving in North America but outside the boundaries of the United States.

Until that time, the only ribbons sported by young officers were the yellow ones signifying pre-Pearl Harbor service. I was to find my American

Theater Ribbon a source of considerable curiosity once I left the 131st. But more of that later.

Troops not on duty at gun posts continued infantry training. I was informed that my platoon was scheduled to become adept on skis and snow-shoes. We got as far as learning how to strap 'em on before the ground disappeared beneath north-Michigan snows, and I never used them in my short time with the regiment thereafter.

We sent motorized patrols into the predawn hours each day to scour the immediate countryside for any evidence of impending attack on the locks by whomever. Needless to say, they all returned safely. The only excitement during my tour with the 131st occurred when a bear went though an outpost on Neebish Cut, a narrow stretch of the river well downstream from the post. In the dark of night it refused to halt as ordered, provoking spirited bursts of small arms fire in the process. If there was an After Action Report telling what happened to the bear, I never saw it.

Shortly before Christmas I received my long-awaited present from regimental headquarters. "Lieutenant Sefton, here are your orders to report to the 501st Parachute Infantry Regiment in Camp Toccoa, Georgia. Ten-day delay in route."

It had been an interesting ten months since I had joined the Army with the Airborne goal in mind. The timing of my orders allowed me to stop off at home for Christmas, much to mother's delight. Pete had volunteered for service during the past summer and had been accepted at his World War I rank of captain. Considered too old for infantry duty in that grade, he was assigned to the Army Air Corps, where he was commanding a headquarters squadron of ground personnel in a bomber group.

Pete and Kathleen had been engaged before he had left for France in World War I, and he had written her every day, whether the letters could be mailed or not. He continued the practice when his Air Corps unit went to North Africa and then on to Italy. Because he could not mention military activities, he described duck-hunting episodes, poker games, sight-seeing, etc. One of her reciprocal replies became a highlight in family annals:

"You have a nice time, honey. This is the last war you're going to!"

I reported to 501st headquarters early in January. The regiment had been activated in November at Camp Toccoa, a former CCC (Civilian Conservation Corps) camp in the northeast Georgia foothills near the small town of Toccoa. It was designated a one-regiment training facility for parachute infantry. The 506th Regiment had been the first unit to train there before leaving for Jump School at Fort Benning.

Colonel Howard R. Johnson, the original 501st commander. He was killed in action in Holland. (Photo, courtesy of Mark Bando, 501st PIR Historian.)

The regiment was still filling up when I arrived. We received Airborne volunteers directly from reception centers to be trained from scratch. Most were marched on arrival directly to the 40-foot-high mock tower, strapped into a chute harness attached to a steel cable slanting away outside, and told to jump. Anyone refusing to do so was promptly shipped back from whence he came.

Actually the mock tower was kind of fun. Used to teach and practice proper exiting techniques for leaving a plane, it let the departer drop little more than halfway to the ground before reaching the end of the static line attached to the steel cable, then glide diagonally to earth 20 yards away. Yet I recall one seasoned lieutenant who found himself emotionally incapable of leaving the tower and therefore left the regiment.

This make-'em-prove-their-guts-quick-or-ship-'em-back-fast policy reflected the personality of our regimental commander. Colonel Howard R. Johnson was a flamboyant character who gloried in his role of preparing elite troops for battle. A zealot on the subject of physical fitness, he would personally conduct calisthenics for the entire regiment before breakfast. Physique also was important. When I joined the regiment, all three battalion commanders were well over six feet tall, and one was a former professional wrestler.

The highest foothill near Camp Toccoa was Mount Currahee. It was three miles to its peak from the center of the camp up a dirt road. Any officer who couldn't get up there and back in 50 minutes flunked Johnson's eligibility test — which meant running virtually all the way if you wanted to stay in the regiment.

Fortunately for some, the time taken to run Currahee was recorded by the honor system. Officers would run it after drill hours, then list their times on a special sheet in battalion headquarters. Having heard an unsubstantiated report that the best time ever recorded was 40 minutes, I decided to prove my superior running ability by taking a crack at that record. I put on my old basketball shoes and took a couple of warm-up laps around the small camp while some two dozen other officers were starting their runs. I passed the one in the lead who had slowed to a plodding pace 50 yards short of the peak. Then I barreled all the way down despite shin splints, side stitches, and other related discomforts. I had run it in 45+ minutes.

At the finish line I sat for five minutes, primarily to keep from vomiting. Those I had passed on the trip were straggling in when I felt I had recovered enough to head for the showers. Later I went to battalion headquarters to post my time. All of the others who had started out ahead of me had already done so. Every mother's son of them had logged it in less than 50 minutes. I never again took the Johnson eligibility test seriously.

The Tables of Organization for a parachute infantry regiment specified two lieutenants per platoon in anticipation of heavy losses during an airborne assault and the difficulty of replacing them promptly. The platoon leader slot called for a first lieutenant with a second lieutenant assistant. There not being that many firsts on hand, I was assigned as leader of the third platoon of Fox Company. Shortly thereafter, 1st Lieutenant Huey Hendrickson assumed command of the company.

Huey was an Army brat, the son of a Regular Army non-com. He knew

Army from A to Y but had never seen an American Theater ribbon. He eyed mine circumspectly for several days before finally broaching the subject.

"Just what is that ribbon you're wearing, Sefton?"

"It's the American Theater ribbon, Sir."

"Yes, of course, but how did you win it?"

"By going across the river to pay the troops, Sir."

At every Officers Club party thereafter, Huey would delight in calling me over to an uninformed group to "Tell 'em how you won that ribbon by paying the troops." And I always enjoyed the opportunity.

Huey was short, bowlegged, balding, and socially somewhat unpolished. But we F Company junior officers considered him a rock-solid commander. For whatever combination of reasons, however, he was relieved by Captain William Pelham, a chemical warfare officer with no infantry troop experience. He did stand several inches over six feet, however, and seemed determined to prove that his lack of infantry background was no detriment to being a hard-ass commanding officer. If he had a sense of humor at the time, he was careful to conceal it. Nor did he betray any vestiges of the enlisted man's point of view.

I was not destined to become his favorite platoon leader. Our relationship was aptly illustrated when Lieutenants Bill Osborne, Bill Morgan, and I were detailed to booby trap foothill trails for a night training exercise. The deal was to plant small charges well off to one side of the trails and connect them via trip-wires to batteries on the other side. The charges were simply detonator caps wrapped in a few inches of explosive prima cord, which could be used in sufficient quantity to wrap around trees and blow them down across roads.

Bill Osborne, who had started his military career by enlisting in a prewar Army cavalry unit, had been to demolition school and seemed to relish our assignment. Morgan was unabashedly uncomfortable with explosives. I was cheerfully ambivalent, happy to be away from our CO's critical presence.

The three of us squatted on a foot trail as Osborne demonstrated how to wrap the detonator and sever one strand of the trip-wire, leaving the other intact. He stripped the insulation from each severed end and bent the bared wires into small hooks, spaced well apart along the surfaces of the severed strand which remained unstripped. Then he brought Morgan into the act.

"Stick your hand in here, Bill, so the bared ends can't touch while I connect the charge." I did wonder idly why he had already hooked up the battery, but then he was the one who had been to demolition school.

Just as he was making that final arrangement, I saw a squirrel running up a tree nearby and stood up for a better look as the other two remained squatting over the charge. It went off with an impressive bang, most likely because Morgan's hand was sweating enough to complete the circuit from the end of one bared wire to the other. Morgan's hand was badly gashed and bleeding profusely. Osborne had fragments of detonator cap in his face and in one eye. My legs were well peppered with similar tiny missiles, as attested to by the blood starting to seep through my fatigue uniform pant legs. Oddly, my watch gained two hours in the 15 minutes it took us to return to camp.

Our first stop was the infirmary where Osborne and Morgan were held for treatment. My legs were daubed with iodine, and I was assured that the cap fragments hadn't penetrated all that deeply and would eventually work their way out. That left me to report the incident to Captain Pelham, bloody pant legs not withstanding, as I stopped at attention in front of his desk and saluted.

"Sir, there's been a bit of an accident. Morgan and Osborne are over at the infirmary."

He glared and summed up our relationship: "SEFTON, WHAT DID YOU DO TO THEM?"

Chapter 5

Jump School

The regiment completed basic infantry training at Camp Toccoa and entrained for Parachute School in Fort Benning, Georgia, arriving early in the already hot month of May.

Jump School normally involved four one-week stages. The first was A Stage, comprised of rigorous physical training designed to discourage the faint of heart. You ran, not walked, everywhere you went during duty hours. Big sergeants with bulging muscles in white tee shirts conducted every exercise including push-ups, sit-ups, excruciating sessions with Indian clubs, and lo-o-o-ng runs in tight formation, among many others.

The sergeants recognized no rank within the classes they conducted throughout the four-week period. Anyone, from field grade officer to private, was addressed simply as "You there!" so far as I ever observed. Any infraction of rules or routines would result in "You there, gimme twenty-five!" or perhaps "fifty" meaning the specified number of push-ups to be performed promptly and in full. The penalty for inability to accomplish the total prescribed was the humiliation of sprawling, exhausted, at the instructor's feet in view of fellow classmates.

Due to the emphasis on physical fitness the regiment had undergone throughout the 13 weeks of basic training at Camp Toccoa, we skipped A Stage. The one time I personally experienced the "You there, gimme fifty" for some minuscule lapse of attention, I did them all in rapid-fire order and bounced up without breathing very heavily. Almost any man in my platoon could have done the same. To say we were physically fit would have been a bit of an understatement.

B Stage involved the prolonged practice of exiting and landing techniques. We exited from mock-ups of C-47 fuselages, wearing dummy chute backpacks filled with sawdust. We hooked up our canvas strap "static lines" to the overhead cable running the length of the fuselage using the left hand and keeping the strap over — never under — the left arm. We shuffled toward the door, pivoting on the right foot upon reaching it, and placing the left foot on the threshold. Then we crouched and extended our arms to grip the outer surfaces of both sides of the aperture. At the command "Jump," we would kick out with the right leg, leaving the "plane" in the process.

In theory, the extended right leg would catch the "slipstream" generated by the plane in flight, forcing the jumper's body into a quarter left turn and a feet-first descent while awaiting the "opening shock" of the chute. This occurred when the static line ripped the cover off the backpack, deployed the chute, and let the weight and momentum of the jumper break the 300-pound test cord that had attached it to the apex of the canopy. The theory never worked worth a hoot for me when we jumped from real planes on reaching D Stage.

Practicing landing techniques meant mounting a platform some 12 feet high and snapping a canvas strap attached to our harness to a fixture on a cable slanting toward the ground. When we stepped off to glide away, an instructor trotted along below and behind us with a release line attached to the fixture. He would trip it at whatever point of descent he chose, letting us drop to the ground with the approximate impact of a parachute landing.

Our job was to go into a right or left front tumble, absorbing the impact in the process. The idea was to avoid breaking a leg or spraining an ankle. B Stage routines also continued the emphasis on physical fitness, of course, with liberal doses of calisthenics and running in formation.

In C Stage, normally the third week of the Parachute School course, the 250-foot towers came into play. Each tower featured four arms extending from the top of the steel frame structure. A cable on each arm lowered and raised a metal ring 32 feet in diameter to which the outer edges of a chute could be attached. The trainee would be hoisted to the top and released with the chute already open to return to mother earth.

By way of indoctrination, we first were introduced to the "controlled-tower" process. This meant being lifted to the top and allowed to descend without the ring attached to the cable actually releasing the chute. Thus the descent was straight down with no possibility of the oscillation (swinging to and fro) normally experienced in a jump, thanks to control of the cable. The speed of the descent still approximated that of a live jump, and the proper landing technique was stressed by the instructors.

At that time, the Parachute School was teaching us to land with our feet the width of the hips apart and to execute a downward pull on the risers just before the moment of impact with the ground. The four risers were sturdy canvas straps, each ending in eight "suspension lines" secured around the periphery of the canopy above. The downward pull supposedly lessened the impact of landing. Within months of completing the course, the prescribed landing technique was changed to keeping both feet snugly together and eliminating the downward pull. It seemed the previous theories were resulting in excessive injuries when landing under tactical conditions.

From the controlled tower we progressed to the "free towers," meaning the chutes were released from the rings at the top, allowing us to drift to earth as if we had jumped from a plane. For obvious reasons, only those tower arms not upwind of the tower structures were used.

In C Stage we also learned to collapse a chute still open after landing because of wind conditions and dragging its jumper. This exercise involved huge fans, which generated enough air current to drag the trainee across the field at a goodly pace. The technique was to pull the two bottom risers in toward the body, causing the chute to collapse from the top edge as the lower edge was drawn out of the airstream.

The most memorable phase of C Stage for me personally was the "nerve test," which meant being raised to the top of a tower with no chute attached to the ring. You wore a dummy emergency chute in the usual position, across the front of the body where it could be activated by pulling its ripcord.

An instructor on the ground would bellow through a bullhorn, "Pull your ripcord!" When you did so, you would drop a heart-stopping 20 feet or so to the end of a rubberized rope, similar to the Bungee equipment currently in vogue. You were supposed to transfer the handle of the ripcord from your right hand to your left before hitting the end of the rope, thus proving your nerve would not fail in any crisis requiring use of the emergency chute in case your main chute had not opened properly for one reason or another. The prospect of taking that test terrorized me for a rather simple reason. I'd always had a latent fear of heights.

When it was time for my platoon to be tested, I positioned myself at the tail end of the unit, thus providing optimum time for "stiffening the upper lip," "screwing courage to the sticking point," and similar B-movie bromides. When my turn finally came, it was almost time to break for noon mess, so they took me up a mere 80 feet instead of all the way to the top. I pulled the ripcord on command, changed the handle from right hand to left in dropping to the end of the rope, and thanked God for a very large favor. To this day I still wonder if I could have done it 250 feet above the ground.

In D Stage, final week of the course, we had to make the five jumps that would qualify us to wear the prized parachutist's badge — silver wings curved around a chute canopy in descent.

The first jump was, perhaps, the easiest I was ever to make. After all the waiting, all the training, nothing could have kept me in that plane. I approached the door and went out "by the book," even remembering to count "One thousand, two thousand, three thousand" while waiting for the static line to deploy the canopy. Oddly, there was no sensation of falling, only one of floating until the opening shock rattled my molars, proving the "feet first" bit was never going to work for me. Being upside down when the chute opened was like being on the end of a whip as it was "cracked" by the user.

The rest of the trip to earth was downright exhilarating. That big, beautiful canopy was fully deployed. I was drifting, drifting, drifting, gently and serenely. Sounds from the ground were magnified. The earth was rising, slowly at first, to meet me. Then suddenly it was coming up much faster, and I remembered to climb the front risers to reduce my oscillation.

As air spilled out the backside of the now tilted canopy, I went into a bit of a forward glide, somewhat increasing the rate of descent but allowing me to plump into the sandy soil without the added impact of a downswing. I had done it! DONE it! No future accomplishment would quite parallel that glorious sensation.

The first jump was the easiest for many of us because on all subsequent exits we realized how many things could have gone wrong the first time! I still remember our third jump as the one during which I was most loath to leave a perfectly good plane in flight.

President Franklin Roosevelt was coming to visit the post, and we were lined up along his proposed route to our training site for hours, humped over in our jumping gear in the Georgia heat. Preparing for that jump, and any future one, was always to give me the impression that a valve somewhere on my being had been opened, allowing energy and enthusiasm to ebb away.

By the time we actually boarded the planes after the President had passed, I was asking myself, "What is a nice boy like you doing in a place like this?" I managed to get out of the door like a good little paratrooper, but the experience left me physically and emotionally drained.

We made our fourth and fifth jumps within the week as scheduled. Officers were given some basic jumpmaster training in the evenings. The long-sought-after parachutist's wings were issued, and the regiment was ordered to Camp Mackall in North Carolina for unit tactical training. We were to go by troop train.

Leaves for officers and furloughs for enlisted men would be coming up shortly. I learned there were frequent C-47 flights from Lawton Army Air Corps Base at Fort Benning to the Indianapolis airbase 40 miles from my home in Anderson, Indiana. And I could hitch a ride! I found Captain Pelham in the quarters we shared with other company officers and gave him that good news.

"Sefton," he growled, "I live in Macon, fifty miles from here, and the battalion commander just told me I can't start my leave until after we get to Mackall. But you go right ahead and ask him about yours."

So I presented my case to Major Ballard. "After all, Sir, Captain Pelham will have at least three other F Company officers with him on the train. Besides, if I start my leave now, I'll be back for duty at Mackall while they are still on theirs."

It made sense to him — "Permission granted." I was blithely and hurriedly packing to go when Pelham entered our quarters.

"Sefton, just what are you doing?"

"Oh, hi, Captain. Major Ballard said I could start my leave now, and there's a plane leaving for Indianapolis in two hours!"

Silence. Prolonged silence. Then . . .

"Sefton, you're gonna be a second lieutenant a lo-o-o-ng time."

It seemed I had not relieved the strain in our relationship.

Chapter 6

Camp Mackall

Camp Mackall was a training camp still under construction, one of many being rushed to completion for the vastly expanded Army required to fight World War II. All buildings were wood frame with tarpaper roofing, no aesthetics, with a bare minimum of creature comforts. The soil was sandy and wooded mostly with southern pines.

We had hardly started unit training when Captain Pelham was transferred to battalion headquarters as S-3, operations officer. Lieutenant Huey Hendrickson resumed temporary command of F Company, and I was back in hog heaven, leading my platoon in the relaxed atmosphere he generated.

Shortly thereafter, several men of my platoon asked if they could prepare some broad-jumping pits and pole-vaulting stands in the company headquarters area for recreational purposes. Lieutenant Hendrickson had no objection, so they started their project after evening mess, and I stopped by to observe their progress. It was already well underway and looking good. In fact, the results of their enthusiastic labors seemed little short of professional!

Just then Major Ballard chanced by on his way to a battalion commanders' call at regimental headquarters. Since I was the only officer present, he assumed I was in charge of the activities and inquired in his soft Florida drawl as to the objective of such endeavors. I explained the "recreational purposes" bit without thinking to note my merely incidental contribution to the concept. He made some complimentary remarks and went on his way. I didn't know he had assumed that I knew something about civil engineering to warrant my "supervision" of the project instigated and being completed by the men.

The next morning I was happily teaching scouting and patrolling techniques in an area of tall, wet weeds when a runner arrived. And he was running!

"Lieutenant Sefton is to report to the regimental executive officer immediately." End of message, start of frantic examination of conscience.

"What have I done? What have I done?"

Delaying only long enough to change into dry fatigues, I reported to Lieutenant Colonel Ewell as ordered. He promptly let me know why.

"Sefton, you're being assigned to Regimental Headquarters Company as police and prison officer."

(Police and prison officer? What in hell is a police and prison officer?)

"But, Sir, what about my platoon?"

Colonel Johnson's office adjoined Ewell's, separated only by a flimsy partition ending well short of the ceiling. His gravelly voice had no trouble negotiating the obstacle.

"Is he a platoon leader? I wanted an assistant platoon leader for that job."

"This is the man the battalion commander recommended, Colonel."

(End of Colonel Johnson's interruption.)

"Er, just what am I supposed to do in this assignment, Sir?"

"Police up this area, Sefton. The ditches are eroding, there are too many dead trees around, the company streets are potholed. Spruce it up and do it fast."

"Uh, how much help can I have?"

"Just tell Captain McReynolds [regimental adjutant] what men and equipment you need, Sefton, and you'll have it."

"Thank you, Sir. When I've got it all done can I go back to my platoon?"

"Get it done right and we'll talk about that. Now get with it!"

"Yes, Sir, on my way, Sir."

That same day I sent Captain MacReynolds a requisition for 80 men and 8 trucks, to be available the next morning. His outrage apparently was tempered by Ewell to the extent that I did get 60 men and 6 trucks. I appointed work-crew leaders among the non-coms included in the detail and started assigning projects in order of assumed priorities.

As need for materials arose, I learned to "scrounge" on a large scale (scrounge being an Army euphemism for stealing in a good cause). I would take a truck with a detail of husky troopers, pull right up to the construction company loading dock, and pick up whatever we required. The trick was to do so with aplomb, leaving any witnesses to assume we had every right to be there.

The one time the stratagem almost didn't work involved a large pile of crushed limestone I had discovered in an outlying area of the post. Thinking

how nice it would look on the half-moon drive in front of regimental headquarters, I soon had a detail loading it onto a truck. We had most of what I
wanted aboard when a civilian car screeched to a stop and a construction
company executive demanded to know who had authorized removal of the
stone.

Patting my shirt pocket as though it did, indeed, contain an approved requisition, I replied as casually as possible, "Why, the A. J. Jones Company, of
course."

"We'll see about that!" he snapped, jumping back into his car and roaring
off toward the post.

"Men, we've got five minutes to finish loading and get th'hell out of
here!" The limestone looked great in front of 501st headquarters, and there
were never any repercussions to my knowledge.

Within a very few weeks, we had revetted all eroding ditches, filled in all
potholes, removed all dead trees, and even whitewashed some unsightly
boulders in the regimental area. I reported accomplishment of the assigned
objectives to Lieutenant Colonel Ewell in high hopes of getting back to my
platoon.

"Very good, Sefton. Now we need a guardhouse." It seemed some 20
Geronimos were serving court-martial time for various offenses, so the
"prison" aspect of my title was about to come into play.

I was assigned a building near headquarters. It was big enough for about
30 cots, a guard detail room, and a small office for me. I used the prisoners
for routine police (cleanup) of the regimental area and other chores assigned
by the S-1 as need arose. A nice, trouble-free routine, wot? In a pig's eye it
was!

I was told to have two prisoners mop the floors in the regimental officer's
club. So I sent an armed guard with them. They returned in less than two
hours with one prisoner staggering along while carrying the other passed out
over his shoulder. The perplexed guard had no idea how they had managed
to get drunk. It turned out he was just another victim of paratrooper ingenu-
ity. One prisoner had distracted him while the other copped a bottle of
whiskey off the shelf behind the bar and dropped it into the mop bucket.
Then they took turns, one diverting his attention while the other retrieved the
bottle and guzzled a stiff gulp of the booze. Only a subsequent check of the
mop bucket explained the circumstances.

Then there was dealing with the indignant complaint from headquarters
that the prisoners raking pine needles were working with their fatigue
blouses unbuttoned, their sleeves rolled above the elbows, and hat brims
turned jauntily upward. Furthermore, they had been observed whistling at
passing PX girls and, in general, appearing to enjoy life more than the troop-

ers in training.

"Put a stop to such conduct immediately, Sefton!"

So I lined them all up in formation that evening and, with the sergeant of the guard as a witness, read an order to cease and desist those specific infractions under threat of an additional court-martial.

A particularly recalcitrant character, Russo by name, was standing in the front row. He took one pace forward, ripped open his fatigue blouse, turned up his hat brim, shoved his sleeves above the elbows and yelled, "So go ahead and court-martial me!"

Which I obligingly did. He got another three months of detention and reduction in pay. That did nothing, however, to keep him from being a persistent disrupter of guardhouse routine. The need for sterner measures was glaringly obvious — such as solitary confinement, for instance.

I had an appropriate facility constructed in back of the guardhouse. It was tall enough for a man to stand, or he could sit on the floor. But there wasn't enough room to lie down. There were no windows, just a slot in the door to accommodate flat pans of food. The occupant would be allowed a canteen of water upon entering. Unventilated, it would become a sweatbox under the North Carolina sun. Russo soon gave me good reason to have him placed therein.

Toward noon of his very first day in the contrivance, I looked out my office window to see our Catholic chaplain, Captain Francis Sampson, listening at the slot as Russo poured out his tale of woe. Moments later, the good padre was looming in front of my desk, thundering, "Sefton, you can't treat a fellow human being that way!"

"Just a minute, Father, you've heard Russo's side of the story; now listen to mine." And I proceeded to recite the litany of offenses with which Russo had been plaguing my attempts to fulfill a role I'd never sought and delaying my return to the job of leading my platoon that I so ardently desired.

When I looked out the window again, Father Sam was back at the slot, reorienting Russo as to his responsibilities as an American soldier. While I could not hear that particular sermon, it must have been a doozy. My problem trooper became a model prisoner, eventually leading the other Catholic inmates in evening rosaries!

There was another prisoner who was also a hard case. No amount of discipline or punishment could change his determination to violate every rule governing guardhouse behavior, including remaining in custody. One night he cut through the window screen and escaped unobserved by the guards. We were never to see him again.

For weeks I had been requisitioning iron bars for those windows to no avail. It was time to go scrounging again, but not even the construction com-

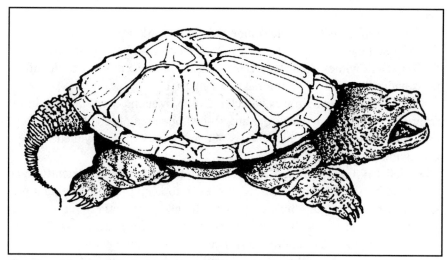

Snapping at the chance to be traded for guardhouse window bars.

pany had any in stock. The only viable source I could discover in the area was a road crew working on a highway bridge just outside the camp entrance. They had steel reinforcing rods, 12 feet long and an inch in diameter. Perfect, just damned perfect! Unfortunately, they were never left unattended during working hours and were locked up in a construction trailer when the crew went home.

I was standing on the bridge pondering the problem when I noticed a commotion near the bank of the water below. Two very sizable snapping turtles were mating in the shallows. On impulse, resulting from my predatory youth, I went down and grabbed them both by their tails. They must have weighed upwards of 15 pounds each. Carrying them back to the bridge, I encountered the road-crew foreman who eyed them with avid interest.

"Man, where did you get them turtles?"

"Oh, they were down there in the water. Do you like turtles?"

"Man, there ain't nuthin' better 'n snappin' turtle soup!"

"Would you like to have these turtles?"

"Man, I would lo-o-o-ve to have them turtles!"

"Well, Sir, if I could be real sure six of those reinforcing rods would be laying in that ditch when I come back here tonight, you've got yourself the makin's of a lotta snappin' turtle soup."

"Man, you gotcherself a deal! Just gimme them turtles now and come on back here tonight."

He was as good as his word. I retrieved the rods after dark, had the motor pool mechanics cut them into proper segments, and was having them installed in all guardhouse windows when Lieutenant Colonel Ewell came along.

"Sefton, where and how did you get those bars?"

I gave him a snappy salute and an honest answer. "I traded two snapping turtles for them, Sir."

He gave me one of those I-don't-really-want-to-know-about-this looks, turned, and walked away without comment. But no more prisoners escaped the guardhouse during the brief remainder of my tenure as police and prison officer.

Shortly thereafter, I was re-assigned to F Company, now commanded by Captain Sammie Homan. But I wasn't to be there very long. Major Ballard, soon to be a lieutenant colonel, summoned me to battalion headquarters.

"Sefton, we want to give Lieutenant Carrol more troop-leading experience, so I'd like you to relieve him as our S-2."

S-2, of course, was the designation for battalion intelligence officer. And Lieutenant Carrol was the younger brother of Lieutenant Colonel Carrol who commanded the first battalion of the regiment. In my naiveté it never occurred to me that he might be on his way out of the job due to less than satisfactory performance. So when he briefed me on my new duties, I took his advice at face value, especially that regarding the care and distribution of photomaps of the various tactical training areas.

"They're kept in this rack of compartments," he explained, "and you've gotta be real firm about insisting that whoever takes any out puts 'em right back where they belong."

My first clue as to the validity of his advice came about a day or so later when I found several photomaps tossed on my desk. I asked the operations sergeant who had put them there.

"I believe it was Captain Pelham, Sir."

"Well, Sergeant Mero, then he's the one who hasta put 'em back." And I plunked them down on Pelham's desk as I was leaving the office; he was away at the time.

When I returned, they were back on my desk, and Pelham was leaving. My back was toward the door as I was indignantly putting them on his desk again. But there was an extra-sensory tingling on the back of my neck. I turned to behold his face framed in the small window six feet above the ground beside the door. It was not a happy face. In about three strides he was back inside, towering in barely controlled rage while making several cardinal points perfectly clear.

First there was the colossal difference in rank between captain and second lieutenant. Then there was the awesome importance of the S-3, compared to the S-2, in the tactical training mode. And finally, there was the never-again-to-be-questioned fact that he would damned well take whatever photomaps he damned well wanted, whenever he damned well wanted them, and the S-2 would damned well put them back in the racks.

I was off to a great start on our new relationship as fellow staff members. Thank you, Lieutenant Carrol.

A more pressing problem, however, was that while the TO&E (Tables of Organization and Equipment) for a parachute infantry battalion called for an S-2, there was no provision for an S-2 section at that point in time. Or at least that's what I was told.

In a regular infantry battalion, an S-2 section included personnel to man observation posts, accompany patrols, and gather and compile indications of enemy capabilities and intentions. Major Ballard solved the TO&E problem by levying each of the four company commanders for "two good men" — a request too often interpreted in military circles as an opportunity to unload two "eight balls."

Any readers questioning the "four company commanders" bit are advised that a parachute battalion was comprised of three rifle companies, but no weapons company, per se. Battalion Headquarters Company filled that role by including an 81mm mortar platoon and a light machine-gun platoon, as well as conventional administration, training, and supply sections.

The eight men selected by their company commanders for the new S-2 section included some interesting characters. One had been a cook until contracting a mild social disease. Another was one of those intelligent but often oblivious types who could sign for issued equipment and forget to carry it out of the supply room. There was a pallid youth who would remark, "S-2 woiks while the woild sleeps." Never having encountered a Creole accent before, I at first thought he was from Brooklyn instead of New Orleans. I did get one New Yorker whose "street smarts" compensated for the lack of outdoor experience common to troopers from smaller communities.

The least physically imposing assignee was Joe Newman from Kokomo, Indiana. Inches below average height and weighing maybe 135 pounds soaking wet, he was later to prove that size had no relationship to courage in combat.

The corporal who was to head the section came from Fort Wayne, Indiana, and may have been released by his CO because of his advanced age. He was 29 and nicknamed "Pop"! But I lucked out in getting him. The remaining two were competent troopers who displayed no adverse reasons for their transfers to S-2 beyond merely luck of the draw.

We spent the remainder of that summer learning to function as an S-2 section with heavy emphasis on observation skills and reconnaissance patrolling techniques. We participated in battalion-scale tactical exercises, including night jump assembly procedures. In the process, we developed rapport and pride of accomplishment within the section.

By the time the regiment was alerted for maneuvers in Tennessee, we were eager for the challenge.

Chapter 7

Tennessee Maneuvers

In September the regiment went to Tennessee for Second Army maneuvers, which lasted through October. Each week featured a four- to five-day tactical problem involving the entire unit. Then we would move by truck convoy to a non-tactical bivouac in the area selected for the next scenario.

The first to reach the new bivouac area would be the unit billeting parties who would lay out the tentage sites, motor parks, etc. Negotiating with nearby farm wives for quantities of fried chicken and biscuits with which to supplement the first evening mess also quickly became battalion SOP (Standard Operating Procedure) for them.

These treats purchased by the battalion staff were usually consumed in the dark around a small campfire after all organizational chores, including the evening mess line, had been completed. The chicken would arrive in whatever cardboard box the farm wife providing it might have on hand. Protocol required each staff officer reaching into the box to take the first piece his fingers encountered, be it breast, thigh, wing, or neck. In short, no groping about or rejection of the initial draw in favor of another try at the moment.

One memorable night, there was a thunderstorm brewing in the distance, and Captain Pelham was openly grumbling about "Sefton's luck" in retrieving a choice piece of chicken each time I dipped into the box. It did not occur to him that I was sitting close enough to the container to glimpse the top layer of contents with each split second of the approaching lightning and gauge my next dip accordingly; nor did I feel it would enhance our relationship if I explained my technique.

The regiment was becoming more cohesive with each successive week of the maneuvers. My S-2 section was accomplishing its varied roles with steadily increasing competence. The fact that the results of enemy actions were decided by umpires rather than by live ammunition, however, did keep the lessons from being as effective as those to be learned later in combat.

There is a military axiom to the effect that "the only constant in combat is confusion." Even in maneuvers that seemed to apply to communications regarding locations. My "walkie-talkie" once picked up the following radio exchange between a major and a lieutenant in a recon unit.

"Just where in the hell are you, Lieutenant?"

"Sir, I am standing at the main crossroads in Bell Buckle."

"That's impossible, Lieutenant. I, repeat I, am standing at the main crossroads in Bell Buckle!"

While I could envision them just around the corner of the same building from each other, their voices faded from my radio band before I ever knew for sure.

About midway through the maneuvers, our battalion mission was to accompany a column of armor in a surprise attack on an enemy-held bridge. The head of the column overshot the side road leading to the objective by a sizable margin before Captain Pelham could call it to a halt. I was standing at the road where we should have turned when he came roaring back from the head of the column.

Reacting to the pressure generated by the crisis, he spotted me, pointed to the nearest tank and yelled, "Sefton, get in that one and start down that road!" I knew he was planning to restructure the column en route, but it would take some doing. So I tried to ask what was, to me, a necessary question.

"Yes, Sir, Cap'n, but how far do you want me to . . ."

"Sefton, I said get in that tank and GO!"

"Yes, Sir, but . . ."

"I said go NOW!"

Piqued by the exchange and insensitive to his urgency to straighten out a mess for which he was operationally, if not personally, responsible, I climbed into the tank and told the crew, "Start down that road and open her up!"

We roared away in a cloud of dust and had gone far enough to be in sight of the bridge, thus obviating any chance of surprise, before a jeep came tearing up from behind with Pelham standing up and gripping the windshield. He ordered the jeep driver to cut in front of the tank so sharply it was a wonder we didn't crush the smaller vehicle.

He was so angry his mouth was moving without any words coming out. I seized the opportunity to yell, "Captain, I did just what you told me to do!"

whereupon I dropped into the tank and sealed the turret cover above me. His only reaction was to go back and bring up the rest of the column for belated continuation of the mission.

Oddly, that incident was to be a favorable turning point in our relationship. While we would never become close friends, it was our last real confrontation and the beginning of harmonious cooperation as fellow staff officers.

Meanwhile, the appetite for fried chicken was becoming widespread throughout the regiment, even though many of the troopers were running out of funds with which to pay for it. This led inevitably to a masterful night raid on a poultry farm by an unknown number of unidentified Geronimos.

Early the next morning, the farmer appeared at the regimental headquarters tent, demanding payment for a large number of birds he claimed were taken.

"There are a lot of troop units bivouacked in this area," Colonel Johnson protested. "What makes you think my boys would do a thing like that?"

"Cuz this is whar the trail o' feathers ends," the farmer noted with unshakable conviction.

So Johnson ended up by levying every enlisted man in the regiment 13 cents and each officer a larger amount to satisfy the plaintiff. Only those who had not enjoyed any of the chicken felt that the universal levy was a bit unjustified, but recollections of the incident became one of those many diverse bonding agents that somehow helped structure the regimental spirit of derring-do.

One of the less glamorous yet important aspects of the maneuvers was that of field sanitation, particularly involving the disposal of human waste. Whenever a unit was to remain in a given location for a day or more — especially if bivouacking — "straddle-trench" latrines were prepared. These were simply mini-ditches, a foot or so wide and two or more feet deep, over which users would squat while answering calls of nature.

I still recall the remark of our battalion mess officer regarding his intent to inspect those facilities. "I gotta see if they're fillin' up fast enough, or should I put more soap in the soup."

Then there was the regimental surgeon the week we were at the Tullahoma Air Base preparing for a jump later canceled due to weather conditions. After seating himself on a conventional toilet in the officers' latrine, he observed a bit uncertainly, "I'm not sure it's safe to go ahead, not being down any lower than this!"

The closest we came to making a parachute jump during the maneuvers was when we were to defend against an air drop by another parachute regiment. The maneuver scenario had us positioned in the general area of the "enemy objective" without knowing the specific location of the Drop Zone to be used.

The regiment was strung out along a fairly steep slope with the trucks we were to use lined up on the road below. It was mid-afternoon. The attacking unit was to make their jump after dark.

Colonel Johnson, in his never-ending penchant for dash and drive, had us rehearse the "entrucking" procedure several times during the daylight hours. A whistle would sound and we would all scramble madly down the hillside to clamber aboard our assigned vehicles while the CO timed our effort. We repeated the exercise until he was satisfied. Needless to say, we were not nearly so proficient when we had to do it after dark.

Shortly after all light had faded from the sky, we heard the rumble of C-47 troop carriers approaching. This was promptly followed by the voice of Colonel Johnson screaming at the regimental S-3, "Allen, where's my map?" and then the persistent blowing of the whistle. The scramble for the trucks ensued.

We did manage to find the enemy airhead and engage them with defensive tactics, but I cannot recall how our efforts were critiqued by the umpires.

It was the following week that we went to the Tullahoma Air Base to make our own jump, but mother nature intervened. In words overheard from a southern trooper, "It's rainin' like a cow pissin' on a flat rock!"

That being the final week of the maneuvers, the regiment returned to Camp Mackall.

Chapter 8

Preparing to Go "Over There"

The weeks remaining in 1943 were spent in a blur of preparations for deployment to the ETO (European Theater of Operations). Every trooper had to be qualified on the firing range in the weapon he carried or served. Every man had to have the prescribed number of preventative shots for the gamut of potential germs to be encountered and had to pass a final physical exam.

Some aspects of those physicals may have been a trifle haphazard. The sight test, for example. A medical detachment corporal came around, pinned the customary chart of letters on a barracks exterior wall, and drew a line in the sand at the proper distance. Then he handed the examinee a 3" x 5" card.

"Cover one eye and read the fourth line." Then, "Now cover the other eye and read it again."

When it was my turn to be tested, I was aware that my right eye was somewhat weaker than the left, so I covered it first and read the line promptly.

"20/20," the medic noted. "Now the other eye."

With inspiration born of the moment, I changed the card from my right hand to my left and placed it over my right eye again.

"20/20 both eyes," the corporal recorded with a nod of satisfaction.

We worked long, arduous hours to meet all preparation requirements. One particular memory involves Thanksgiving Day, on which we departed for the small arms range immediately after breakfast. Each man was handed a paper bag containing lunch — a slice of cheese between two dry slices of bread and an apple. We were more than a tad hungry by the time we'd finished firing, but the evening was looking good from my point of view.

Lieutenant Verne Mertz, whom I didn't really know all that well as yet, had issued an intriguing invitation. "I've lined up a coupla dolls in Rockford," he advised, "and they're gonna serve us a home-cooked Thanksgiving dinner. I've borrowed Lieutenant Shorr's car."

After finally getting back from the range, we showered, shaved, got into our Class A uniforms, and jumped into the car. It sputtered, smoked, and finally started with an obvious lack of enthusiasm. It limped as far as F Company area before refusing to go further.

Mertz surveyed the situation and made a command decision. "I'll go see if I can find a motor pool mechanic," he announced. "Why don't you see if there is anyone around here who might help while I'm gone?" he said as he departed.

One of my former platoon members by the name of Starr was in his barracks, and he admitted he knew a bit about motors. After half an hour of tinkering, he got it started again, by which time Mertz had returned with no mechanic in tow. This time we got as far as the highway outside the camp before the motor conked out for good. It was nearly dark, and we obviously were not going to make it to Rockford for that home-cooked Thanksgiving dinner.

"We can still get to the Officer's Club for dinner if we run fast enough," Mertz observed, "and it's only three miles from here!"

We arrived there in a bit of a lather, only to find they had been sold out and were no longer serving. "Maybe there's something left at the battalion mess hall," Mertz improvised. So we ran another mile and a half only to find a single cook getting ready to leave for the night.

"There's one chunk of turkey left in that canister," he advised, "and I can give you a coupla slices of bread, but that's absolutely all I've got."

"We'll split it," Mertz observed judiciously.

Mertz and I developed a lifelong friendship, which endures at this writing. But it was well after the war that he confessed he really hadn't gone looking for a mechanic that evening. Instead, he had eaten a full meal in the battalion mess hall, just in case Shorr's car failed to get us to Rockford.

Among other administrative requirements for deployment overseas was the matter of baggage markings. One officer, 2nd Lieutenant Woods, was assigned to attend an extensive briefing on the subject, and one officer from each battalion was designated to receive instructions from him for benefit of the companies in their respective units.

In most cases, these could well have been the only commissioned personnel involved in the mundane instructions to be given. But this was the 501st. Colonel Johnson felt it imperative that every officer attend the first briefing by Lieutenant Woods, and it was scheduled late of an evening after another long, hard day.

All of the officers were present, with the battalion commanders seated in the front row on a makeshift bench of planks on cement blocks. Lieutenant Woods was stammering his way through the intricacies of marking symbols to be used, sweating profusely in the process. Most of the audience, including the senior officers in the front row, were starting to nod off in a mixture of boredom and exhaustion.

It was at this point that Lieutenant Woods recalled how instructors at the parachute school had dealt with any vestige of inattention during their relatively few lectures. They would suddenly shout "Jab!" at which command everyone present would slam their right fists against their chests. Anyone falling a split second behind the others in doing so would be doing push-ups immediately thereafter.

So Lieutenant Woods shouted "Jab!" and the battalion commanders knocked themselves backward, right off their improvised bench! If my memory serves, Woods was still a 2nd Lieutenant at the end of the war, despite some spectacular troop leadership while attacking with tank support in Normandy.

Eventually, of course, we completed all deployment requirements and entrained for Camp Miles Standish north of Boston on New Year's Day, 1944. We arrived during a bitter Massachusetts cold snap accompanied by heavy snow.

About half of the officers in the regiment were from the South, the rest from Northern states. During our basic training phase at Camp Toccoa, we Yanks would complain about the rawness of the late winter and early spring temperatures which seemed to cut right through our field uniforms.

"Shucks, Yank," the Rebs would reply, "it gets a whole lot colder up Nawth!"

"Yeah, but it's a dry cold — doesn't bother you near as much."

At Miles Standish, company grade officers were housed in conventional barracks buildings with a communal latrine and shower facility some 40 yards away. The intervening distance featured a foot or so of snow being whipped by a howling wind. An officer of Northern origin was peering through the door window, clad in bathrobe and boots, debating the true need of going for a shower at the moment.

"Go right on out there, Yank," a Southern drawl advised, "it's that *dry* cold and it ain't gonna bother you much!"

Any leisure time in the officers' barracks was inevitably spent refighting the Civil War. As one such debate on the relative merits of the respective armies raged, it was interrupted by Lieutenant Hugo Sims from South Carolina who was maybe 5 foot 6 inches tall and weighed some 130 pounds.

Clad in long-john underwear and pistol belt with an Army .45 dangling at his right hip, he strode down the aisle yelling, "Ho-o-o-ra-a-y for Jeff Da-a-a-vis! C'mon you damn Yankees, stand up and salute!"

Throughout our stay at Miles Standish, we were forbidden to reveal jump boots or any Airborne insignia where we could be observed by the public. The fact that another parachute regiment was headed for England was definitely Top Secret. So when we marched to the dock to board the ship *George W. Goethals* on January 19, we were in regular OD — olive drab — uniforms with our pant legs unbloused to conceal our boots and had no insignia showing. Colonel Johnson was at the gangplank to welcome us aboard. He was in full jump suit, with his boots unconcealed and his parachutist's chin strap dangling from his helmet!

We sailed in convoy and heavy weather. I didn't really get seasick until I stepped off the gangplank and onto the ship. Aside from the misery of the crossing, I have two particular memories.

One was the fact that our own .50-caliber machine-gun crews would man the anti-aircraft defenses en route. And Colonel Johnson took a personal hand in their training for that mission. About halfway across the ocean, he called the entire regiment on deck to witness the crews' expertise. A weather balloon inflated with helium to some eight feet in diameter was to be the target.

When it was released from the deck, Johnson restrained the gun crews. "Hold your fire, hold your fire!" When it was maybe a thousand feet in the air, he commanded, "Shoot 'er down!"

The gun crews fired, and fired, and fired. The balloon soared, and soared, and soared, until it was finally lost from sight. I, for one, could not help wondering how the gunners would do should we be attacked by Stuka dive bombers when we had sailed far enough to be in their flight range.

The other memory involves Lieutenant Hugo Sims with whom I shared a cramped "stateroom" on the voyage. We were discussing postwar plans on the blithe assumption that we would both survive combat. Hugo was one of those relatively rare individuals blessed with a facility for planning far, far ahead. "I think I'll go into politics," he predicted. In fact, Hugo became the youngest member of the U.S. Congress in 1948.

Our convoy arrived in Scotland on January 30 and entrained for England where we were to be attached to the 101st Airborne Division. Our battalion, along with regimental headquarters units, was to be billeted in tents near Newbury, some 40 miles from London.

I arrived there as a 1st Lieutenant. My promotion had come through at Camp Miles Standish.

Chapter 9

Getting Ready for D-Day

We were billeted on the Craven estate. Lady Craven reportedly was an American whose knighted English husband had drowned in a yacht race on the Channel. It was an impressive manor, including some huge trees and park-like areas with deer and pheasants much in evidence. The ground beneath our battalion tents was solid chalk under the topsoil, but there was plenty of acreage for company unit tactical training. For regimental exercises and use of live ammunition, we would be convoyed to designated sites elsewhere.

My immediate personal concern was intensified training of the S-2 section with major emphasis on night patrol proficiency. I also was concerned about the capabilities of Private Allan Hurd, the "intelligent but oblivious type" assigned to the section at Camp Mackall. Could he really move quietly enough in the dark to avoid betraying the presence of a reconnaissance patrol?

I set up a tactical night compass course to be followed by each section member individually, starting off at 15-minute intervals. One leg of the course was along a blacktopped countryside road about midway through the estate. A gravel path paralleled the road with a stone wall alongside. It made a nice place for me to sit, lean back, and observe the passage of each man without being detected.

The night was dark and very quiet. Despite the rubber soles and heels on their jump boots, I could hear each of the first four men coming from my right for several yards before they passed unaware of my presence. Later there was a very slight sound from my left. A cat was coming along the gravel path. When it was just a few feet away, it jumped atop the wall and sat.

I was still looking up at the cat when I heard a .45 being cocked a few inches from my right ear and Private Hurd saying softly, "You're dead, Lieutenant." He had swathed his boots in gunny sacking to assure a soundless approach and was the only one to have spotted me in the darkness.

He had answered any and all questions concerning his qualifications for night patrolling.

There was a non-military side benefit to our night training episodes. Lady Craven's pheasants tended to roost on low branches of small trees, and one S-2 section member contrived a sling that shot small darts with considerable accuracy. Ever mindful of the Tennessee chicken incident, he made sure there was never a trail of feathers leading to the S-2 section tent, whatever his inroads on the pheasant population.

There was a typical English pub not far away which became well patronized by many battalion and regimental officers. It had plenty of beer, which it sold at room temperature, and lots of gin, but hardly ever any Scotch. Major Bottomly, our battalion exec, had been apprised of this condition by returnees from England before we had left the States. He had also learned that anyone requesting a gift package with Scotch via letters to stateside spouses or friends would have such pleas snipped from their correspondence by APO (Army Post Office) censors. But there was a solution to that problem, according to his informants.

"The code word," they had explained, "is 'blueberry juice.' Before you ship over, tell 'em to send you some Scotch whenever you write for blueberry juice!" Bottomly had loyally passed this good word on to Lieutenant Colonel Ballard, who sent his wife a V-Mail note accordingly upon finding the Scotch shortage in our area.

A few weeks later, a package from Mary Ann Ballard arrived for him. It gurgled! It also was accompanied by a letter advising that others were now en route to arrive at regular intervals. There was just one small glitch in the process — it really was blueberry juice!

Late in February, I was sent to London to attend the British Order of Battle School. The curriculum involved identification of enemy combat units, and the instructors were monumentally impressive. They even knew the names of German company commanders fighting on the Russian front!

The "Little Blitz" air attacks on London were taking place at the time. Limited numbers of bombers would come over at night in reprisal for British air strikes on German cities. As one consequence, every evening there would be an influx of civilians into the cold, draughty underground (subway) stations, lugging pallets and blankets with which to shiver through the night.

Barrage balloons were placed on steel cables throughout the city, and anti-aircraft batteries were emplaced in every park or other open areas. British night fighter planes were aloft. But these precautions did not prevent all bombs from striking indiscriminate targets.

During one noon-hour break, I had met an attractive shop clerk who was amenable to a dinner theater date the following evening. She lived with her widower father in East Hounslow, some 20 miles outside the city center, and would take the train home after our date. The air-raid sirens were wailing before the first act was over, but the audience was too inured to such occurrences to bother leaving the theater.

After the performance concluded, I escorted her to the station only to learn that one of the bombs dropped that night had landed squarely on the one train line to East Hounslow!

I had more than $50 worth of English pounds in my wallet, but no London cabbie would consider the trip. What with the petrol rationing and all, they could make several times that amount in the same time frame by taking free-spending GIs on short hops from one after-hours club to another.

The problem was further complicated by the fact that Cynthia and her father had been bombed out of residences twice and were without telephone service in their small apartment. There was no way to let him know that she was safe but wouldn't be getting home as early as expected. It was easy to imagine the depth of his concern.

London was blacked out, of course, and we were standing on a corner pondering our dilemma when a British army weapons carrier pulled up, its blue "cat eyes" lights glowing dimly in the darkness. The WAC driver was lost and asked for directions, which Cynthia was able to provide.

"Thank you veddy much! Is there anything I can do for you?"

"Not unless you're going to East Hounslow, lady."

"Oh, but I am! I'm quartered out there — just 'op in the back!"

Our progress through downtown London was diverted several times by air-raid wardens detouring traffic past burning buildings. In each case, the firelight reflecting on the glass fragments made the streets appear to be paved in diamonds.

There was another stop farther along, and we could hear the driver telling someone else to " 'op in." It was a British Tommy in uniform, holding an unconscious infant with one eye lying on its cheek.

The man's face was virtually expressionless.

"Sorry to bother you, chaps. My 'ouse was bombed and my wife lost 'er arm and I just now found the baby. Your driver will be dropping me off at the 'ospital."

The incident was to be one more piece in the mosaic of my admiration of English stoicism and endurance under conditions our American populace was so mercifully spared — all the while complaining of rationing and trivial shortages.

The driver dropped us off at Cynthia's address. Her father's expression of relief was almost emotional, and they invited me to spend the rest of the night on a sofa in their cramped living room. I explained the need to be back in class come morning and started hiking for London with hopes of catching a ride on the way.

Some enemy planes were again attacking the heart of the city, and I could see the rising streams of ack-ack tracers in the sky ahead. My casual-observer status changed abruptly when a sizable chunk of descending shell fragment clanged loudly on the pavement directly behind me. Discretion being the obviously better part of pointless valor, I ducked into the nearest doorway each time the guns opened up thereafter.

Near dawn I finally caught a ride that got me to class on time.

Our training was intensifying to include frequent overnight tactical exercises on a regimental scale. I recall one night jump in which I hit the ground so hard I couldn't walk for the better part of an hour. There was a lot of emphasis on night assembly and troop deployment in securing an airhead.

There was the week that we convoyed to Imber Range for tactical exercises with live ammunition. The "enemy" was half-silhouette targets deployed in defensive positions. The exuberance of our troops was demonstrated in two incidents I still remember vividly.

One was occasioned when a large Belgian hare decided to cut across the front of D Company as it advanced to attack. The brisk, if one-sided, fire fight resulting involved every line weapon short of mortars. The other incident concerned a large water tower well off to the right of the designated training area. It proved too tempting a target for a goodly number of riflemen and was spurting uncounted streams of its contents before the perpetrators were brought under control.

There also is a somber memory of Imber Range. The mail orderly handed me a letter from home. While holding it yet unopened, I somehow knew my maternal grandmother had died. The letter confirmed that she had passed away unexpectedly.

Sometime after mid-May, our battalion staff officers were "Bigoted," the code word designating those who were told the place and date selected for the invasion of Europe. The briefing materials included aerial photomaps of our Drop Zone near the village of Angoville Au Plain on Normandy's Cotentin Peninsula. The DZ was some four miles behind Utah Beach, the northernmost of the five seaborne invasion sites.

There also was a full-color terrain board of the area, constructed of some rubbery substance, which featured every building, hedgerow, ditch, tree, and even bomb crater! I could only assume there was a similar board depicting the initial objectives of each unit involved in the invasion.

To make doubly sure that every man in the S-2 section would be able to orient himself on the ground, I had them carve replicas of all key terrain features out of soap. They also studied the photomaps until they claimed they saw them in their sleep. And each boned up intensively on his individual assignment upon assembling after the jump.

The battalion assembly plan called for Pathfinders, jumping an hour ahead, to guide the planes in with radar and mark the DZ with flares. When we had landed, the adjutant would hoist a green lantern at the battalion headquarters assembly site. Headquarters staff personnel, including my S-2 section members, would be disbursed among different planes in the serial on the flight and would assemble on the lantern.

Section assignments included the prompt scouting of specified locations beyond the DZ perimeter where the presence of enemy troops would pose the most immediate threat to the assembly process. We would have two folding bicycles, developed by the British Airborne, for use in this regard, if feasible. The bikes would be dropped with a special chute to expedite their recovery on the ground.

Every jumper would have a toy "cricket" (a clicker) suspended on a string around his neck. On encountering anyone unrecognizable in the dark, it was to be clicked in challenge. If the other person said "Flash!" you were to respond, "Thunder!" and expect him to reply "Welcome!" indicating you had found a friend, not a fight. Every officer also was to have a large luminous button which could be clipped to the back of his collar for the benefit of any troops following him in the darkness.

We were soon to learn what can happen to best-laid plans when aggressive enemy action is factored into the equation.

Suddenly the training and planning phases ended. Basic loads of ammunition for all weapons were issued and distributed. We were headed for the marshaling areas at the air bases from which units would enplane for Normandy.

The 501st Regiment, less the 3rd Battalion, went to Merryfield. The 3rd Battalion had been designated Division Reserve and would take off from Welford with the jumping echelon of division headquarters.

Our marshaling area was surrounded by barbed wire and guarded by MPs. There was room within the enclosure for limited activities — I recall a soccer game of sorts with S-2 section personnel. But we were well sealed off from any civilian contacts.

The grand plan for Operation Overlord called for us to take off for Normandy late in the long English twilight of June 4. As history has recorded, adverse weather forecasts postponed the invasion by 24 hours. We got that word a few hours before the originally scheduled departure.

The reaction to that news, which remains most firmly entrenched in my memory, is the one reportedly voiced by Lieutenant Colonel Ewell. As the story goes, one flustered officer approached him saying, "Colonel! Colonel! The invasion has been called off for another twenty-four hours!"

To which Ewell pragmatically replied: "Well, what do you expect me to do about it? Throw myself on my goddam sword?"

No one seemed to consider the delay as providing one more day to live.

Chapter 10

Jumping into Normandy

Early the afternoon of June 5, we learned that the invasion would proceed. Colonel Johnson called us all together, mounted an improvised stage, and delivered an impassioned address. It started with, "Men, we've come a long way from Toccoa," then stressed at some length our superb readiness to decimate any German units unfortunate enough to get in our path on our way to Berlin.

In dramatic conclusion, he whipped out his throwing knife, held it aloft, and proclaimed, "By this time tomorrow, this knife will be plunged deep in the back of the blackest Nazi in Fra-a-a-nce!" While the cheers were still resounding, he started shaking hands with everyone in turn. I was perhaps 150th or so in line, but even by then he was wincing from the unrestrained grips of his hyped-up troopers. And he still had well over 1,000 to meet!

After an early evening mess, we started blackening our faces with burnt cork and gearing up to go. It took a while to get into all of our equipment.

We were an awkward-looking lot with the hump of main chutes on our backs and musette bags slung beneath the reserve chutes in front. Our web belts were festooned with canteens, ammo pouches, entrenching tools, first aid packets, emergency D rations, and bayonets. Leg pockets bulged with K rations, grenades, and Hawkins land mines. Trench knives and extra aid packets were strapped to ankles. There were gas masks in their canvas carriers on our left sides and inflatable "Mae West" life preservers across our chests. Coils of jump rope dangled from shoulder straps for use in case of tree landings, and our switchblade jump knives nestled in small pockets near the top centers of our jump suit jackets. All were topped by steel helmets with leather chin-cup straps.

Men armed with M-1 rifles carried them partially disassembled in canvas Griswold cases wedged at an angle between reserve chute and torso. Those armed with the shorter carbines simply stuck them under their harness straps. Crew-served weapons and their ammunition would be dropped in equipment bundles.

As an officer, I was further encumbered with binoculars, wire cutters, an escape kit, and the .45-caliber automatic pistol my father had carried through World War I, plus ammo pouch for same. I also carried an Airborne carbine with folding stock and ammunition for it, plus the dime store cricket on its string and the luminous button, of course.

We were dressed almost as excessively as we were equipped. Jump suits impregnated against gas attack were worn over wool OD shirt and pants, which in turn were worn over long-john underwear. Extra socks, ponchos, toilet articles, and mess kits were packed in the musette bags.

The airfield was roughly a half-mile from our pyramidal tent quartering area. There were 90 C-47 Troop Carrier Command planes scattered around the perimeter. Their fuselages and wings were painted in broad black and white stripes. Except for the runways, the field was covered with mustard weed in full yellow bloom.

We would take off in two serials of 45 planes each with our battalion in the second one. There would be approximately 1,050 jumpers in each serial, which would leave the field a few minutes apart to head for their respective Drop Zones in Normandy.

We marched out in company formation, but on reaching the near edge of the field we split off into 18-man sticks and crossed to our designated aircraft, wherever it was parked.

About halfway there, the road dipped slightly so that we were at eye level with the surface of the field and its panorama of mustard weed in bloom. Troopers from the battalion ahead had already split into sticks. At that distance, they looked like files of amphibious ants crossing a golden pond toward toy planes gleaming with black and white stripes.

Our battalion staff had been dispersed among the unit aircraft to minimize odds of losing many of the headquarters group en route to the Drop Zone. So I was riding with a squad from D Company and would jumpmaster the stick, hooking up my static line to the overhead cable near the open door, but jumping last.

As our plane was taking off I could look back down at the stream of planes to follow, barreling along the runway. A roaring river of black and white stripes! I had the impression someone had thrown the "On" switch of a monstrous machine, and there was no way of stopping it.

We would fly around the Cotentin Peninsula, skirting Cherbourg en route, and come in from west to east toward the seaborne invasion beaches. It would be eight minutes flying time from the West Coast to our DZ. Four minutes later, the planes would be over the English Channel again, heading back to the airfield.

I almost always got sleepy on airplanes. Unless, of course, I got sick. In this instance one of my tentmates had playfully doused my jump jacket with Tabu perfume before we dressed to depart for the airfield. I suspected Lieutenant Leo "Big Bird" Malek of that perfidity, but he was grievously wounded right after the jump and out of the war before I could accuse him.

I dozed off strapped in my seat, head resting on the reserve chute, before we were half an hour in the air. The perfume did contribute to some uncommonly pleasant dreams. I was awakened by the thump of heavy but ineffectual flak as we rounded Cherbourg, only to fall asleep again. Suddenly the squad leader was shouting in my ear. "Lieutenant, we're coming over France!" It was one helluva wake-up call.

The red light beside the door came on shortly thereafter, meaning we were 5,000 yards offshore. Time to stand up and hook up, giving us the chance to abandon ship in case the plane was disabled by coastal anti-aircraft batteries. Looking out of the door and under the left wing, I could see the black coastline sliding toward us. I bellowed the sequence of commands above the roar of the plane and its open door.

"Stand up and hook up!" The 17 men beyond me unbuckled seat belts, stood, and snapped their static lines to the steel cable running the length of the fuselage.

"Check equipment!" Each man checked the jumper in front of him, making sure the static line was securely snapped and held with the left hand, running over — not under — the arm. The man at the far end was, in turn, checked by the man ahead of him.

"Sound off for equipment check!"

The responses came down the line. "Number seventeen OK!" "Number sixteen OK!" etc., until all had verified their readiness. Now they would stand hunched in the aisle and wait.

As we came over the coast, I was watching the ground for muzzle flashes. There was not so much as the flare of a match; only total darkness below. The plane started dropping toward our jumping altitude of 300 feet. We now had less than eight minutes to go!

I stayed in the door, looking ahead under the left wing. Soon I could see fires burning on the ground in the distance. "We're in great shape, men! The Air Corps has bombed hell out of things!" It never occurred to me that those fires could be burning planes shot down from the serial preceding us, which they were.

The squad's light machine gun, ammunition boxes, and other supplies were packed in an equipment bundle on the floor near the doorway. It was nearly six feet long and about two feet in diameter. The static line for its attached chute was already hooked to the overhead cable. We would shove it out when the green light beside the door came on, and the squad would follow.

There should be less than two minutes to go. The plane crew chief was helping me edge the bundle closer to the door. Suddenly I sensed something different was happening outside, so I stood up to see what it was. The night sky was lacerated with streams of tracers from ground fire, groping for our C-47 lumbering 300 feet overhead. Instinctively, I ducked aside from the door.

That was a bad move from the troop morale angle. The men closest in line started cringing toward the floor, pulling lengths of static line from the backs of their chutes in the process. I hadn't stopped to think. But OCS principles of leadership prevailed, and standing fully in the door with a bravado feigned if unfelt, I shouted, "It's okay. They can't hit us!" In the same moment, a burst of automatic fire went through the plane somewhere near the front, sounding like rapid blows of a sledgehammer and severely damaging my pose as a prophet.

By then I could see our Drop Zone just ahead, recognizable even in the intermittent light of the partial moon peeking between cloud banks. I looked at the two-button light panel beside the door, which was controlled by the pilot. The red light, which had come on 5,000 yards offshore, was still glowing. When it went out and the green one came on, I would yell, "Go!"

I could see the dirt crossroads on the near boundary of our DZ. It was sliding away under the plane. The red light still glowed balefully. That posed one hell of a quandary. Had the pilot been hit by the ground fire? Had he simply forgotten to turn on the green? Or did he know there was another plane immediately below, ready to grind us up in its propellers? Meanwhile, we were flying at full throttle toward the seaborne invasion beaches, less than four minutes away.

Then I saw dark puffs in the sky nearby. They were the camouflaged chutes from planes to our left. Everyone else was jumping! I took one more look at the red light and yelled, "Let's go!" The lead man and the crew chief helped me slide the equipment bundle through the door. It got halfway out before the slipstream caught the front end and twisted it to jam in the doorway. We cursed, kicked, and clawed until it finally departed. The first five men followed in rapid-fire order.

As the number six man reached the exit, the plane yawed wildly, throwing him against the side of the aperture. The barrel of his carbine, protruding from under his webbing, broke through the paper tape covering the two thicknesses of the aluminum door jamb, holding him firmly in place. The men behind him simply kept coming until their aggregate pressure popped him out like the insides of a squeezed grape.

The exit of Geronimo number 12 was expedited by the plane, which chose that moment to turn up on its left wing, jettisoning him without need to jump and causing me to look directly down at moonlight reflecting in water. The C-47 righted itself immediately, but not before my fleeting glimpse recorded whitecaps on the surface! While I had hardly been timing the sequence of events since overshooting the DZ, it seemed highly likely that we had exhausted the four minutes of flying time from there to the English Channel.

The remaining five men had been thrown off stride but were now storming down the aisle toward me. I crouched in the door and screeched, "Stop! We're over the ocean!" The first man hit me like a Notre Dame fullback going through a Peewee team line and went right on out the door. I bounced off the door of the toilet compartment behind me and landed on my knees in time to try stopping the next man. Same impact, same result, with him and the other three still coming. None had the slightest intention of remaining in that plane. And I was getting downright tired of bouncing off the biffy — the toilet — door.

Suddenly I was all alone in the empty C-47 passenger compartment. Even the crew chief was gone! I had a momentary impulse to go up to the cockpit, tap the pilot on the shoulder, providing he was alive, and say, "I didn't have a chance to get out, Mac. Do you mind making another pass at the field?" I decided against it.

They had made it perfectly clear in England that to return to base with the plane would constitute desertion in the face of the enemy. A capital offense by military justice standards. Then there was the prospect of disgracing the family name, what with my father back in service and all. Obviously, I had to jump, then and there, regardless of consequences.

I was, of course, wearing a Mae West inflatable life preserver. And we'd been assured one could live four hours in the Channel before succumbing to hypothermia. Surely the seaborne invasion fleet would pluck me from the water before then.

We had been trained with repetitive monotony on how to exit a plane. You crouched and placed your left foot on the door sill, hands with fingers and thumbs gripping the outer skin of the fuselage. Then you kicked out the right leg, extended to let the slipstream turn your plummeting body one-quarter way to the left, thus lessening the opening shock.

Our battle cry going into Normandy was supposed to be "Bill Lee," in

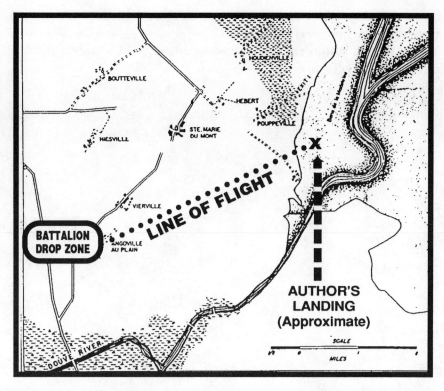

Missing the Drop Zone by miles. (Adapted from *Rendezvous with Destiny, The History of the 101st Airborne Division,* enlarged edition (Sweetwater, TN: 101st Airborne Division Assoc., 1948), 98.

respect for the major general who had pioneered the Army Airborne program. He had come to England in command of the 101st Airborne Division, welcomed our 501st Regiment on its arrival, then was invalided home due to a heart attack.

Having decided to jump, regardless, I stood bolt upright in the door and toppled out stiff and straight as a pine log. I did utter a battle cry: "Oh, shit!"

It took 83 feet for a static-lined chute to open; then you looked up immediately to see if your canopy was fully deployed. The opening shock rattled my molars, but I did look up in an instant and simultaneously plowed into solid earth! The plane could not have been flying more than 90 feet above the ground.

Had I landed on an island in the Channel? Before I could even grapple with that question I heard hobnail boots pounding the ground in my direction and glimpsed moonlight glinting on bayonets.

My folding stock carbine was wedged inaccessibly under my webbing, but my father's World War I .45 automatic was holstered on my hip. Unfortunately, I had secured it with baling wire to prevent its loss on the jump. I clawed at it to no avail. I would not take a single Nazi with me to that Last Roll Call in the sky!

Chapter 11

The Assembly

I was lying on my left side, still clawing at the .45, when the hobnail boots skidded to a halt two feet in back of my head. I rolled over to face my fate — whatever — and found myself staring into the eyes of a cow, backed by several others of her species. The moonlight shining on her horns still made them resemble bayonets. She shied away before I could kiss her on the nose, her hooves still sounding like hobnail boots.

I fumbled at the snaps of my chute harness, but they refused to cooperate. So I yanked my trench knife from its leg sheath and started slashing. Through the chute harness, through the jump suit, and into the ODs. Fortunately, I calmed down before reaching any arteries.

While I was slashing away, a wild-eyed trooper came charging out of the darkness. No helmet, no weapon. He paused long enough to ask, "Are you okay?" I mumbled an affirmative and he sprinted off again. So far as I know, he is still running somewhere through Europe.

Any authoritative history of the Normandy invasion will tell you the Douve River had flooded all low-lying fields alongside, thus creating a shallow lake some 18 miles long. Yet not a single aerial photo interpreter had deduced this fact from the hundreds of shots taken of the area by Allied aircraft as recently as the day before we jumped.

When our plane had tilted on its left wing, I had seen the moonlight reflecting in that water. The unsubmerged tops of grasses waving in the breeze were the "whitecaps" that convinced me we were over the ocean. So much for the accuracy of fleeting observations under the stress of a combat jump.

My "hobnail boots and bayonets." (Illustration by Jim Jones)

I had landed a mile short of the invasion beach, and it was time to get on with the war. I got to my feet, loaded my carbine and pistol, retrieved two hand grenades from my leg pockets and hung them on the front of my webbing. Twenty yards away another trooper was thrashing around, also having trouble getting out of his parachute harness. I identified myself, cut him loose a bit more carefully, and helped him up.

He asked a rather logical question. "Lieutenant, what's your plan?"

Not having the slightest semblance of one at the moment, I struck my most steadfast Infantry School pose and replied, "Follow me!"

Just a bit further on, three Geronimos were considering how to cross a deep, water-filled ditch. Such obstacles crisscrossed the low ground, each swollen with a surfeit of water which shelved into the adjoining fields. So we had to wade through water up to our ankles or knees before reaching the edge of each ditch, which could be six to eight feet deep.

We challenged the three troopers with the prescribed "Flash!" and heard "Thunder!" in return. We responded, "Welcome!" Way-to-go lads — precisely by the book!

They seemed considerably relieved at finding an officer present and showed their gratitude by asking, "Lieutenant, what's your plan?"

This time I countered with a question of my own. "Are your weapons loaded?" They were not. Nor had any of them hung grenades where they would be handy. I was to gather more than 30 men in the next half-hour before finding one who had thought to put a round in the chamber of his weapon. But I did not encounter anyone who failed to ask, "Lieutenant, what's your plan?"

Nor did I find one who seemed dissatisfied with my answer, "Follow me." At the very least, it kept them from remaining alone in the dark.

The terrain was very flat, consisting of pasture land laced with those flooded ditches. The moon had retreated behind more clouds. Far off in the night I could see tracers streaking along the contours of higher ground. The sound of the firing was arriving several seconds later. The fighting seemed to me to be at least three miles away. I assumed the Drop Zone and assembly areas were over there somewhere.

There had been a "Plan B" in arranging for the assembly of our battalion. "If things get all screwed up, just head for wherever the fighting is!" So far as I was concerned, Plan B was now in effect. I led off headed for the noisy high ground, gathering more and more Geronimos as we went.

By trial and error, we developed a technique for crossing the ditches: Wade out in the shelving water until you could see where the grass stopped, which meant you were standing on the near edge of the ditch. Look ahead to where the grass started again. That was the far edge of the ditch. If you could make it in one jump, you would not get your ass and everything else wet. The moonlight, even diffused by the clouds, was bright enough for such observations.

It was slow going, but we were progressing from field to field, the size of our group growing steadily en route. Crossing one field, a machine-gun team joined us. The larger of the two was carrying the tripod. The smaller man, hunched under the weight of the gun, fell into our casual column right behind me.

When we reached the next ditch, I waded without pause to where the grass stopped, noted that this one was relatively narrow, and crossed it with one short jump. The little machine-gunner failed to note my technique; apparently it was his first ditch. He took a normal stride and disappeared in the water.

I waited for him to come thrashing up, but the only thing breaking the surface was bubbles. I got down on my knees and reached arm's length into the water. I could feel the top of a helmet. He was standing on the bottom with the gun still on his shoulder. He seemed to feel I had gotten him in there so it was my job to get him out.

Fortunately, he had his chin strap fastened. I gripped the front edge of his helmet and lifted. He came up rather easily, considering, but none of his ensuing remarks smacked of gratitude. He apparently felt that only a very lousy leader would lead him into a ditch!

The high ground was getting nearer. There was but a short time interval between seeing a string of tracers and hearing the staccato report of the weapon that spewed them. There were maybe a hundred men strung out in a column of fuzzy clusters behind me. Things were still all screwed up, but we were less than half a mile from the fighting.

There was another challenge from the darkness ahead. I recognized the voice of Major Dick Allen, our regimental operations officer. Thank God! He would certainly know what to do next.

Allen had maybe 30 men with him. He also had a question. "Sefton, what's your plan?"

I explained my intention of moving onto the high ground and finding something to shoot at. He concurred with the concept and proposed an amendment.

"You take twenty men as the point, and I'll bring up the main body."

That made good tactical sense, and I was relieved to have the well-respected Allen assuming responsibility for my hodgepodge assortment of ditch-dampened warriors. But I wasn't sure how many ditches he had crossed, so I offered an amendment of my own.

"Fine, Major. But when I reach that clump of trees out there, I'll wait for you to come up. Then I'll move out again."

I had already learned how flooded ditches could disrupt the control and progress of even a small column moving across that terrain in the dark. But since lieutenants do not give majors oral exams on such subjects, I was hedging my bet in the interest of assuring a cohesive formation behind me before going into an assault.

Allen agreed with the proposal, so I led 20 men off toward the clump of trees, about midway to the high ground by my calculation.

Approximately halfway to the trees, we encountered the granddaddy of all ditches to date. It was a good 20 feet wide and presumably quite deep. There was, however, a log of telephone pole dimensions positioned across it — not exactly a two-lane bridge, but what the hell. We edged along the log, using our weapons like tightrope walkers' balancing poles, and crossed without anyone falling off.

A hundred yards later I looked back. The main body had done a column left at the ditch and was disappearing off to that flank in the darkness. So much for that plan, and so long, Major Allen.

The immediate area was thick with scattered Geronimos in search of a mission. Very shortly I had more than 60 men again, plus two other lieutenants, none of whom disappointed me by failing to ask for my "plan." The high ground was looming just ahead. Some light artillery rounds were starting to fall. It was obviously time for a more detailed decision.

I stopped the column, sending men to the front, flanks, and rear as local security. "If anyone approaches, challenge 'Flash' — if they don't answer 'Thunder,' start shooting!" All according to the book.

I called the two officers into a council of war. Rank among lieutenants has been likened to virtue among whores, but neither questioned my right to decree their immediate fates.

"I'll take twelve men and move out as the point. Each of you take half of the rest and follow fifty yards behind. If I hit anything I can't move through, you flank it from both sides — fast! Are there any questions?"

There were none. So I counted off 12 men and informed them they were the point. Then I asked for two volunteers to precede the point as scouts. The silence was embarrassing. Finally a 1st sergeant said, "I'll be one scout, Lieutenant." No one else said anything.

I remembered the luminous button, took it out of my breast pocket, and hooked it on the back of my collar. "If you lose sight of this button, the Krauts will get you. Call in those guards from the flanks and rear; we'll pick up the man ahead as we go. Move out, Sergeant!"

Two months later, back in England, I was watching a truckload of men who had been wounded in Normandy returning from a hospital. One of them suddenly was at my elbow, red-faced and highly indignant.

"Lieutenant," he demanded, "do you remember me?"

"You're in Easy Company, aren't you?"

"Yeah. But do you remember me the first night in Normandy?"

"I'm sorry, trooper, but I don't have the foggiest recollection of you the first night in Normandy."

"Well, you damned well *should*! You put me behind a bush and LEFT ME THERE ALL NIGHT!"

So much for assuming every order you give in combat will be executed as expected. He was probably the local security guard I had sent to the rear. Or maybe to one of the flanks. In any case, he was voicing a pent-up but well-justified bitch.

Meanwhile, back to the war.

The ground was definitely getting higher and drier — the sounds of fighting closer and closer. I halted the point momentarily. "Drop your packs and fix bayonets!" We left 12 musette bags neatly aligned on the Norman landscape. So far as I know, none of us ever saw them again.

We moved ahead. A figure was crawling on the ground. It was my own S-2 section sergeant, Pop Dornick. He couldn't walk because he'd banged up both ankles on landing. He was giggling inanely. "They tried to kill me! They tried to kill old Pop!" It was a sensation widely shared that night.

The Tables of Equipment called for Pop to be armed with a Thompson submachine gun, making him the envy of the section. Since he couldn't walk — and I was going into the assault — I "suggested" we trade weapons. He was in too much pain to argue with that logic. I found a spot on my web belt to hook the pouch of Tommy-gun magazines as we concluded the transaction.

Then Pop remembered to tell me something. "Colonel Ballard is right over there by that hedgerow." We had been about to assault our own battalion assembly area.

I reported in to the colonel, virtually doubling his forces at hand, then joined him in trying to round up more men.

We went along the hedgerow; there was a bomb crater in the field just beyond. The moon had come out again, and we could see a soldier sitting on a bushel basket-sized lump of earth thrown up by the bomb, obviously an American.

The colonel called out, "What unit, trooper?"

"Dog Company, 501!"

"Well, this is Colonel Ballard. Come over and give us a hand."

"Love to, Colonel, but I broke my leg on the jump."

He was sitting there with his rifle across his lap, waiting for any target in a coal scuttle helmet. Just because he couldn't move didn't mean he couldn't fight.

After-action analyses purportedly showed that our battalion had the most compact drop pattern of any in the 101st Airborne Division. God help the others! We spent the remaining hours of darkness pulling together semblances of units and searching, mostly in vain, for equipment bundles.

Most of the shooting was being done by the Germans, sitting in their prepared positions and laying fire on the areas where they assumed us to be. Some of their assumptions were pretty good. I was discussing the situation with Lieutenant Ed Allworth, our battalion adjutant, and another officer when a small mortar shell broke up the conversation by landing right in the middle of our group. We were all knocked flat by the concussion. Both of the others were lightly wounded by fragments.

The imminence of dawn was finally starting to lighten the eastern sky. And the awesome significance of hedgerows was becoming increasingly apparent. Each was an earthen wall, at least four feet high and three feet thick, with brush growing on top. They bordered virtually every field, breaking the battleground into a checkerboard of seemingly endless obstacles.

Our troops huddled behind those bordering the assembly area, peering through the foliage on top. Vision was inevitably limited by the next hedgerow, often less than a hundred yards away. If we wanted to take that one, we would have to assault across a pasture completely innocent of cover or concealment. Since the battalion was still missing two of the four company commanders and maybe 80 percent of the troops, we were hardly in a position to make a coordinated dawn attack.

The colonel had the only radio in evidence, having jumped with it strapped to his leg. Since no one else seemed to have one, he might as well have left it in England. We hadn't found any field phones or reels of wire yet, either.

The light was growing stronger, approaching full dawn. The colonel assigned a mission to me: "Take a patrol and find the 1st Battalion." They were supposed to have shared the DZ with us. Neither of us could know they were scattered over 60 square miles of Normandy.

Four of my S-2 section scouts had found the assembly area. I rounded them up and started on the patrol.

Chapter 12

A Pond Can Be a Nice Place to Visit

If any significant elements of the 1st Battalion had landed north of our position, there would certainly be sounds of them fighting the Germans who were firing on us from that area. The best bet seemed to be the low ground to the south. A hedgerow ran off in that direction, so I started the patrol alongside it.

I had two scouts leading and two behind me, with intervals of ten yards or so between patrol members. The hedgerow was on our right, open terrain to our left. It was not yet fully dawn. A voice seemed to emanate from the earth, almost at my feet, addressing one of the two scouts who had already passed the spot.

"Hey, trooper, what's going on?"

I recognized the voice of Lieutenant Clair "Horrible" Hess, an F Company platoon leader. He was rolled up in his camouflage chute and lying against the hedgerow. The scouts had nearly stepped on him. And I probably would have.

"Hey, Horrible! There's a war going on. Get up and give us a hand!"

"Can't do it, Sefton. I've got a buncha machine-gun holes in my legs." Which, of course, he did, having been hit before he could get out of his chute.

He had already treated the wounds with his aid packet, so I explained that we were on a mission and assured him that the medics would undoubtedly be along very shortly. They did find him — two days later.

A bit farther on we encountered Lieutenant Brasil just emerging sopping wet from a ditch blocking our route. He'd been pinned down by a machine gun from the moment he had landed until the gliders came in at first light.

When the gun crew shifted their attention to the gliders, Brasil had rushed the position, hurled one grenade, and kept right on moving — briskly!

I told him the hedgerow would take him right into the battalion assembly area and started to move out again.

"Watch the ditch, Sefton, it's a *deep* mother!"

Having long since awarded myself a Master Ditch Crosser Badge, I waded out to where the grass stopped, gauged the distance to where it started again, and leaped hard. Unfortunately, the grass on the far side was floating a deceptive two feet toward me from the submerged bank of the ditch.

Brasil watched me disappear that much short of the far bank and was still gaping at the spot when I surfaced, treading water. Only one course of action made sense in those circumstances. I kept my expression as deadpan as possible and observed: "You're right. It *is* deep."

The rest of the patrol crossed more wisely, and we continued along our hedgerow. Suddenly the air was filled with the characteristic snap-snap-snap of machine-gun rounds fired from a distance but passing *very* close overhead. We all hit the ground, hugging the protection of that wonderful earthen embankment between us and the gunner somewhere off to our right.

Time frequently loses all relevance in combat. I'll never know whether I lay there mentally pinned down for two minutes or ten before a dazzling thought occurred: *Hey! I'm allowed to shoot back!*

Cautious peering through the hedgerow foliage revealed a large farmhouse — almost a chateau — some 400 yards to the right. Aha! Movement in the front yard shrubbery!

The Tommy gun was useless at that range, so I commandeered an M-1 rifle from one of the scouts, rested it across the top of the hedgerow, and squeezed off my first shot fired in anger. Damn! That was more like it!

The recoil of the weapon felt good against my shoulder. The satisfaction of finally being able to smite back at the bastards created a feeling of near-euphoria. I expended the eight-round clip, raking that shrubbery fore, aft, port, and starboard. There was no more movement, and no return fire. Considering the odds against wiping out a gun crew with one clip at 400 yards, there was probably none there to begin with. But at least I *felt* a lot better.

This was all taking place within a few yards of the point where our hedgerow ended. Beyond that was the low ground — crisscrossed with ditches, naturally. There was another hedgerow going off at 90 degrees to the right of the direction we had been taking. But it started some 30 yards short of the one we were behind. Since I had been unable to see anything resembling the 1st Battalion in the low ground ahead, I had already decided to execute a column right of sorts and reconnoiter in that direction.

That maneuver was complicated a bit by the fact that a ditch ran along the near side of the intersecting hedgerow and widened into a small pond — actually an overflow of the widening ditch, itself — effectively filling the gap between the two hedgerows.

On the far side of the pond, squarely in the gap, was a hummock resembling a muskrat den. A solitary GI lay behind the hummock yelling repeatedly, "Go back! Go back!" He offered no explanation as to why we should heed his advice. He just kept yelling, "Go back!"

Undeterred by such obvious and unbecoming temerity, I told the lead scouts, Joe Newman and Maurice Sanquist, to hie themselves to the next hedgerow while I provided fire cover. They negotiated the pond by trotting along the near edge until it narrowed back into more ditch-like dimensions at the start of the intersecting embankment, then leaped it at that point and ducked behind the new cover.

Well and good! I sent Lewis Frey off to do likewise, continuing to bang away at the inoffensive shrubbery as he departed. One burst of German machine-gun fire crackled nearby, but it seemed to come from well to the right of my target area. I tried to spot the source of the fire and took a few random shots at likely clumps of foliage without perceptible result. Finally, I could see that Frey had joined Newman and Sanquist. In fact, he was lying on the ground at Joe's feet. But since he had every right to follow the soldier's creed of resting whenever possible, I attached no particular significance to his prone position.

Instead, I handed the M-1 to the remaining scout, said, "Cover me, will ya?" and loped off in a "maneuver crouch" to join the others. I was at approximate midpoint along the water's edge when a burst of machine-gun fire from my right flank — the direction from which we had come — all but removed my nose and eyelashes. That explained what the GI pinned down behind the hummock had been yelling about.

A well-trained, heads-up infantry officer will always decide on the best course of action in the stress of combat emergencies, according to Fort Benning OCS instructors. *My* very prompt decision was to jump into the pond.

That particular course of action resulted in a sitting position on the bottom of the ditch, some eight feet below the surface. The sun was penetrating the water in green and gold shafts. It was very quiet, obviously a nice place to visit, even if one couldn't live there, at least not for long. Especially if one had neglected to fill his lungs with air before descending, as had been the case in this instance.

My immediate reaction to the situation was to mentally assume the role of a detached observer — a sensation I was to experience time and again in

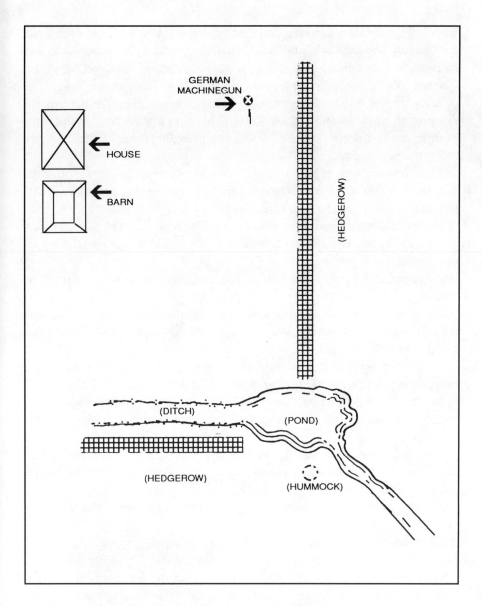

future combat crises. It was as though I were standing safely aside and analyzing my predicament with casual interest.

"This is not really the proper way to fight a war, Sefton," the observer remarked. "For one thing, you have no plan. And no air in your lungs. Your first ploy, obviously, is to go up and get some air so you can reason this thing out in the prescribed military manner."

Having spent countless boyhood hours playing underwater tag while skinny-dipping in Indiana gravel pits, the problem of reaching the surface was easily solved. I assumed a crouching position on the bottom of the ditch and lunged upward, breaking head, shoulders, and belly button into the Normandy atmosphere. Fortunately, I surfaced facing the direction of the German machine-gunner, so I could see the beaten zone of his next burst plowing up the turf as it progressed with startling rapidity in the precise direction of my semi-submerged position. I had no trouble at all in deciding to sink immediately back to the bottom as succeeding rounds roiled the surface I had just vacated.

The observer was mildly amused. "You've screwed up royally, Bucko. You still have no air in your lungs and no plan. You have to go up again and *this* time be *sure* you get some air."

So I repeated the previous maneuver, gasping a satisfactory lungful of air and retreating below the surface just as the gunner all but creased the top of my helmet.

Newman, observing from behind the hedgerow, reported to Frey and Sanquist, "They just killed the Lieutenant."

It seemed unlikely the gunner would miss again. But at least I had enough air to permit some thinking time, provided, of course, I thought fast. I decided to fool the bastard.

The water shelved out beyond the edges of the ditch into the fields beyond, as previously noted. Ergo, it should be possible to climb the side of the ditch nearest the gun position, rest my hands on top without breaking the surface and slo-o-o-o-wly ease my nose into breathing position undetected. Helluva plan!

I started crawling across the bottom toward the side of the ditch. The water was becoming murky from the mud I was stirring up. I felt the bag of Tommy-gun clips slip off my web belt.

"You're supposed to practice supply economy, Sefton," the observer noted.

Obediently, I turned and groped for the ammo bag, found it, and reattached it to my belt. Then I proceeded to ease up the side of the ditch until I could rest my hands on top, albeit still under several inches of water.

There was a patch of green scum floating on the surface at that point. As kids, we had called it frog shit. I inched my face to the surface, fully draped with the slimy substance. Never had anything so foul smelled so sweet!

I would never hazard a guess as to just how long I hung onto that bank, breathing through the scum, before calling out, "Newman, Joe Newman!"

There was a prolonged silence from the patrol member who had reported me killed to Lewis Frey a short time earlier. I called out again. Finally, I heard a very hesitant and tenuous reply, "Lieutenant? Where *are* you?"

"Over here. Can you see me?"

"Lieutenant, your own *mother* couldn't see you!"

"Well, stay put. I'm gonna work my way down *slowly* in your direction."

For the next 25 minutes or so, I inched my way along that bank, keeping hands well under the water and face barely above the surface, still adorned by the mask of scum. The water was very cold. My legs were drawing up in cramps. It seemed to take forever to reach the point directly across from Joe at the start of the intersecting hedgerow.

"Joe, my legs are too cramped to use."

"It's okay. I've got a jump rope." He reached around the edge of the hedgerow and tossed a length of his jump rope toward me.

I let it sink, holding onto the bank with one hand and reaching underwater toward the rope with the other arm. I felt it slip off the end of my fingers.

Joe pulled it back and tossed it harder. This time it reached me easily. But by now, the cramps were numbing my hands. I was unable to fashion so much as a granny knot. I did, however, manage to wrap the rope around and around the small of the Tommy-gun stock.

"Joe, when I count three, I'm gonna let go of this bank and I'll sink to the bottom like a sack of bricks. When I do, you start pulling like hell on that rope!"

I counted and sank as predicted. The rope grew taut. I held the Tommy gun across my chest, cradled in the crooks of my arms and crawled across the bottom with my elbows. I hit the far bank of the ditch and crawled right on up, aided by the pull of the rope. My head and shoulders broke water at the edge of the ditch, five feet from the safety of the hedgerow, at which point both ends of the Tommy gun jammed in the roots of submerged vegetation. I couldn't move another inch.

I could feel my back getting wider and wider as a target for the gunner.

Newman was bracing one leg against his side of the hedgerow and straining at the rope with all of his 135 pounds in the effort to pull me loose. My back felt at least two acres wide, and the gunner *had* to be sighting on it with leisurely delight. Joe strolled out like it was a Sunday afternoon in the park at Kokomo, got a firm grip on the collar of my jump suit, heaved me out of the water, and pulled me behind the hedgerow.

And not a shot was fired!

Lewis Frey was still there in the prone position. It turned out that he had also taken the water route and been pulled out by Joe while I was banging away at suspected gun positions. And he also had emerged from the experience severely cramped. It was to be nearly an hour before both of us could walk well enough to continue the patrol.

When Frey and I were able to navigate, we moved out again, with Newman leading. I'd ordered the fifth man back to the assembly area, rather than have him attempt to negotiate the pond and join us.

We hugged the hedgerow which would pass some hundred yards below the barn and outbuildings of the farm where I had first fired at the suspected machine-gun position. A trooper from the 506th Regiment was lying beside the embankment. Gravely wounded, he was already turning the gray-green pallor we would come to know as the color of death. He was beyond coherent speech and any help we could give him.

Farther along was a 501st man with a finger shot away. And a few hundred yards out in the low ground, some other troopers were visible. Since both Frey and I were still somewhat hobbled by cramps, I sent Newman out to see if they were part of the 1st Battalion. The nine-fingered man opted to go with him in the hope of finding a medic.

At this point we were directly below the two-story brick barn of the farm we had been approaching. Joe and the wounded trooper had left the protection of the hedgerow by some 50 yards when the air was filled with the crackle of rifle fire. I looked out to see Joe standing in the open field with bullets kicking up the ground all around him. The wounded man was rolling at his feet.

"Hey, Lieutenant, this poor sonavabitch has been hit again!"

I suggested somewhat peremptorily that Joe get his lucky ass back to the hedgerow and bring his less fortunate friend along. Said friend now sported a bullet hole in the calf of his leg, but he made excellent time on the return trip, regardless.

Meanwhile, a mortar shell had penetrated the roof of the barn, setting the building afire. I was watching smoke fill the barnyard when three Germans materialized from the burning building. The range was only 100 yards, but the Tommy gun proved useless. The prolonged submersion in water and muck had rendered it inoperable.

I screamed at the others, "Get 'em! Get 'em!" But they couldn't spot the targets through the smoke. I remembered the .45 pistol on my hip, whipped it out and blasted away. A cow 30 degrees off the line of fire ran a small circle and dropped dead. Helluva shot!

The Krauts disappeared in the direction of the farmhouse.

About 200 yards ahead, the hedgerow ended at a cluster of houses identified on the maps as Bse. Addeville. Arriving there, we found it occupied by the regimental commander, Colonel Johnson, and a mixed bag of troopers from various units. Major Allen was also there with the main body of our impromptu command from the preceding night. A screen of Geronimos was deployed at the base of the adjacent high ground in the general direction of St. Come-du-Mont. The Germans, of course, held the high ground. There was sporadic sniping, but no significant fire fights in progress.

I reported in to Allen and learned they had established radio contact with Colonel Ballard. I used the radio to tell Ballard where I was — and where the 1st Battalion wasn't. He estimated it would take two hours for the battalion to move to our position as Colonel Johnson had directed.

I stretched out on the grass behind one of the houses and fell into a glorious sleep.

Paratroop patrol in Normandy, June 8, 1944, a French churchyard at St. Marcouf. (Photo, National Archives, 111-SC-189929)

Chapter 13

Getting on with D-Day

I awoke two hours later, feeling somewhat guilty about not yet having won the war. No one else seemed to be doing much about it, either. Ballard had reported difficulty in moving the battalion to join us as ordered. I learned later that they had attempted the same route we had taken and had bogged down at the pond.

Feeling I really should be doing *something,* I decided to take a couple of my scouts and see if we could find someone to shoot at. We moved off in the direction of the high ground, "snoopin' and poopin' " in true S-2 tradition. The protective screen of troopers apparently had a few holes in it, because we encountered no friendlies on the route we were taking.

We approached a house about 80 yards ahead. I had no way of knowing it was occupied by Lieutenant John McNulty, my closest friend in the battalion. He had two men and a machine gun with a ruptured shell casing in the chamber, and no extraction tool for removing it. He had been skirmishing for some two hours with Germans trying to evict him from the residence.

I was carrying a carbine found unclaimed in the village, having discarded the useless Tommy gun. We were still some 70 yards away when four Germans suddenly emerged from a ditch, sprinting at an angle from left to right across our front in a determined assault on the house. I emptied the clip of the carbine ammo at them as they disappeared behind intervening foliage near the building.

In comparing notes with McNulty later, I learned that they had shot the lock off the front door with machine-gun fire and hurled a concussion grenade through the entrance. Mac had flattened himself against the wall and opened his mouth to avoid rupturing of his eardrums. He could see the Germans charging just before the grenade exploded, slamming him against the wall with no serious damage. The door swung shut from the force of the blast, and he expended a Tommy-gun magazine through it. When it swung open again, two of the enemy were down and the other two were dragging them into the safety of a ditch.

I always claimed I got 'em with the carbine. We never did settle the argument.

Having determined the enemy was, indeed, present in more force than I personally commanded at the moment, I found my appetite for mortal combat temporarily sated. And complete ignorance at the time of Mac's plight in the house ahead left me bereft of motivation for heroics in that direction. It seemed an excellent time to go back and inquire as to any further word from Colonel Ballard. After all, I was *his* intelligence officer.

We got back just in time to find Major Allen casting about for the makings of a combat patrol. "Ah, Sefton! Take some men and secure those buildings over there."

He was pointing across the field toward the same farmhouse and outbuildings we had spent so much of the morning skirting. The objective was about 200 yards away across a pasture exposed to fire from high ground.

I recruited a machine-gun team and a rifleman to augment my awesome striking force of Newman, Frey, and Sanquist. We crossed the field via a very shallow but dry ditch, drawing no fire en route, and reached the shelter of the first outbuilding. It was a two-story brick affair. The farmhouse itself was across a driveway which ran back to the still burning barn.

Since the Germans who had fled the barn earlier had disappeared toward the house, we eased up to the door, intending to fling it open and leap in, firing if required. The door was securely locked. So we shot it open and leaped in anyway, finding ourselves in a large kitchen, completely innocent of German soldiery.

Considering the significant size of the establishment, I posted the machine-gun team outside the door to cover the approach from the enemy-held high ground. Then I organized the rest of the patrol for a methodical securing of the building. Joe Newman and I would leap into rooms — the others would provide backup in the event we had leaped into trouble.

Hollywood would have loved us! We kicked open each door and sprang through the doorway, Joe to the right and I to the left, crouched, weapon stocks clamped against hips, ready to spray instant destruction into any corner. After leaping into some eight or ten empty rooms, we began to feel a little silly.

By the time we reached the second floor, we were reasonably sure there were no Germans cluttering up the premises. Otherwise, there would have been some serious resistence to our progress thus far. So we separated, Joe going down the hallway to the right while I took the rooms to the left. I had just leaped heroically into the last empty room in that direction when I heard Joe calling from the other end of the hallway.

"Hey, Lieutenant, c'mere!"

He was pointing his weapon into a front bedroom from which a babble of voices was chorusing "Seeveel! Seeveel!"

There were at least three generations of French people in that room, numbering approximately 15 at first glance. Joe had already deduced that "Seeveel" probably meant "Civilian." But they kept shouting it, just the same.

Since they obviously posed little threat to our military security, I decided to return to the ground floor and check on the machine-gun team. One of the family opted to accompany me and assist in the war effort. It was the grandmother. Upon reaching the kitchen, she appointed herself mess officer and put on a large pot of tea.

The machine-gun team had scooped out the semblance of a position in the backyard, a few feet from the door. The gun was mounted on its tripod and pointed up the driveway. The gunner and his assistant were shielded from enemy observation by a small section of picket fence.

The driveway intersected the road from Bse. Addeville about 50 yards in front of the house. At that precise point, the road made a left turn and proceeded straight up the high ground. The gunner had sighted his weapon along the center line of the road and was attempting to pick off an occasional German who dashed across it some 200 yards up the hill. It was like trying to hit a deer in mid-leap crossing a firebreak, but the gun team was enjoying the challenge.

For the next two hours, we took turns drinking tea in the kitchen with Grandma and sniping at Jerries through the palings of the fence as they flitted across the roadway. And, while we did not observe any confirmed hits, we did contribute noticeably to their alacrity in making the crossing.

It was a rather enjoyable little war until someone shouted from inside the house, "Lieutenant! Joe Newman's been hit!" He had been peering out of a second floor window. A single round had hit him just below his collarbone and exited nastily through a shoulder blade. We carried him down to the kitchen and stanched the profuse blood flow with aid packet compresses.

Anticipating that initial shock would soon turn into considerable pain, I took a morphine Syrette from the aid packet, inserted the needle into his arm, and started squeezing the tube. I squeezed and squeezed to no apparent avail as Joe calmly observed my efforts. Finally, he offered a suggestion.

"Lieutenant, would it help if you broke the seal?" Which, of course, I hadn't thought to do.

Having no direct communication with Major Allen in Bse. Addeville, I sent a runner across the intervening field to request more skilled medical assistance. He returned with a battalion surgeon and an aid man, coming under a hail of small arms fire just as they reached the shelter of an out-building.

The medics checked our bandaging job, placed a bottle of plasma on a table, and tapped the dispensing tube into a vein in Joe's arm, securing the needle with tape. Then, noting that they had no stretcher with which to evac-uate him, they departed across the field, this time crawling in the shallow ditch which they should have utilized on their initial crossing.

The afternoon was wearing into evening when Allen sent a runner to advise us he was pulling the troops out of Bse. Addeville to join Colonel Johnson, now at the La Barquette locks on the Douve River. Seizure of the locks was one of the initial objectives assigned to the 501st. Johnson had occupied the site with a small force from various units earlier in the day and had been seeking reinforcements ever since.

I sent the runner back with word that we had a badly wounded man requiring evacuation and would appreciate the time and assistance required for the job. The runner may or may not have made it. In any event, the next time I scanned the village through binoculars, none of our troops were in evidence.

Dusk was rapidly approaching, and enemy fire from the high ground was increasing, indicating movement in our direction. I started preparing to with-draw, taking Joe along in the process. He wasn't being cooperative.

"Lieutenant, you're gonna endanger the patrol! You've gotta leave me here."

"Shut up!" I responded.

There was a low brick wall across the front yard of the house. I moved the machine-gunners and riflemen up there and opened up with every weapon, hopefully suppressing German ardor for the moment. Then we began to vacate the premises.

First we placed Joe on a blanket from the house, with one man holding each corner. It split down the middle, dumping him on the ground. Two men then tried the "fireman's-carry" technique. That didn't seem to work either. Time becoming of considerable essence, I hoisted him over my shoulder, and, with a man trotting alongside to hold the plasma bottle aloft, we all withdrew briskly.

We pulled straight back from known enemy locations, passing the barn behind the house and getting over the hedgerow with which we had become so familiar that morning. Using it as cover and concealment, we emerged just south of Bse. Addeville which still seemed deserted. I sent Sanquist in to check. He returned in the semi-dark to report.

"Father Sam is still there with a buncha wounded, and the Krauts are starting to come in from the high ground." It was decision time regarding Joe Newman, who had not enjoyed our retreat thus far.

"Joe, I don't know where we're going from here, but we'll sure take you along unless you'd prefer to stay with Father Sam."

He opted for the latter course of action. Sanquist pointed out the small building where he'd seen the chaplain, and Joe headed unsteadily off in that direction.

He was to join 13 other wounded there. They would be threatened but unharmed by the Germans; two would be killed by our own artillery later. Father Sam would be awarded the Distinguished Service Cross for his actions.

By now it was fully dark, but we could determine Allen's route to the locks by the trail of discarded equipment, primarily gas masks. Less than 1,500 yards later, I almost stepped into the foxhole just completed by Lieutenant McNulty. I was cordially invited to spend the night.

Having slept less than three hours in the past 40 or so, I disposed of my followers nearby and accepted his hospitality.

Chapter 14

The Fight at the Locks

McNulty and I were awakened at misty dawn by German 20mm shells spattering mud from the parapet of our foxhole. When the firing lifted, Mac peered cautiously over the edge and made a profound observation.

"Bill, this La Belle France is not so damned La Belle!"

Colonel Johnson had seized the La Barquette locks, one of the 501st objectives, early D-Day morning with some 50 men accumulated from various regimental units. There were no German troops in the immediate area, but the low flatland made the position vulnerable to artillery and mortar fire from higher ground as well as to determined attack by as few as a company of enemy infantry.

Johnson could hear continuing small arms firing to the north, indicating friendly forces engaged within a 1,000 yards or so. When a patrol arrived with word that Major Allen was holding Bse. Addeville on the higher ground in that direction, the colonel withdrew his troops from the locks and headed out to join him, intending to return with a combined force to hold the locks more securely. He arrived in that village shortly before I had reached it with my own patrol.

Allen argued that withdrawal from Bse. Addeville would make the locks position yet more vulnerable to the enemy his men were containing, but Johnson insisted on his own point of view. He took the bulk of Allen's contingent back to the locks, leaving him with a cover force and orders to bring them to the locks at dusk. Since I had by then left the village to occupy the farmhouse where Newman would be wounded, I was unaware of those decisions.

By the time I stumbled into McNulty's foxhole that night, Johnson had

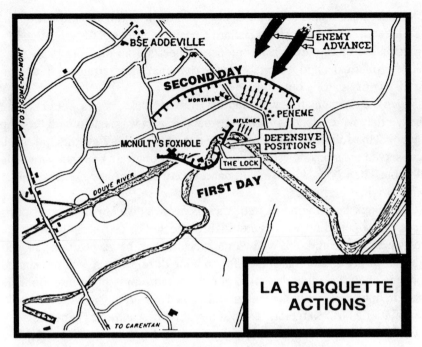

(Adapted from *Rendezvous with Destiny, The History of the 101st Airborne Division,*
enlarged edition (Sweetwater, TN: 101st Airborne Division Assoc., 1948), 145.

some 250 troopers deployed in a shallow U, the bottom of it across the
Douve River on the far side of the locks to the south and the wings extending roughly northeast and northwest. Mac's position was near the end of the
right wing, facing west toward the causeway running south from St. Come-
Du-Mont to Carentan. The 20mm fire harassing us was from enemy dug in
along that causeway, a bit over a mile of flat landscape away.

During the night a small group of Germans had attempted to enter the
perimeter, whether by accident or design. They were readily repulsed, leaving two of their dead behind.

Since one S-2 function is to determine unit identification of any enemy
contacted, I went over to check the bodies for evidence. The first one I
reached had been carrying a "potato masher" grenade with the handle tucked
into the front of his belt. One of the rounds striking him had detonated the
warhead. The gory results of the blast convinced me there was no real point
in searching his front pockets.

What no one at the locks knew at the moment was that a battalion of the
German 6th Parachute Regiment was approaching from the northeast, to the
rear of our defensive perimeter. They were withdrawing from the Utah

beachhead area, sticking to the marshy lowlands with the intention of reaching Carentan. They had skirted Ballard's position earlier in the morning, losing 20 killed or captured in the process. They had no idea the locks were held by Americans and were laboring across the soggy terrain without benefit of security patrols out front.

When the Germans first were spotted from the locks, no one could be sure whether they were friend or foe. Once that question was settled with the help of binoculars, Johnson hastily redeployed the bulk of his force, including all crew-served weapons, to face the oncoming but unaware German parachute battalion. The troops with McNulty and I were among the few left in place on the original perimeter.

Our troops held their fire until the enemy was well within small arms range, then opened up with demoralizing effect. The Germans returned the fire as best they could, but we had the advantage of better positions as well as initial surprise. The fight raged for an hour, during which Johnson started worrying about the rapid depletion of our limited supply of ammunition. He also felt, however, that the enemy morale was deteriorating and that he could hear faint cries of "Kamerad" from some of them wanting to surrender.

In view of these developments, the colonel ordered a cease-fire and asked for two volunteers, one man who could speak German and another who would carry an orange flag used to identify American troops during the invasion. The three of them started out toward the enemy lines, only to crawl back after firing from both sides broke out again.

Less than an hour later, he tried again. This time, two wounded Germans met him with hands in the air, explaining that most did want to surrender, but that officers had been shooting those who voiced such intentions. Johnson sent one of them back to their battalion commander with an ultimatum. "Surrender within the next thirty minutes or our superior forces will wipe you out." Or words to that effect. The ploy worked. Twenty minutes later, small groups of enemy started straggling out with hands clasped behind their heads and weapons left behind. By 6:00, even the battalion commander had joined the growing procession, insisting on his right to "negotiate" the surrender. His demands were not honored; he had waited far too long.

Oddly, those of us who had remained on the other side of the restructured perimeter knew very little of what was happening only a few hundred yards away. My personal participation in the battle consisted of carrying mortar rounds from our immediate area to the gun pits in the center of our position. Since enemy artillery fire from the direction of Carentan kept coming in, I did not dawdle in completing my task. I never so much as glimpsed the enemy we were fighting in the process.

Altogether, some 350 Germans were captured at a cost of 10 Americans killed and 20 or so wounded. While there was no accurate count of the enemy dead left in the marshes, it was estimated to be another 150. It was the most significant victory for the 501st to date.

As those surrendering entered our perimeter, they were herded together behind a little stone house in a small orchard. Unfortunately, the growing crowd was observed by German gunners on the high ground near Carentan who may have assumed they were Americans. In any event, they opened up with 88mm guns and mortars. The first barrage killed or wounded 13 of the prisoners. A subsequent shell killed Captain MacReynolds, our regimental adjutant, who was organizing the holding compound.

Ever since arriving at Bse. Addeville the day before, Johnson had been calling by radio for Ballard to bring the 2nd Battalion to the locks. Even though actively engaged with the enemy near the DZ, Ballard attempted to comply. He started a patrol along the same route I had taken at dawn to see if it would be possible to circumvent the intervening enemy positions. The intensity of fire it received in the vicinity of my favorite pond proved that route was firmly closed to further travel. Throughout D-Day and D+1, the severely understrength 2nd Battalion fought against superior forces while Johnson continued to call for their help at the locks. Then they were ordered to form the general reserve for a dawn attack on St. Come-Du-Mont by the 3rd Battalion 501st plus two battalions of the 506th Regiment and one of the 327th Glider Infantry Regiment. Eight light tanks from the beach were to support the assault. Thus Johnson and his victors of La Barquette were left at the locks, ducking German artillery fire but facing no more ground troop attacks throughout D+2. I was not to rejoin Ballard's staff until the following day.

The attack on St. Come-Du-Mont had succeeded in driving all remaining enemy south toward Carentan. When I finally caught up with the 2nd Battalion, they were preparing to march to billets in the village of Vierville, just north of St. Come-Du-Mont. McNulty's platoon was leading, so I hiked along beside him. We were so busy recalling our respective D-Day experiences that we overshot the road where we should have turned right. By the time the error was realized, the head of the column had reached "Dead Man's Corner," the junction of our road with the one running south across the causeway to Carentan. It was so named because of the light tank still sitting in the intersection with a hole the size of a softball in its side. The commander had been killed by the panzerfaust rocket,which had stopped it there during the attack by the 501st 3rd Battalion.

While waiting for things to be sorted out, Mac and I sat shoulder to shoulder on the right side of the road, leaning comfortably against the mossy bank of the paralleling hedgerow. A company of 101st troops was skirmishing against a German rear guard unit some 300 yards away in the low ground flanking the causeway. There was a lone house well beyond the enemy's position.

Suddenly a single bullet buried itself energetically into the mossy bank precisely between our heads. Hardly a spent round, it obviously had been damned well aimed! Mac and I slid promptly into the ditch at our feet. A sergeant equipped with binoculars flattened himself against the opposite hedgerow and studied the scene below.

"I see the bastard!" he yelled. "He's shooting from a second floor window of that house! He shoots and then ducks away!"

I had acquired a discarded Springfield rifle en route from the locks, a weapon considered much more accurate than the M-1 for long-range sniping. So I assumed a prone position next to the sergeant and had him identify the window concerned, then set the rear leaf sight for 500-yard range.

"I've got a bead on the window," I advised. "Just let me know when he pops up again."

Seconds later the sergeant said, "There is he is!" and I squeezed off a round.

"You got him!" the sergeant exulted.

I knew it was unlikely that I had so much as hit anywhere near the window and that the odds of clobbering a human head at 500 yards with an unzeroed rifle were ridiculously remote. But who was I to disclaim a feat that so obviously boosted troop morale? I modestly acknowledged the plaudits of all who accepted the sergeant's assessment of results.

The battalion ended up enjoying several days of recuperation in Vierville. Early on during that interval, I reminded myself of the S-2's duty to collect any enemy documents available. Taking several section scouts, I set out to find the former enemy headquarters in St. Come-Du-Mont. While I could recall some words from my two years of high school French, they did not include the one for "headquarters." But I figured I could always improvise.

Stopping a civilian on the street, I asked, *"Ou est le chambre de le Boche Commandant?"* At first I wasn't sure he understood my French, but when I'd repeated the question twice, his puzzled look cleared up.

"Ah, le chambre de le Boche Commandant!" (It sounded somewhat different coming from him.) He motioned us to follow and led us to a house in an obviously residential section which he indicated dramatically was, *"Le chambre de le Boche Commandant!"*

He accompanied us as we barged into the house and led us up a staircase where he pointed to a closed door. *"Le chambre de le Boche Commandant!"*

I shoved it open and charged in, followed by my Geronimos. The only occupant was an exceptionally attractive young female in a slinky black negligee supine on a four-poster bed.

The reaction of my scouts was an enthusiastic chorus of "Search her! Search her!" It was clear to me, however, that she could not possibly be concealing any German documents in that outfit. Nor were there any other items of Intelligence interest in the room or the rest of the home. But there was no doubt in my mind that we had, indeed, found the chamber formerly occupied by the German commander.

Chapter 15

Taking Carentan

While recuperating in the billeting area, the battalion grew in strength as troopers landing astray on the jump came trickling back, each with his own tale of survival. Lost weapons were replaced and basic loads of ammo restored. We were ready to continue the war.

Meanwhile, the 101st Airborne Division had been ordered to capture Carentan, the largest town on the Cotentin Peninsula aside from the port of Cherbourg at the northern tip. Carentan had a population of only 4,000, but it boasted four highways and three rail lines serving the area. It also offered the best routes of approach for any German counterattack from the south aimed at denying the junction of Utah and Omaha bridgeheads.

The attack on Carentan started in the pre-dawn hours of June 10, D+4. The 502nd Parachute Regiment attempted to proceed directly down the causeway from St. Come-du-Mont. It was a miserable route of approach, featuring four bridges, one of which had been partially destroyed by the Germans. And the last half mile of the causeway was virtually devoid of cover from fire by strong enemy positions to the right, despite preliminary reports that the town would be lightly defended.

The 327th Glider Infantry Regiment crossed the Douve River well to the east of Carentan that same night and started their attack toward the town along the south side of the stream. They, too, found heavy going against well-prepared opposition.

The 502nd took horrendous losses, and, despite launching the first bayonet attack by American forces during the invasion, was stopped well short of Carentan. The 327th also failed to attain the optimistic objectives of its attack on that first day of fierce fighting.

The next day, Sunday, D+5, we learned that our regiment and the 506th would spearhead the final attack on Carentan. It was to kick off at dawn the next morning with our regimental objective being Hill 30, the high ground beyond and east of the town. The 506th, having relieved the 502nd in the positions it had attained, would help take the same high ground from the west if all went well in attacking the town itself.

The 501st would attack with two battalions abreast, the 3rd on the right and us on the left. To reach Hill 30, our battalion would have to cross the Canal De Vire Et Taute and its flooded approaches. Rubber assault boats were brought forward for that crossing.

I still vividly recall the first stages of our attack, the lead troops struggling to drag the heavy boats through waist-deep marsh en route to the canal. Enemy mortar rounds sent up geysers of water around and among them resulting in cries of "Medic!" from many wounded. Up ahead, H Company of the 3rd Battalion, having taken a somewhat easier route, was struggling up the base of Hill 30 under heavy fire.

I was with the battalion command group immediately behind the attacking units. The entire battalion was effectively pinned down. Feeling I had nothing of significance to contribute to the attack, I took some of my S-2 scouts and sidled off to the right, intending to gauge any threat of enemy attack from that flank. Passage of the 3rd Battalion through their zone had left no friendly troops between us and the adjacent buildings of Carentan.

The route I took reached the Vire Canal several hundred yards north of where our battalion was supposed to cross it in the boats. There was a railroad bridge at the spot, known to have been blown by the Germans. I was surprised to find that only part of it had fallen into the water and that an easy six-foot jump from the near bank made it readily passable. (Much later I learned that H Company had used the bridge to get to the base of Hill 30.)

We crossed into Carentan unopposed. A number of buildings were burning from artillery fire as we warily made our way deeper into the town, poised to return fire from any direction. We shortly were "reinforced" by a peg-legged Frenchman, obviously a World War I veteran, who stumped along behind the patrol waving a bottle of wine and singing, "It's a long way to Tipperary" in broken English.

Suddenly a ground-level window of a building to my right was thrust open. I whirled to engage any target emerging, only to see a young mother carrying a runny-nosed baby crawl out. She rushed up, holding her child out to kiss me on the cheek. It was a nice gesture, even though neither the kid nor I enjoyed it all that much.

Just a block or so farther, we rounded a corner to meet some 506th troopers coming into town. Leaving our French reinforcement to continue his celebrating with them, we headed back to the battalion. It was still pinned down short of the designated canal-crossing area.

I flopped down beside the CO and advised, perhaps too casually, "There's a bridge over there, Colonel, where we can cross without getting wet."

His reply carried a slight note of exasperation: "Well, Sefton, why don't you just show me where it is?" (Looking back over the years, I should have reported the passability of the bridge promptly upon determining it. At the time, however, it simply did not occur to me that Ballard would consider abandoning the assigned crossing point in the interest of expediency. So much for being a junior officer in his first days of combat operations.)

To the best of my recollection, the entire battalion ended up crossing the railroad bridge and sweeping south astride the highway leaving Carentan toward the village of Le Billonnerie just beyond Hill 30, which was already under control of the 3rd Battalion. We found that area rather hotly contested by counterattacking enemy units.

We took over the hedgerows flanking the highway on both sides of the village, entering immediately into fire fights with the enemy. The battalion staff group was observing the action from the second floor of a house immediately overlooking the fighting on the left side of the road. Colonel Ballard and the mortar platoon leader, Lieutenant Bill Russo, were leaning out a window, noting targets to be engaged. Major Bottomly and Captain Pelham were likewise surveying the battlefield.

Seriously doubting that all of the approaching Germans were blind, I suggested to Ballard the likelihood of their imminent reaction to our obvious exposure. (After all, an S-2 is supposed to evaluate enemy capabilities.) His reply was merely a glance which caused me to wonder if he felt I was becoming a "Nervous Nellie."

My hunch that disaster was about to befall grew stronger by the second and was promptly verified by an 88mm shell demolishing the roof above us. Although I was standing nearest the head of the stairwell at the moment, all four of the others passed me before I could hit the first step going down. Pelham was particularly spry in the descent, being motivated by a slight nick on his jaw from a small fragment of shell or debris.

We established the battalion CP in another house across the highway as the troops completed digging in against further counterattacks, which started in earnest the next day. Hitler had ordered his army commander in Normandy to retake Carentan, using a fresh SS Panzergrenadier division in addition to the other units we had been fighting. Their objective was to drive the 101st back to the Utah beachhead.

SS troops hit us aggressively just as we were launching an early morning attack of our own. The fighting was fierce and fluid. A tree burst shredded the nerves in one of Lieutenant McNulty's wrists, putting him out of the battle and subsequently the war. His platoon sergeant, Joe Bass, was knocked down by a rifle round that went through his helmet. He put his hand to his head and withdrew it covered with blood. The blood also covered some small lumps of gray dirt he had acquired while crawling around. His dazed first impression was that the lumps had come from inside his head.

"They always told me I didn't have any brains," he told me later, "but there they were, right in my hand!" Joe survived the war, winning a DSC before being killed in Korea.

The attack shattered F Company's position, but elements of Headquarters Company stopped it at the next hedgerow. My S-2 scout, Allan Hurd, was shot through the shoulder in that rallying action.

On learning a number of F Company men had withdrawn beyond the Headquarters Company line, I went back toward Carentan to find them. German artillery was pounding the highway, so I stuck to the fields alongside, scrambling over hedgerows in the process. In one such instance, I landed on the far side only to find a German machine-gunner aiming directly at me from some 30 yards away. Fortunately for me, he had been shot neatly through the forehead and died while sighting over the gun.

Just short of Carentan, I found 1st Sergeant Hershel Parks rounding up his F Company men who had ended up in that area; he was heading them back toward the lines. So I returned to the battalion CP, ducking artillery bursts en route. The fire fights were still raging when I arrived.

D Company was heavily engaged on the west side of the highway some 300 yards beyond the CP. Deciding to get a close-up reading on their situation, I started up a shallow ditch paralleling a hedgerow that intersected the one from which they were firing at the enemy holding the hedgerow just beyond. The ditch would bring me to the left flank of their position. It was less than half a foot deep. The hedgerow it paralleled was on my immediate left. To my right, the side of the ditch sloped gently up to the edge of the field it bordered. If I raised my head at all, it was at eye level with a flat expanse of short grass.

About 100 yards short of D Company's position, I reached a point where the zone of interdictory machine-gun fire was plunging into the ditch. It was obviously unobserved and coming from some distance beyond the front lines, but it kept striking the same yard of ground just ahead of me in short, sporadic bursts, at an erratic pace.

I could never later recall how many times I steeled myself to cross that beaten zone. I remember vividly, however, that in each instance the plunging fire resumed precisely as I was set for the attempt, leaving me with less and less desire to continue my self-imposed mission of reaching the front line hedgerow.

Suddenly two troopers were rushing back from D Company toward me. They were running upright alongside the ditch, each clutching the upper arm of a comrade who had been shot through his head or neck. The sun was shining on the bright red blood streaming down through his hair as his toes bounced along the ground behind the racing pair. The imagery of horses pulling a Roman chariot flashed through my mind, followed immediately by the realization that they were but a few remaining paces from where the interdictory machine-gun bursts were once again ripping into the ground.

The most recent burst ended just as they hit the beaten zone, and they dashed on toward the rear. In the brief glimpse I had of the casualty as they passed, he appeared comatose, if not already dead.

Had I been assigned the mission of getting up to D Company, I would like to think that I would have kept trying. As it was, I turned meekly around and crawled back to the battalion CP. In retrospect, it was the first time since landing in Normandy that I asked myself, "Is this trip really necessary?" Up to now, my mind had simply blocked out the horrors of combat in the interest of accomplishing the jobs for which we had trained so intensively. In this particular instance, the instinct of self-preservation had prevailed.

Late that afternoon we were reinforced by Sherman tanks of the 2nd Armored Division, fresh from the beach and ordered to attack. The tankers were magnificent! The commanders stood upright in their turrets as they rammed through the hedgerows with our troopers following like chicks behind mother hens. The Germans broke and retreated with our combined force in hot pursuit. We drove them 2½ miles before stopping.

Carentan was not to be threatened by counterattack again.

Chapter 16

On Static Defense

We ended up on the near edge of a gentle valley with the Germans on the other side, a mile or so away. The highway we had been astride since Carentan ran straight as a die from us to them with the usual pattern of hedgerows on each side of it. It was nearly dusk when we arrived and set up defensive positions.

Lieutenant Ed Allworth, our battalion adjutant, suggested we dig a slit trench for the night together. He had picked a site immediately behind a hedgerow a couple of hundred yards behind the rifle company positions. We started to hack at the rooty soil with our entrenching tools. It was going to be hard work, and I was already very weary. It was a good time to remember my S-2 responsibilities.

"Gee, Ed, I've gotta go see how the section is coming along on the observation post. But I'll get back as soon as I can."

Work on the OP did, indeed, seem to warrant supervision; but I had every confidence Ed would proceed on the slit trench without me. The job of S-1 in combat tended to make any battalion adjutant appreciate the perils of enemy mortar and artillery fire. He was four feet down and going strong by the time I returned to render what little help was required. Neither of us had any trouble falling soundly asleep in the completed slit trench.

I was awakened at dawn by Ed jabbing me in the ribs and pointing at the six-inch trunk of a tree lying across the open top of our shelter instead of growing out of the hedgerow where it was when we had retired. It had been sheared off by an artillery round during the night and missed plunging butt-first into our hole by less than two feet. The fact that neither of us had been awakened by the blast was convincing testimony to the depth of fatigue combat can engender.

There is a military axiom to the effect that the only constant in combat is confusion. This was illustrated by an incident I did not personally witness, but which was so widely related as to give it considerable credence.

It seems one of our machine-gun teams in the new defensive position was still soundly asleep that first dawn when a German NCO in dress uniform awakened them with a tirade regarding their negligence. He apparently was returning from a sojourn to the rear, unaware that the front had suddenly moved 2½ miles in his direction, and thought he was berating a German gun crew in the early morning twilight. His second mistake was in trying to make a run for it when he realized his error.

The respective front lines continued to remain a mile apart, well beyond small arms range, so action was limited to exchanges of mortar and artillery fire. One morning I came across Lieutenant Russo stretched out on a vantage point alongside the highway, peering down the road through binoculars. Curious, I flopped down beside him.

He had been watching occasional enemy dispatch riders motorcycling several hundred yards along the distant reaches of the highway before turning onto a side road. One of his 81mm mortars had been registered on a specific spot on their route just short of the turnoff, and he was in radio contact with the gunners standing by at their weapons.

Within moments, another rider came into view. Russo guessed at his speed for about three seconds, then barked a command, "Fire one!" We could hear the mortar in the rear cough as the high trajectory round started on its 20-second journey. When it landed, it blew the rider off his machine! Sniping with a mortar? If I hadn't seen it happen, I would never have believed it.

As the static situation continued, the troops kept improving their individual positions, extending and elaborating foxholes to include sleeping room and overhead protection. I recall one featuring a hand-printed sign, "For Sale — Dirt Cheap." Aside from that, they had little to do beyond avoiding incoming shells. Something akin to boredom was becoming evident.

About halfway between us and the Germans, there was a lone house along the highway, visible well above the intervening hedgerows. Suspecting the enemy might be manning it as an observation post, I asked Colonel Ballard if I could take a combat patrol and seize it for our own use in that regard.

"Sure, Sefton. Just ask for some volunteers."

It took all of five minutes to find 20+ Geronimos looking for something to do. We set off tactically but briskly to negotiate the hedgerows between our outpost line and the house, encountering no opposition en route. If there had been any Germans observing from there, they must have been sufficiently impressed by our number to make discretion the better part of valor. The fact that we attracted no mortar or artillery fire indicated we had arrived unobserved.

It was a very fine house, indeed, two stories high and solidly built. The only problem lay in the fact that all ground floor means of entrance were on the sides facing the highway and German lines. Any observation team we established there would have no means of withdrawing safely if attacked. I radioed back for a demolition team. Lieutenant Jesse Tidwell arrived with his men in short order, carrying a container the size and shape of a foot locker.

"So what's this mission, Sefton?"

"Well, Jesse, I need a 'mouse hole' blown in the back wall of that house so our observers can crawl in and out without exposing themselves to the Krauts."

The house was shaped like a shoe box with the wide front side facing the highway. The wall I indicated was on the narrower end toward our lines. Jesse's men propped their container against an appropriate spot a foot or two off the ground.

"Whatcha got in that thing, Jesse?"

"Oh, this is our demo charge."

"A bit on the heavy side, isn't it?"

"Naw, this is a brick house."

With that he pulled on a wire extending from the container, and they all took off running hard as a thin wisp of smoke appeared. I was lying against a bordering hedgerow some 25 yards to the side and wondering about their hasty departure when the charge went off.

There was a horrendous flash and roar, followed by timbers and chunks of masonry soaring impressively aloft. I immediately realized that all of those objects would soon be starting back down.

Back at the battalion CP, Ballard thought we had run afoul of a booby-trapped ammo dump!

The soaring debris attained its apex and seemed to come raining back down for minutes. Fortunately, none of the patrol members were struck by anything larger than the size of a walnut, but everyone on the downwind side was coated from head to foot with black dust.

The only parts of the house left standing were the far wall on the other narrower end and ragged remnants of the sidewalls extending from it. When I revisited the site 45 years later, not even those vestiges remained.

Somewhere along the way since Carentan, our battalion supply officer, Lieutenant Jerry Mullins, had acquired a big German army motorcycle.

Lieutenant Colonel Robert A. Ballard who led the 2nd Battalion in Normandy and Holland. He assumed command of the regiment in Bastogne and ended his military career as a major general, Florida National Guard. (Photo, courtesy of Mark Bando, 501st PIR Historian)

While I had occasionally rented motor scooters in civilian life, I'd never ful-
filled my desire to ride a full-sized machine. It was obvious to me that this
one could hardly be used for hauling supplies, but it would be ideal as an
S-2 reconnaissance vehicle. Not really expecting Mullins to agree with me,
however, I decided on a more subtle approach.

"That's really a beauty, Jerry! Does it work the same way as the Harley I
had back home?"

"Of course it does. Lemme show ya." With which he proceeded to
demonstrate starting, accelerating, and braking procedures.

"Mind if I take a little spin?"

"Naw, go right ahead."

I climbed aboard the beast and got off to a jerky start, but felt downright
adept after a couple of laps around the field. Then, giving the former pos-
sessor a friendly wave, I yelled, "Be seein' ya, Jerry!" and roared off through
a gap in the hedgerow made by a tank. It really did make more sense to have
the bike for S-2 operations.

Besides which, I outranked him.

Chapter 17

Winding Down

Shortly thereafter, on June 26, the 501st was ordered to a tactical bivouac area 15 miles south of Cherbourg as an advance element of the 101st Airborne Division. American VII Corps had by now captured the port and were mopping up remnants of German units still holding out on the tip of the peninsula well northwest of the city itself.

Three days later, the entire division — including the 501st — moved up to just south of Cherbourg. The mission was to defend against any highly unlikely enemy attack from the south, there being no German units of any significance left on the peninsula in that direction.

By this time I was majorly in love with the motorbike, having ridden merrily up and down the truck convoys to our new positions. In justifying its use for S-2 missions, I took Section Sergeant Pop Dornick on a meandering tour of the area in search of any German documents overlooked by the VII Corps victors.

We were puttering along on a narrow farm lane with Pop astride the seat behind me. The lane ran along a limestone base, covered by a few inches of slimy mud. The rock tended to break off into shallow shelves paralleling the direction the lane was taking. Unexpectedly, the front wheel slipped off one such ledge while the rear wheel remained at the three-inch-higher level, and I was suddenly going 180 degrees in the opposite direction. It struck me as a humorous development.

"Howdja like that turn, Pop?" I asked with a laugh. No answer. I looked back to see my section chief sitting in the slimy mud precisely where the change in direction had occurred. He was voicing numerous remarks quite audible above the sound of the motorcycle. Most of them had to do with my biking techniques, but several touched on my ancestry as well.

We never did find any overlooked documents, but one of my scouts later came across an automatic rifle of particularly interesting design. It may well have been a Russian weapon because some German units in Normandy actually were comprised of Georgians who had defected to the Nazis, apparently preferring to fight for Hitler rather than for Stalin. In any event, we took it down to the beach to see how it worked.

I was driving a jeep along a narrow dirt trail leading to the ocean. There were German *"Achtung Minen"* signs warning of anti-personnel mines in the fields alongside, but American white cloth engineer tape on each side of the trail indicated it had been swept for vehicular land mines. When we were yet a good hundred yards short of the beach, I had one of those sudden hunches that said, "Stop right here."

So I did, offering only the terse comment that we were going to walk the rest of the way. We fired the strange weapon into the sea, learning only that it worked, and I backed the jeep out to the start of the trail as we returned.

The next day an American soldier wandered into a mine field bordering the trail we had used and was killed by a "Bouncing Betty" mine that sprang three feet into the air when triggered and sprayed him with the steel balls it contained. A jeepload of medics went racing to the site. Ten feet beyond the spot where we had stopped, a land mine blew them all into the hereafter.

I was to experience a number of such hunches in subsequent combat situations and never failed to observe their warnings.

As we sat tactically twiddling our thumbs, combat rations were becoming less and less popular with the consumers. Ballard, ever concerned with troop morale, assigned me an oddball mission.

"Sefton, take a jeep and trailer back to the beachhead and scrounge us some of that good Navy food."

My initial move was to drive back to the areas where we had fought those first two days and salvage every piece of German equipment I could find. This included discarded enemy gas masks, parts of uniforms, ammo pouches, a few bayonets, and an occasional shoulder weapon. There was also a goodly number of German helmets which I made sure sported a hole from a shot with my carbine before tossing each into the trailer.

In the course of my scavenging, I went down a farm lane bordered on each side by the ubiquitous hedgerows. A grave for a German soldier had been dug into the side of the one on my right. His comrades had carved a wooden headboard featuring his name, rank, decorations received, and date of birth and demise. I was genuinely touched by such evidence of their painstaking regard for a brother-in-arms; then I noticed the toe of a boot protruding at the foot of the grave. It seemed they had been forced to withdraw before digging it any deeper.

No, I did not attempt to add the boot to my growing trailerload.

The trailer was almost full when I happened to look into a foxhole and discovered a European hedgehog, a cousin to our American porcupine, which had fallen in and couldn't climb out. On impulse, I scooped it up carefully with my entrenching tool, deposited it in the trailer, and departed for the beachhead.

The beach was a beehive of activity, but I managed to find the driver of a DUCK, an amphibious cargo vehicle, willing to take me and the trailer out to a fairly sizable naval craft riding at anchor in the distance. When he understood the purpose of my visit, the skipper gladly hoisted the trailer aboard and summoned his officers to the bargaining table.

We sat in a circle on an upper deck as I presented the "Invasion Combat Souvenirs" one at a time. It was evident from the start that the officers' respective craving for something to show the folks back home was exceeded only by the ship's larder of choice edibles with which to dicker the deals.

Within half-an-hour we'd agreed on enough cases of goodies that the infantry never sees in combat to fill my trailer to the heaping point. My stock of combat souvenirs being exhausted, it was time to bring out the hedgehog.

"What th'hell is THAT?"

"Why, Cap'n, this is a European hedgehog, fightin'est animal in the world. Can lick its weight in wildcats! And for just three more cases of those canned peaches, you can be the only ship in the Navy that has one for a mascot."

"What do we feed it?"

"Just about any table scraps you have on hand." (Not a bad spur-of-the-moment answer, considering I hadn't the foggiest idea of its dining preferences.)

"Okay. Three more cases of peaches."

The Navy helped me tie down the overload in the trailer, and I returned to the battalion in triumph with more than a quarter-ton of their dietary delicacies. I would like to think the exploit had nothing to do with the high rating subsequently registered on my Officer's Efficiency Report, but then it probably didn't hurt it any, either.

On July 9 we were alerted to prepare for return to England. The notice also specified that no German army vehicles were to be taken along. So I posed a theoretical question to Colonel Ballard.

"Sir, what would happen if we got back to England and discovered a motorcycle like this one mixed in with our battalion equipment?"

"Oh, Sefton, I'd have a nice motorcycle and you'd have a court-martial."

End of discussion. I would have to leave it at the beach.

The next day the entire division was loaded on truck convoys, ready to head south in a prescribed schedule of unit serials. Our battalion was drawn up on a side road, waiting to be inserted into the stream passing by on the highway. When the proper moment arrived, Ballard pulled out in the lead vehicle but was followed by only six of our trucks before another battalion, arriving early, cut into our column.

By the time I learned what had happened, Ballard was several miles away, thinking all of the trucks following immediately behind carried his command. It was a great excuse to roar after him on the motorcycle and advise him of the situation. He had our six trucks pull off to the side and told me to go bring up the others.

I was going down a long hill on the return trip when the motorcycle started to sway. The rear tire was going flat! There was nothing to do except pull off to the side where a lone GI from some infantry unit happened to be watching the convoys go by.

"Hey, soldier, how about holding this thing steady for a minute?"

I unstrapped my carbine and musette bag from in back of the seat just in time to flag down Major Allen coming along in the jeep. I jumped in and waved goodbye to the soldier, still holding the handlebars of the German motorcycle.

The rest of the battalion caught up of its own accord, and our column arrived at the beach intact. It was the end of our part in the invasion and of my love affair with motorbiking.

Chapter 18

Summer in England

The 501st Regiment had jumped into Normandy with 168 officers and 2,175 enlisted men. On July 13 we landed back in England having lost 213 killed in action or mortally wounded, 490 who were to survive wounds or injuries, and 195 missing or captured for a total of 898 — a bit over 38 percent of the command.

The casualty rate, as is normal in infantry combat, was highest among company grade officers, platoon leaders in particular. I was missing a painful number of close comrades among those left behind.

Upon reaching our pre-invasion billets on the Craven estate near Newbury, leaves and furloughs became the order of the day. Most of the officers took their leaves immediately. Ed Allworth and I opted to take ours when they had returned. I was put in temporary command of F Company for the interim.

One of the more onerous chores for unit commanders was that of censoring the troopers' outgoing mail. In discharging that responsibility, I found myself scanning two letters by the same man, one addressed to his wife and the other to his fiancée in towns 50 miles apart! Knowing I had thus become aware of his situation, he came to my office of his own accord to discuss it.

He was a most unlikely looking Lothario, young, freckle-faced, and obviously in an emotional quandary. I did not press him for details as to how he had gotten himself into the mess, but I did ask how he intended to resolve it.

"There's only one thing for me to do, Lieutenant. I've gotta get myself killed in our next operation." Which he did, by walking into an open field in Holland and challenging a German tank with a bazooka, according to his buddies. It was too late to wish I had violated the confidence of our discussion by disclosing it to Father Sam when he returned from his leave. He might well have counseled the lad toward a less permanent solution.

For several weeks before D-Day, Ed Allworth and I were among a number of regimental officers who had dated nurses assigned to a hospital unit some 40 miles from Newbury. That unit was now at the southern shore of England, staging for movement to France. It seemed to us an excellent idea to spend our upcoming leaves there.

The lovely village of Seaton was on the sea in the shire of Devon. We rented a bedroom in a lobster fisherman's cottage with a trellis of red roses in full bloom forming an arch over the short walkway leading to the front entrance. It was easy to establish rapport with the elderly lobsterman. He was a pipe smoker, as was I, and a gift of my tobacco proved much preferable to any available to him in wartime England. His wife, however, remained unthawed by our Yankee charm.

We promptly located our nurse friends and settled in to enjoy our leaves. Never having swum in the ocean, I was intrigued by the action of the four-foot waves breaking on the sharply shelving beach. It would be great fun to don my trunks and sit down amongst 'em. Su-u-u-u-ure it would!

As I would soon learn, each wave breaking on the gravelly beach created a brisk undertow. Within seconds, I was being tumbled tail over teacup in rapid succession, unable to break to the surface for air. The idiocy of drowning after surviving Normandy flashed through my mind before both feet found the bottom, permitting an upward lunge through the waves and enough frantic strokes to reach shore. I was bleeding from a dozen minor cuts inflicted by the sharp stones and fully disaffected of any further desire to swim in the Straits of Dover.

After the four of us had dinner the next evening, my date and I opted for a stroll along the beach in the long summer twilight. It was well after dark by the time we ended up at her quarters, and I headed back to the lobsterman's cottage. It was a bit of a surprise to find Ed and our luggage awaiting me on the sidewalk.

It seemed that he and his friend had returned to our room, only to have the host's wife intrude in high dudgeon and cast them out forthwith.

"Hell, Bill, we were just sitting there talking without so much as having our shoes off!" he maintained indignantly.

"Sure, Ed. Let's go find a hotel that's still open."

The leave ended all too soon, and we were back to duty on the battalion staff. My wounded scout, Allan Hurd, had not yet returned from the hospital, so I found out its location and went to visit him. He was fully recovered but was not being released for an interesting reason.

"You've gotta get me outta here, Lieutenant. The nurses are trying to get me transferred over as a ward boy!"

"We won't let 'em do that, Hurd. By the way, how did you happen to get hit?" (Having already heard the story, I was interested in his version.

"Well, they were comin' across the field at us, and I 'boloed' on the rifle range, ya know, so I was kneelin' on top of the hedgerow to get better shots and they musta got wind of me."

It was true that he had once failed to qualify in firing for record with his rifle during training, but in combat he was to dispatch an inordinate number of enemy by making sure of shots not apt to miss. There was no way we would surrender him to a hospital for duty as a ward boy, his soft voice and friendly, helpful manners notwithstanding. He was back with the S-2 section shortly thereafter.

I also located the hospital where Lieutenant Malek was being treated for his massive "friendly fire" wounds. A salvo from a Navy destroyer supporting our battalion had fallen 200 yards short on D+1, killing or wounding nearly a dozen F Company personnel preparing to launch an attack. I wasn't sure the guy on the bed was Leo Malek until I heard him speak.

His formerly robust frame was reduced by some 40 pounds. The skin on his face seemed stretched against the bones beneath. He invited me to stick my hand through the ten-inch gap between the calf muscles and shinbone of one leg, but I declined the offer. He was eager for details concerning the combat he had missed. In filling him in, I recited the litany of all other casualties among our mutual friends. His most memorable comment was, "And you got back safely, huh?"

I was not to see Leo again until attending a 101st Airborne Association Chapter fling one weekend in New Jersey, *circa* 1970. His very first question was, "Are you rich?" He obviously expected to hear that my lucky star had continued shining. He walked with a limp and had undergone an operation two years prior to remove a final piece of jump boot still in one ankle, previously overlooked in other surgeries. When I tried to contact him a few years later, I learned he had died.

By July 25, we were back to full training routine in preparation for our next mission, wherever and whenever. The schedules were intensive, but we did have Sundays off. On one such morning, I was relaxing in my tent when Colonel Johnson came striding down officer's row growling, "Awright, who wants to make a jump?"

Twelve us were too slow in sneaking away under the backs of our tents. It seemed the CO had established social relations with an English landowner a few miles away and wanted to give his family a demonstration of parachuting techniques. His jeep driver would spread a yellow equipment chute in a field in front of their manor as a target. We would split into four three-man teams, each jumper putting an English pound note in the kitty to be awarded to the team that landed a man closest to the chute. Johnson would jump last as a one-man entrant in the contest.

By the time we boarded the C-47 he had arranged for, a number of the other officers were insisting that if the Colonel wanted to jump as a one-man team, he should put three pounds in the kitty for the privilege. He finally agreed. We circled the target field a time or two, and then the first team made its jump.

Lieutenant Jim Patton would lead the next team. A big, good looking officer, he was standing in the door looking ahead under the wing for the target chute. He didn't know the pilot had adjusted the course to the left, having noted the first jumpers had drifted more to the right than anticipated. Jim was still trying to spot the chute when the green light beside the door indicated the plane was abeam of the target.

Johnson, standing beside the two team members near the door, yelled, "Green light, Patton, jump!" He had overlooked the fact that he couldn't possibly be heard over the roar of the slipstream. His next action was to grab the overhead cable in both hands, scream, "Dammit, I said JUMP!" and boot Jim vigorously out of the plane! His two teammates did not wait for such incentive.

The remaining three-man teams made their respective jumps on the next two passes over the field. One of them (not mine) landed a man squarely on the yellow chute. Then it was the Colonel's turn. He had the pilot drop to 300 feet altitude. It was a lovely summer day with the sun creating a gentle updraft as it reflected from the field. When his chute opened, he neglected to look up and check the canopy, which had one suspension line looped over the top, giving it the characteristic double bulge suggesting an ample female bosom.

The minor defect was not increasing the very slow rate of his descent, but I felt it was inappropriate for a regimental commander to appear negligent of correct jump procedures so I yelled, "You've got a 'Mae West,' Colonel!"

He might have corrected it by flicking his risers. Instead, he pulled the ring of his reserve chute which promptly fell straight down below his feet. Although now less then 150 feet from the ground, he pulled it up and threw the armload of nylon straight out with the same result. With hardly 50 feet to go, he pulled it up again and this time threw it upward, only to have it cover him completely!

He was still clawing at it like a cat in a bag when he landed gently on one leg a few yards from where I was standing. Finally freeing his head from its folds, he glared at me, demanding, "What're ya tryin' to do, Sefton, SCARE ME?"

Obviously I had missed a golden opportunity to keep my mouth shut!

Following their return from Normandy, all airborne divisions in the European Theater had been assigned to the First Allied Airborne Army. They were to plan for 13 different operations before we finally jumped into Holland on September 17.

For two of those, which were to be aborted, we actually went to the marshaling areas prepared to take off. The first one was dubbed Operation Serin, a serin being a European thrush. We were to jump at Chartres, short of Paris, but Patton's tanks got there first. Our division commander, Major General Maxwell Taylor, addressed the assembled troops upon learning the operation had been canceled.

"Men," he consoled, "don't be disappointed. I promise you another mission!"

He was a brilliant general, but quite a bit short on the enlisted man's point of view. He obviously felt that every trooper shared his regard for further combat experience as an asset to military career advancement.

Our second trip to the marshaling area involved a proposed jump into Belgium, just behind the Maginot Line. Again, the ground troops made our trip unnecessary. On September 16, however, we were marshaled for Operation Market-Garden, the liberation of Holland.

Our English summer had ended.

Chapter 19

Jumping into Holland

It would be the largest airborne assault in history. Two American divisions and a British division, with a Polish brigade in Reserve, were to seize and hold bridges and other critical points along 60+ miles of the highway from Eindhoven to Arnhem. Montgomery's Second British Army would break through the reeling German lines eight miles south of Eindhoven and race across all significant water barriers between there and the Westphalia Plain north of the Lower Rhine River. Then Allied armored divisions could pour into the Ruhr industrial area, shortening the war by months.

The mission of the 101st Airborne was to utilize three Drop Zones along 16 miles of that highway. The 506th Regiment would jump on DZ C, five miles north of Eindhoven, and the 502nd on DZ B, a couple of miles beyond. Our 501st Regiment would use DZs A and A1 near Veghel, approximately 25 miles beyond the front line. We would seize and hold the highway and railroad bridges across the Willemsvaart Canal, a major water barrier.

Sunday, September 17, was a pleasant day in England. By mid-morning we were assembled on the airfield, waiting to board our planes. A young trooper limped up to me, blood oozing from one boot.

"Lieutenant, my carbine went off accidentally and the round went through my foot. Whadda ya think I ought to do?"

First off, there was no reason for his weapon to have been loaded. Of greater significance, however, was the jaundiced view any court-martial board would take of such an "accident" occurring just before taking off to face the enemy. Noting that likelihood, I gave him the best advice I could.

"If I were you, soldier, I'd get on that plane, make the jump, then head for the nearest aid station and tell 'em a German shot me."

He didn't take my advice. Much later I was told he was serving hard time for the duration of the war with a Dishonorable Discharge to follow.

Just before it was time to clamber aboard the C-47s, a jeepload of Army nurses came down the line with the latest rumor. "Monty has already jumped off and broken through the lines!" It sounded good to us.

Ballard had dispersed his staff throughout the serial again, so I was jumping with another rifle squad. Since their platoon leader also was aboard, he would jumpmaster the stick. For reasons I can no longer recall, I was the fourth man in the lineup.

After crossing the Channel and Belgium, we stood and hooked up well before approaching the front line south of Eindhoven. It had not been the smoothest of rides, and I was already feeling the onset of air sickness. As we passed over the front, there were several moments of ground fire and flak, but our plane was not hit.

Because of the flat, open terrain around Veghel, I had decided to carry an M-1 rifle instead of a carbine. But I didn't want to jump with it disassembled in a Griswold case, so I mentally developed an alternative procedure. I'd hold the weapon in my hands, go out the door in the "long thrust" stance of bayonet drill, then come smartly to "present arm" while waiting for the chute to open.

The long-thrust-out-of-the-door bit worked like a charm. Apparently, however, I was a bit slow in presenting arms. Somehow a suspension line wrapped around the front sight of the weapon, ripping it out of my grasp and dangling it on the periphery of the canopy all the way to the ground. It plunked to earth right beside me.

Thanks to the broad daylight, dedicated troop transport pilots, and lack of enemy presence anywhere near the DZ, it was a "parade-ground jump" with a tight landing pattern. Everywhere I looked, troopers were freeing themselves of chute harnesses. Quite a few of them were cutting souvenir scarves out of the canopies, a self-established prerequisite of the assembly procedure. The Dutch Underground was present in force, helping to gather equipment bundles and loading them in carts.

My S-2 scouts were to meet me at the objective, so I struck out toward Veghel, well over a mile to the north, ignoring the tumult of troop leaders assembling their units. Rounding a barn en route, I encountered a farmer who must have stood six feet six inches in his wooden shoes. He promptly handed me an apple, which I munched, appreciating the gratitude we were to find endemic in the populace. While the apple was delicious, eating it brought the nausea that had been impending on the flight to full flower. Fortunately, I was beyond his sight before my stomach rebelled and relieved me of its contents. I went on, feeling much better.

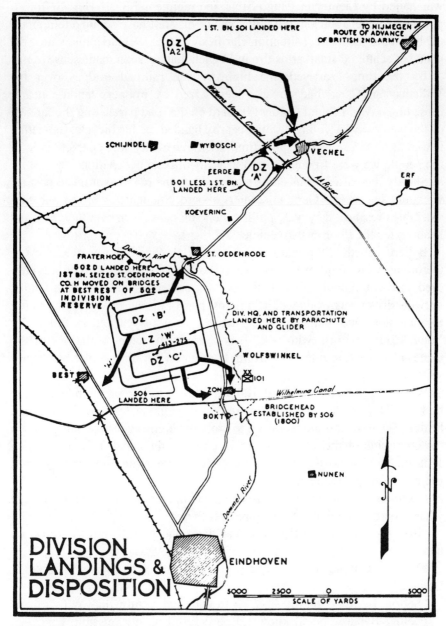

DIVISION
LANDINGS &
DISPOSITION

(From *Rendezvous with Destiny, The History of the 101st Airborne Division,* enlarged edition
(Sweetwater, TN: 101st Airborne Division Assoc., 1948), 266.

With half a mile yet to go, I passed through the village of Eerde where I was hailed by Lieutenant Hugo Sims, the regimental S-2. "Hey, Sefton, if you see Colonel Johnson, tell him some of his staff have set up a temporary CP here until the tactical situation clarifies." Since we could already hear the sound of scattered small arms fire in Veghel, that decision made sense to me.

By the time I arrived, the highway and railroad bridges over the Willemsvaart Canal had already been seized by troopers landing nearer those objectives. I found Colonel Ballard on the road paralleling the far side of the waterway. A young civilian nearby handed me his bicycle, indicating it was mine to use as transportation. Such generosity was characteristic of the people we were freeing from four years of Nazi occupation.

Shortly thereafter, a bus came tearing down the road. As it raced past us, we could see several German soldiers aboard. Suddenly aware of our considerable presence, they were pulling their soft caps down over their ears and heading for the floor of the vehicle.

Ballard yelled, "Stop that bus!" precipitating eager compliance by every Geronimo who could bring his weapon to bear fast enough. Within a hundred yards, it veered into a ditch, its back end thoroughly riddled. Oddly, only the driver was wounded, having lost part of his ear in attempting to run the gauntlet. One of the prisoners taken was a 14-year-old in full Hitler Youth Corps uniform who was so arrogant as to tempt violations of the Geneva Convention rules of warfare. Fortunately for him, cooler heads prevailed.

When the excitement abated, Ballard told me to hop on the bike and see how far D Company had progressed in organizing to hold the railroad bridge. The easiest route would be to cross the highway bridge and go down the other side of the Willemsvaart. In crossing the canal, I found Colonel Johnson amid a dozen or more troopers on the bridge and remembered Lieutenant Sims' request.

"Colonel, part of your staff has set up a temporary CP in that little village where you can see that church spire over there."

"Fine, Sefton. Get in that little car there and go tell 'em to get on up here!"

"Yes, Sir, Colonel, but first I have to check on Dog Company for Colonel Ballard."

"Sefton, I said go get my staff." And with that he turned away.

Feeling Ballard should know I'd be delayed on my mission, I pedaled quickly back there to advise the reason. He was less than sympathetic.

"Sefton, I said go down to Dog Company. Get going!"

My fond hope of getting across the highway bridge without Johnson spotting me proved futile.

"Sefton, haven't you gone yet? Get in that car and go NOW!"

The last I'd heard, a full colonel still outranked a lieutenant colonel. Besides which, I saw no virtue in straining relationships between my regimental and battalion commanders, especially not with me in the middle. Furthermore, Eerde was hardly half a mile away, so the trip shouldn't take more than ten minutes.

The "little car" I was to use was not only small, it also had a flat rear tire, plus several bullet holes and copious bloodstains attesting to the marksmanship of the troopers who had surprised the German former occupants. A member of the regimental S-2 section was sitting at the wheel. The vehicle had an unbloodied rumble seat, so I chose to sit there.

The road to Eerde was also the highway from Eindhoven to Arnhem. From Veghel it went straight for 400 yards before angling slightly to the right. At that precise point, one of our two-man bazooka teams was occupying a foxhole just off the right side of the pavement. As we approached, they waved frantically and shouted, "Get off the road; there's a tank coming!"

The driver reacted immediately, executing a sharp "Column right" and plowing the nose of the car into the far side of the ditch just short of the bazooka team. Despite a lifelong innocence of training in acrobatics, I did a complete forward flip, propelled by the abrupt stop, and landed on my feet atop the bank. At the same moment, one of the bazooka men yelled again, "It's okay; it's a Limey tank!"

Recalling the pre-takeoff news brought to us by the Army nurses concerning Monty's early success in breaking through the enemy lines, I was not at all loath to believe our Allies might be reaching Veghel on the first day of the attack rather than on the second as scheduled. So I stepped into the center of the highway to welcome the vanguard.

It was a medium-sized tank, barreling toward me at maybe 35 mph, still nearly 200 yards away. The commander was standing erect, protruding halfway above the turret, and waving at me with his right arm. Since my greeting to him could mark a mini-historic moment, possibly reportable in *Stars and Stripes,* I was trying to think of something as memorable as "Dr. Livingston, I presume" to say. Meanwhile, part of my consciousness was assuming the "detached observer" role reminiscent of the Normandy pond episode.

"That's a funny color for a Limey tank," the observer noted. "Theirs are painted solid olive drab like ours, and this one has camouflage stripes. But he's a Limey, alright, he's wearing a black cap. No, they wear black berets. What army wears black c-a-a-a-a-ps?"

The answer came to me suddenly. First, there was the black Teutonic cross now readily discernable despite the camouflage striping of the front

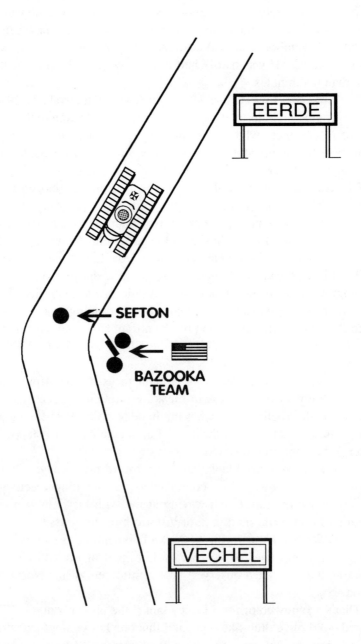

A case of mistaken identity. It was not one of Monty's tanks.

armor plating. Then there was the startled look on the tank commander's face as he realized I was not a fellow German. Finally, there was the fact that the hand on the arm he had been waving was holding a Luger pistol.

The tank was less than 50 yards away and still coming full speed ahead. The German was aiming the Luger at me, as I tried to get my M-1 rifle halfway into firing position. I heard the passage of his round snap in the air by my left ear a split second before I fired, virtually from the hip, at an upward angle of perhaps 120 degrees. He threw up his arms and disappeared down the turret as I leaped aside to keep from becoming road kill.

I was never to know whether I drilled him through the navel or missed him by a yard.

Meanwhile, the tank roared past the bazooka team at a range of 30 feet. The gunner was triggering the weapon, but nothing happened. I could see they had not hooked the battery wire to the coil spring at the rear end of the tube to complete the firing circuit and was bellowing for them to do so. The assistant gunner hooked up the wire before the tank had gone 50 yards beyond them. This time the weapon fired.

Standing only slightly to the right rear of the firer, I could see the flight of the rocket as it struck the tank's turret, then ricocheted toward the sky without exploding. They had also neglected to pull the pin that would have armed the warhead of the projectile before inserting it into the tube. The tank roared on toward the bridge and Colonel Johnson.

One way to warn friendly troops of impending armor attack was to fire a series of three shots in rapid sequence. And theoretically it was possible to impede the traversing action of a tank turret by firing 30 caliber rounds into the seam between turret and chassis. The bazooka team was still trying to reload as I banged away three series of three shots with the M-1, aiming optimistically at the turret seam of the rapidly fleeing target. For all the good accomplished, I might as well have taken a nap.

As the tank neared the bridge, Colonel Johnson also assumed it to be the lead vehicle of Monty's onrushing army. He, too, was preparing to welcome the crew until a burst from one of the tank's machine guns suggested he could be wrong. He and the other Geronimos standing on the bridge ended up dangling from the structure's side struts as the tank rumbled across and proceeded into the town.

The fact that no one was hit by the machine-gun fire, then or later, suggested that the weapon may have been loaded with belts featuring the wooden slugs we had discovered in Normandy. We had surmised they might have been used on 1,000-inch ranges where traversing exercises were practiced on paper targets.

The street into the center of town twisted and turned before emerging

Friendly civilians help troopers with directions behind enemy lines, September 18, 1944. (Photo, National Archives, 111-SC-2715351)

where a channel from the canal ended in a square suited to the loading and unloading of barges plying that waterway. From there, the main thoroughfare of the community went northeast toward Nijmegen. It was jammed with joyous Hollanders celebrating their liberation from Nazi oppression in a carnival atmosphere.

One of our officers reportedly was admiring a display of cigars in the window of a tobacconist shop in the square when he heard the clanking of tank treads and turned to see the vehicle's turret gun traversing in his direction. He avoided imminent demise by diving through the plate glass and into the store. Another did a back flip into an air-raid shelter, breaking his shoulder in the process. At least so the stories went.

It is well established, however, that the tank then charged north, straight up the main drag, firing ineffective machine-gun bursts en route. A Pathfinder sergeant was running right behind it, futilely firing a .45 pistol into the plating covering the motor. Private First Class Goble, one of my S-2 scouts, was keeping pace alongside, attempting to jam the barrel of his M-1 rifle between a tread and its bogie wheels. All to no avail. The celebrating throngs parted like the Red Sea for Moses, and the tank was last seen heading north past the city limit of Veghel at a rather lively pace.

For my part in the episode, I proceeded to Eerde once the tank had become the colonel's problem, gave Lieutenant Sims the word to haul tail into Veghel, checked out D Company's progress, and reported back to Ballard accordingly. I did not feel required to elaborate on any other aspects of my sojourn.

The 501st had landed, had assembled, and was ready to get on with the war.

Chapter 20

Holding Veghel

Well before dawn on D+1, E Company was hit by a sharp probing attack from the west along the north side of the Willemsvaart Canal. Lieutenant Joe McGregor's platoon was forced to pull back, and he suffered a head wound while covering their withdrawal with his Tommy gun. At dawn a counterattack restored the position and carried Mac back for evacuation as the enemy force retreated.

Aside from that episode, the first few days in Veghel were passed in a "comic-opera-war" atmosphere, so far as our battalion was concerned. At every outlying village reached by my S-2 patrols, the populace would welcome them with more ripe apples than they could carry. In Veghel itself, some householders attempted to provide sheets and blankets for use in their foxholes! Dutch Underground members, some of them mere boys, kept bicycling into the Command Post with reports on the activities of German units from miles around. The lead columns of Monty's armor reached us on D+2, 24 hours behind the optimistic schedule.

In the daylight hours of D+1, the 3rd Battalion had repulsed two attacks on Eerde, but our units were not involved in those actions. On D+3, the 1st Battalion conducted a brilliant "broom and dustpan" operation along the canal to the northwest. A and B Companies attacked abreast to drive a German parachute training battalion into the guns of C Company which had maneuvered into position behind them. Forty of the enemy were killed, 40 more wounded, and 418 taken prisoner — all at an American cost of 4 killed and 6 wounded. Aside from helping herd some of the prisoners into Veghel, our battalion played no part in that action, either.

Meanwhile, Dutch Underground reports indicated a dangerous build-up of enemy forces in the town of Schjindel, some 2½ miles due west of Veghel. Impressed by the success of the 1st Battalion's sweep, Colonel Johnson ordered both the 1st and 3rd Battalions to attack that community at dawn the next morning, D+4. Suddenly, at 10:00, the order was changed. They were to start their attack immediately! That meant jumping off in the dark with no prior reconnaissance against an enemy of undetermined strength and composition. And it meant leaving us, the 2nd Battalion, to hold Veghel, the primary responsibility of the 501st Regiment.

The impromptu night attack was hairy from start to finish. The troops groped their way through 2½ miles of darkness, encountering scattered resistance en route and capturing various groups unaware of their advance. The commander of the 12 British tanks assigned to support them refused to move his vehicles at night. The 1st Battalion entered Schjindel shortly after midnight, seizing every third home and awakening thoroughly surprised Germans in the process. The 3rd Battalion, attacking on the left of the 1st, met continuous resistance from its front and left flank but got into town at first light. The tanks came up later in the morning.

At dawn, the mop-up continued as Germans awakening in the houses not yet searched put up sporadic resistance before surrendering. By 7:15, German armor and infantry attacks were developing from the southwest, requiring the extended effort of both battalions to repel them. Meanwhile, very heavy enemy forces were descending on 502nd Regiment positions south of Schjindel, but it was developments in Veghel that soon gave Johnson even greater concern.

Early on the morning of D+5, we were receiving increasing reports of German build-ups beyond the village of Erp on the Aa River, a bit over three miles southeast of Veghel. Ballard told me to take our demolition team to Erp to mine the bridge there along with a rifle squad for their protection and then get back to the battalion CP.

We set off in jeeps, following two British armored cars that paused cautiously at each turn of the road while maintaining constant radio contact with their headquarters. Traveling right behind the second vehicle, I was bemused by some of their transmissions that I overheard, one in particular.

"We're just approaching the twisty bit at [map coordinates]. I just saw a Jerry making a reccy with a shovel" (meaning a German soldier was answering a call of nature). Aside from that solitary sighting, however, we had noted no enemy on our way to Erp.

Upon reaching the village, we found no immediate evidence of impending disaster, so I deployed the security squad and told the demolition crew to start mining the bridge, then went back to Veghel.

In the short time it took me to return, the vanguard of the 107th Panzer and 280th Assault Gun Brigades struck at Erp. The security squad wisely "fired and fell back" — all the way to Veghel. The demolition squad barely had time to touch off its preliminary efforts at mining, blowing only a one-inch crack across the bridge's surface. The German tanks had no trouble crossing it and barreling on toward Veghel.

Since Colonel Ballard already knew of the situation from the British in the armored cars, I rounded up my S-2 scouts and went off on a patrol in hopes of determining the depth of the attacking column. We took a route paralleling the road from Erp at a few hundred yards from the enemy's left flank. It didn't take long to realize the attack formation was seriously deep.

Within two miles or so, the sounds of front-line fighting were behind us. It was time to cut left and approach the Erp road for a look. That meant crossing some 300 yards of bare, flat field to a farm road paralleling the German advance at much closer range. There were bushes, trees, and farm buildings along that road.

Squatting in a cabbage patch, I studied the scene through binoculars. Aside from foliage and structures, there was nothing else to be seen — not a chicken, not a dog, no movement of any kind. The longer I looked, the more my cold hunch developed into monumental proportions.

"Going across that field is NOT a good idea!"

A couple of my more intrepid Geronimos were feeling no such apprehension. "Let's get going, Lieutenant. There's gotta be a barrel of Lugers over there!" (Those German pistols were the most prized of all combat trophies.)

Their enthusiasm put me in an awkward position. It would not be good troop leadership practice to share my growing misgivings based on that hunch, despite any visible validation for it. Fortunately, an enemy gun half a mile ahead on our original route chose that moment to fire an overhead round into Veghel. One member of the patrol did happen to have a rifle grenade, so I changed my command decision.

"Let's go knock out that tank first."

What I really wanted to do was to find a less conspicuous route to that farm road. But there was no point in sharing that goal at the moment since the prospect of knocking out a "tank" seemed wholeheartedly endorsed by the patrol. Just as we were starting on, however, F Company came up from behind us. Ballard had committed them to making a flank attack on the column, and they were prepared to do so across that same field! I changed decisions once again.

"Hold up, men. Let's hook on to the right of this counterattack."

The company wasn't 20 yards into the field before they were greeted by rifle and machine-gun fire from along the farm road. Those enemy flank security troops might have let my patrol walk right up to their gun muzzles, but they couldn't allow a full company to get that close without contention.

F Company troops opened up with all weapons, including mortars, quickly achieving fire superiority and advancing across the field. Our patrol kept pace with the platoon on their right. We ended up in a ditch on the near side of the farm road which extended another 150 yards to the right before ending at an intersecting road. One enemy machine gun, if positioned at the end of the ditch, could have enfiladed the entire company line. I told the platoon leader I would secure that flank with my patrol.

The enemy, driven out of position by the attack, had obviously regrouped and had been reinforced. As we crawled along the ditch, twigs clipped off of overhanging bushes by flat trajectory fire kept dropping on the back of my neck. I could find no virtue in peering over the edge to see where they were coming from.

With a third of the way yet to go, I came to a slit trench dug in the bottom of the ditch. It contained four children ranging from perhaps seven to three years of age, all blond, blue-eyed, and meticulously clean. Their response to my dust-stained, unshaven visage appearing over the edge of their shelter was big smiles and a chorus of "Allo! Allo!" A bit further on, their parents were cowering in the bottom of a similar slit trench, the mother holding an infant in her arms.

By this time, the patrol was sheltered from enemy fire by the couple's farmhouse directly across the road. Sending the rest of the group to secure the end of the ditch, PFC Goble and I dashed across to the house for a better assessment of the tactical situation.

As on so many other farms in the area, the house featured an extension comprising a mini-dairy barn. We entered that portion of the structure, which had small Gothic windows providing observation of the enemy front. I pulled a milk can up to one of them and sat down to survey the terrain ahead. At almost the same moment, a German emerged from cover some 35 yards away and went sprinting off at a slightly left to right angle.

"Gee, look at him go!" I remarked in surprise.

"Well, aren't you going to shoot him?" Goble asked with a tinge of exasperation.

"Oh, yeah, of course."

Forgetting I had loaded the M-1 with tracers in case of the need to point out targets of opportunity, I did remember to lead the angling runner like a rising quail in squeezing off the round. The path of the tracer suggested a red finger of fate as it ended somewhere in the seat of his pants, inspiring a flat dive into new cover from which he did not re-emerge.

Goble seemed sufficiently impressed.

Meanwhile, it was becoming apparent that F Company would not be able to advance beyond the farm road without reinforcement, so Ballard ordered them to return to Veghel for deployment against the increasing enemy pressure. I took the patrol back with them and found that the battalion CP had been moved into the basement of a farmhouse on the edge of town facing the onslaught.

There was a British 90mm gun unit in the farmyard, dueling with Tiger tanks clearly visible in the fields beyond. Tank and artillery shells were pounding the area. There was an old silo foundation in the yard, but no one was using it as shelter. I told the patrol members to get in it and stay there, then went into the basement of the house to report to Ballard.

The battle was raging, but momentum seemed to be shifting in our favor. The 2nd Battalion was holding the town. I looked out a ground-level window of the basement CP to see if my scouts were remaining under cover. They were, but two Tommies of the British gun unit were sitting on an orange crate in the center of the yard making a pot of tea over a small fire in complete disregard of incoming shells.

"Those two are gonna get killed!" I predicted to someone nearby. Just as I turned away, the window pane was shattered by the concussion of a shell that must have landed virtually in the laps of the tea-brewers. Their remains were little more than bundles of bloody rags. Yet, ten minutes later, two more Tommies were sitting on the remnants of the orange crate making a pot of tea.

Long thereafter I queried a British soldier concerning his army's obsession with tea-making, even while engaged in combat. I still recall the reply: "I say, Yank, the war's not going to be over tomorrow, so you might as well have a cuppa." Perhaps not, but it certainly was over for those two Tommies in that farmyard.

Before dark that evening, the Germans abandoned that particular attempt to cut the highway by attacking Veghel. But they would probe our battalion twice more before striking in force at Eerde.

Chapter 21

A Very Bad Day at Eerde

At dawn the next day, D+6, the enemy attacked E Company's positions on a smaller scale, inflicting heavy mortar fire casualties before being stopped at 10:00. At 1:30 they struck D Company, but were repelled within an hour.

While we had been holding onto Veghel by our fingernails, Colonel Johnson had pulled the 1st and 3rd Battalions back from their attack on Schjindel. The 1st was now in position at Eerde with outposts in the prominent sand dunes extending approximately one mile from north to south and a half mile to the west of that small community. On the morning of D+7, the enemy struck the area in force from the north.

The attacking units included two battalions of the German 6th Parachute Regiment, the enemy we had battled in Normandy, a battalion of their 1st Parachute Regiment, and a battalion of the elite Hermann Goering Regiment. They were heavily supported by tanks and artillery.

Johnson ordered our 2nd Battalion into Regimental Reserve behind the 1st in Eerde. We suffered numerous casualties from artillery fire en route, and the day didn't get any better after our arrival. Fighting in the difficult sand-dune terrain had come to such close quarters that neither side could employ overhead fire directly on the front lines. As a result, our reserve area was catching almost everything the German artillery had to throw.

Our troops were digging slit trenches with the speed and efficiency that incoming rounds always inspired. Morale was taking a beating as casualties continued to mount with no chance for us to shoot back. In the midst of the chaos, Father Sam appeared, distributing Holy Communion! I received one

Chaplain Francis L. Sampson as a major with the 82nd Airborne Division, 1953. "Father Sam" to all 501 troopers, he was captured at Bastogne and survived POW camp to become a major general and chief of chaplains, in 1967. A year after retiring from the Army, he became president of the USO. His next tour of duty was as assistant to the president of Notre Dame University, in charge of ROTC affairs. Now nominally "retired," he is busy spelling other priests in his hometown of Sioux Falls, SD. His reprinted book, *Look Out Below,* provides engrossing insights into his unique multiple careers.

of the hosts and was immediately transported into a feeling of complete serenity. If this was my day to die, I was as ready as I'd ever be.

Wire communications between battalion and regimental CPs were non-existent, and the radios were proving unreliable. I had brought along the civilian bicycle handed to me the first day, so I told Colonel Ballard I would run liaison between him and regimental headquarters. The first step was to ride off in their direction and find out precisely where they were located.

All roads in that part of Holland were somewhat elevated due to the high water table, with deep ditches along each side. I was still feeling incongruously serene as I pedaled along, but not to the point of foolhardiness. Whenever I heard incoming rounds that were going to hit close, I would dive into a ditch. On one such occasion, I landed squarely on a trooper who was huddled face down at the bottom, literally trembling in terror. The fact that a shell burst on the road at precisely the same moment that I plummeted in from above did not help his nerves much, either.

A bit farther on, I heard the unlikely sounds of metal grinding on metal coming from the ditch on my right. I discovered that the sounds were generated by four troopers, two each side-by-side, face down. There was a handful of dried reeds lying across the ditch directly above them, and each pair was striving strenuously to get under that purely psychological protection. The sound of four helmets grinding together continued in discordant testimony to the impact of intensive shelling on the human psyche.

These events were to comprise my only clear recollections of that terrible day. My feeling of serenity may well have been a God-granted sanity shield against the horrors otherwise prevailing. While the heroics of 1st Battalion units were repelling the attack, we in reserve could but passively suffer our punishment. Casualties among our CP group included Sergeant Joe Mero, who later died of his wounds, and Corporal Bruce Beyer, wounded and evacuated.

By dark the enemy had been driven off, but sporadic shelling continued well into the night. By the time it finally ended, the digging of shelters had progressed to the point where another two feet of depth in some instances would have bordered on desertion.

The next day, as well as I can recall, the regimental front was restructured with our battalion taking up new positions south of the Willemsvaart Canal on the west arc of the perimeter guarding Veghel. There was no enemy in contact with our front. Compared to the experiences at Eerde, the war suddenly became downright peaceful.

Chapter 22

Night Patrol

In combat actions to date, I had always felt most useful and productive when I was leading troops, whether bringing them out of the Normandy marshlands for assembly or taking them on patrols. Upon our return to England in July, I had asked Colonel Ballard for reassignment to a rifle platoon. He had replied that we were too close to our next operation to break in a new S-2.

The fighting in Holland thus far had taken its characteristic toll of company grade officers. In our battalion, Lieutenants Volango and Frase were KIA. Lieutenant Clare Hess had recovered from his Normandy wounds in time to join us shortly after the jump, only to catch a shrapnel fragment across the forehead a few days later. He ended up in a hospital bed right next to Joe McGregor. Lieutenants Gibson and Brash both had fingers shot away. There were other officer casualties I can no longer recall.

As we settled into the relative quiet of our new defensive positions, Ballard indicated his concern regarding the growing officer shortage by telling me to cease personal participation in S-2 section patrol activities. While I appreciated his concern for my continued well-being, the restriction increased my "fifth wheel" perception of staff duty compared to troop-leading assignments.

On each of the next several nights, I sent reconnaisance patrols to sweep the area two miles beyond the battalion front. Their reports never varied: "Nuthin' out there, Lieutenant." By the fifth night, I was developing a good case of the "CP willies" due to the lack of personal activity of any significance.

This next patrol was sure to be another "milk run," and Ballard had never really reiterated the restrictions. The scouts might appreciate the fact that I got off my duff again, and I would be getting th'hell out of the CP, if only for a few hours, more than likely without being missed. How many more reasons did I need?

The night was quite dark with a three-foot blanket of ground fog hugging the soft surface of the terrain. The patrol seemed to float silently above it, disembodied from the waist down. We had left canteens and any other equipment that might rattle behind. We wore soft wool caps instead of helmets. I had removed the stock from a Tommy gun and attached the rear end of the sling to the bolt that had held the stock in place.

With the sling around my neck, the weapon dangled across my front with its muzzle pointed left of my left foot. If I were to squeeze the trigger, the recoils from the burst would cause the gun to swing from left to right in an ascending arc, spraying any enemy ahead at close range. I was keeping my hand on that trigger as we drifted on in the darkness.

Something started to brush against the calf of my left leg. We were angling into a strand of German communication wire that the patrol of the previous night had not encountered. It was stretched a foot off the ground, coming from somewhere ahead and continuing somewhere behind us.

"Hmmmmnnnn!"

Had we sidled past an outpost in the silent dark? Or perhaps something even stronger? The only logical move was to backtrack along the wire and find out. We found the end of it wrapped around a fence post. Whoever planned to hook up a field phone there had yet to do so. The next obvious move was to check out the other end.

Shortly beyond the point where we had first angled into the wire, another one junctured off toward the Willemsvaart Canal, several hundred yards away to our right.

Double "Hmmmmnnnn!"

Either some German communications team was merely practicing wire-laying techniques or serious trouble could be brewing on our battalion front. At this point in time, we figured we could rule out the merely practicing bit.

The wire paralleled a dirt road nearby on our right as we followed along it slowly, all senses on Red Alert. Visibility at ground level was limited to several yards. We could hear no sound of human presence ahead. Not a whisper, not a cough, not a single clank of equipment. We crawled on into the silence with tension building like a wall to be penetrated.

The wire continued through a brushy fence line. Just beyond, another dirt road intersected from the left, forming a T-junction. A small blue light glowed faintly a few feet beyond the intersection to the right of the road we were paralleling. It was less than 50 yards from our fence line to the light source, whatever it might be. We had to get a closer look.

With the rest of patrol disposed to provide cover fire if required, PFC Goble and I crawled to the near corner of the junction and stood up ver-r-r-ry slowly to look across it. The light was coming from one of those small battery-powered lanterns the German army favored. They had various colored lenses, including a blue one for use at night.

All we could see of the user was the side of his face. He was sitting motionless, partially in a ditch beside the road, apparently studying a map or something below our angle of observation. Was he alone or part of a squad, platoon, or what-have-you? All we knew for sure was that he was not part of our Army.

I signaled Goble to follow and started crawling back to the patrol, mulling over the next course of action. Prudence would dictate a quick return to the CP to report our findings. On the other hand, the element of surprise suggested that a hit-and-run assault could be made at minimal risk. While I was still mentally weighing the pros and cons, Goble crawled up beside me to whisper in my ear.

"We're not gonna go back and leave that bastard sitting there, are we?" (Damn these intrepid types who precipitate my decisions!)

"Of course not, but we gotta do it right. C'mon back to the patrol."

Pop Dornick also was carrying a Tommy gun, so I positioned him across the road in the same ditch as the lantern holder and less than 50 yards away. He was to open fire when Goble and I tossed grenades from our previous vantage point. The rest of the patrol was to provide cover fire for our withdrawal, if necessary.

My patrol members carried three grenades, but the cotter pin through the safety handle of one was mashed so firmly in place that we took only the other two. We would crawl back up there, each toss a grenade, empty our own Tommy guns into the position, then get th'hell out of Dodge!

Arriving back at the junction, we could still see only the side of the lantern user's face. He had not changed position noticeably since we had left. On my whispered count of three, we each pulled the pins on our grenades and pitched them across the 20-yard interval to the target.

It was the first time I'd thrown a grenade at night, and I was startled by the unexpectedly loud crack of the firing pin igniting the fuse powder train. It sounded like a .22-rifle shot disrupting the silence. Nor had I anticipated the trail of sparks following it from my hand to the end of its arc to the target.

My reaction to these two "surprises" occurring in the tenseness of the moment was to stand erect, hold the Tommy gun by the forearm and pistol

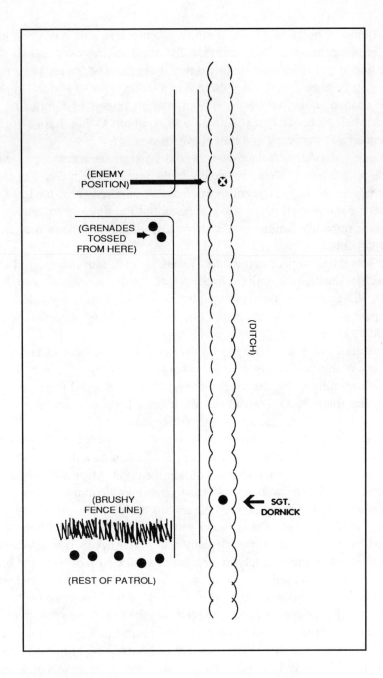

grip, and start spraying the darkness where the blue light no longer glowed. The second grenade had yet to explode! Goble was doing the same along-side. My magazine was empty in a matter of seconds. I told Goble, "Let's go!" and took off in sprint gear.

It should be noted that I had never run so much as a mile of track in my life, let alone hurdles. But I still vividly recall sailing over that five-foot fence line in full stride and looking down at the faces of the patrol members staring up from behind it. They did not require an order to join me in flight.

We dashed some 200 yards without hearing sounds of return fire, so I called a halt to count noses. I came up one short. Goble wasn't with us. Someone had to go back and find him. Guess who?

To say I started back cautiously would be an understatement of monumental proportions. Staying very close to the ground, I kept listening intently for any sound of movement to my front. A hundred yards along I heard someone coming well before I could make out the figure. I squatted in the darkness, reloaded Tommy gun at the ready, directly in line of the oncomer's approach.

He was within a pace and a half of walking right into me before I could see his head against the dark skyline. He was wearing a soft wool cap. It was Goble. His Tommy gun had jammed halfway through the magazine, and he had spent some time working the bolt before deciding to depart without expending the rest of his rounds on the target!

We spread out in a defensive arc to watch for any signs of reaction at the junction. Within half an hour we could see blue "cat's eyes" — dim lights of a vehicle coming along the road to the junction. It stopped there, remained for several minutes, then withdrew. We assumed it was evacuating at least one casualty. Nothing else seemed to be happening.

It was close to dawn when we returned to the battalion CP where only the guards and the duty officer were awake. There was no indication that anyone had noted my personal absence during the night. Meanwhile, I was still pondering the full significance of those new enemy communication wires, particularly the one that junctured off toward the Willemsvaart Canal.

Our battalion's right flank ended just short of the Canal where it was crossed by the railroad bridge. A platoon of glider troops was emplaced to guard the bridge. Immediately to their front, a thick strip of trees and brush, some 50 yards wide, ran west along the waterway for several hundred yards. Any enemy unit strong enough to overrun their position from such cover could blow that bridge and continue on to attack the highway bridge as well as the one constructed by our engineers to facilitate tank crossings.

When I saw Colonel Ballard a couple of hours later, I reported "an S-2 patrol" had discovered the wire, feeling no compulsion to elaborate on its makeup. I also recommended that we send a combat patrol to probe that portion of the canal-side brush strip where it angled into our battalion zone. He agreed.

The patrol did not get far beyond our own outpost lines before stirring up a hornet's nest of aggressive reaction from the brush strip. Within the next hour or so, Ballard had committed both front-line rifle companies to the attack in an attempt to pinch off the brush strip midway and move along. Shortly thereafter, Colonel Johnson committed the battalion on our left, as well. In the meantime, the strip was being pounded with all of the mortar and artillery fire on call. Fortunately for our side, German artillery return fire was relatively light.

In trying to assess the strength of the enemy formation, I followed Lieutenant Billy Heaton as he led his E Company platoon up a ditch that approached the Canal at a point near the far end of the brush strip. The ground was being swept by enemy flat trajectory fire from our right. There was a clump of trees just ahead where the ditch ended at a dirt road. A couple of them, struck by our artillery fire, had fallen across the ditch, blocking observation in that direction beyond the intervening 20 or so yards. Heaton suddenly rose to his feet and started emptying his Tommy gun into the downed trees.

"What'n hell're ya shootin' at?"

"Those Krauts runnin' outta those trees!" They were making such good time I hadn't so much as glimpsed them from my position behind him.

Upon reaching the end of the ditch, Heaton found he could not deploy his platoon without risking heavy casualties. He sent a runner back to report the situation to Lieutenant Frank Gregg, E Company commander. A while later, I decided to go back and report to Ballard. Crouching along in the ditch, I was surprised to catch up with Heaton's runner. He was kneeling on the bottom, holding his helmet above the edge on the muzzle of his rifle and raising his head beside it at frequent intervals.

"Just what are you trying to do, trooper?"

"There's a sniper over there somewhere shootin' at me and I'm tryin' to spot the sonavabitch!"

I pointed out that aside from taking a good chance of getting himself killed, he was also failing to carry out the mission his platoon leader had assigned. Rather reluctantly he continued to the rear.

A bit farther on, an artillery officer was cowering face down in the ditch. He was the forward observer who should have been up there calling in fire orders to support Heaton's attack. My heated verbal suggestions that he get on with his job proved ineffective, but an unrestrained kick in the butt restored his devotion to duty and sent him crawling on up the ditch toward the platoon position.

The attacks ended at dusk without really pinching off the retreat of the Germans along the Canal. If any prisoners were taken, I never heard about them. When I visited the brush strip the next day, the evidence of carnage was impressive. Bodies and parts of bodies were littered among the trees and bushes shredded by artillery and mortar bursts. There were piles of Teller land mines and footlocker-sized boxes of explosives abandoned in place. Purportedly, the enemy force had been drawn from an officer training school with the sole mission of blowing the bridges. Given one more day without being discovered, they might have accomplished much of their mission.

Oddly, the events of that day are not recorded in histories of the 101st Airborne Division or the 501st Parachute Regiment. Nor are they noted in the pages of *Hell's Highway,* a thorough compilation of unit Holland combat records and individual combatants' recollections published by George Koskimaki who served as General Maxwell Taylor's radio operator.

This may be due to the fact that the fight did not involve armor on either side, that our own casualties were very light, and that the threat of an assault on the bridges was unperceived until no longer extant.

Since it was a significant part of my war, however, I've recorded it to the best of my memory.

Chapter 23

Finally Back to the Line

The regimental front was readjusted to encompass the ground taken in the attack. Our battalion remained on the right sector of the new perimeter, but now with our right flank anchored on the Willemsvaart beyond the far end of the brush strip.

Late that afternoon, Colonel Ballard granted my long-standing request.

"All right, Sefton, go down and take over the right flank platoon of E Company." I left the CP with alacrity.

Lieutenant Patton had been leading that platoon temporarily, having been assigned there from his job as regimental demolitions officer. He had deployed the troops precisely on the line indicated by the map accompanying the plans to readjust the battalion position. The men had just finished digging their new foxholes when I arrived to take over a couple of hours before dusk. I took a quick tour of the position and shuddered.

An intersecting dirt road comprised the left flank with Lieutenant Heaton's platoon on the other side. Another road intersected on the right, paralleling the Canal some 50 yards away. Each road had deep ditches alongside with one rifleman dug in beside each ditch to prevent enemy access. Worse yet, another elevated road ran between those two less than 100 yards beyond the front-line positions, effectively limiting our field of flat trajectory fire to that distance.

I called Gregg, now a captain, on the field phone and requested permission to move the main line of resistance up to the road crossing our front and put outposts well beyond. He had no objection. Designating the three troopers nearest the phone to "Stick with me!" I sent them along the line with the news that we were moving up to the road immediately. Having just finished hours of digging where they were, the troops received that word with something considerably less than elation.

By dark the men were bone weary, but I was satisfied. Our platoon machine guns were well positioned on the new main line of resistance. Strong points protected the ditches entering the sector. A communications trench had been dug across the road intersecting on the right to permit crossing it without exposure. Lieutenant Heaton had agreed to outpost the boundary road between our platoons. It was time to thank the three men I'd been using as runners and send them back to their respective assignments.

The first two were both from rifle squads. I complimented them on their help and told them to report back to their squad leaders. The third seemed to have become increasingly surly as the work progressed, so I saved him 'til last.

"What's your name again, trooper?"

"I'm Smitty."

"Oh? And what's your job here?"

"I'm your PLATOON SERGEANT, goddammit!"

Oops! I'd been away from line duty long enough to overlook a major principle of troop leadership in the exigencies of the moment. The fact that Dale Smith and I were to develop a friendship that endured long after the war was eloquent testimony to his forgiving nature.

When Colonel Ballard came by the next morning to find his right flank unit had moved forward beyond its delegated location, his only comment was: "Good strong position, Sefton." His approval was not shared by Lieutenant Verne Mertz, who arrived a few hours later.

Mertz was the machine-gun platoon leader in Battalion Headquarters Company. The afternoon before, he had positioned one of his gun teams to cover the intersecting road on Heaton's right flank. Startled to find it could no longer traverse right without firing into my new platoon line, he came stomping right over. Our conversation went something like this:

"Did Battalion order your platoon to move up here, Sefton?"

"No, I did it so I would have a field of fire, but I cleared it with Gregg."

"Do you realize my gun is now 100 yards behind there and can't traverse to the right without shooting into your platoon?"

"So move it up to my left flank where it can traverse from hell to breakfast."

"My gun stays right where Battalion said to put it!"

"Well, my platoon stays right here where Ballard has now approved it!"

It should be noted that Mertz's military philosophy stemmed in large part from his prewar service in a Regular Army field artillery unit from which he was later commissioned via the Infantry Officer Candidate School. He also was born and raised in Minnesota where even the natives admit to being "a little sot in their ways." The concept of a mere platoon leader juggling part of an established defensive line of his own volition was anathema to his nature as well as to his creed of military protocol.

His machine gun remained in its original position for the remainder of our stay in that area. Our momentary conflict evolved into close comradeship during the rest of the war and continues to this day. But he has yet to agree with the propriety of moving that platoon.

Meanwhile, I was concerned with the need to build the platoon's confidence in their new leader after my unheralded arrival and the precipitous change of position. There also was the fact that it was this platoon that had been overrun during the night attack of D+1. My first step was to initiate a policy that required the platoon sergeant, the radio corporal, and me to rotate two-hour shifts of walking the line and checking the outposts from dark to dawn each night.

There was a lone house with a few small outbuildings located about midway along the road which was now our front line. One of the platoon machine guns was sited alongside it. The day after our move up, one of the gun-team members approached me in confidence regarding the corporal to whom he reported.

"He's been acting real queer lately, Sir. Last night, f'rinstance, our sleeping bags were side by side in that shed. I got up to go check on the guy on the gun and he asked where I was going. I told him and was back in less than a minute. I was just crawling back into my sack when I heard him cock his .45 and felt it jammed in my ribs. He said, 'Who's there?' I really thought he was about to shoot me!"

I thanked him for confiding in me and assured him that I would keep an eye on the corporal. That night I was taking one of my shifts of walking the line. The sky was clear and a full moon was beaming. Just as I approached the house, the quiet was violated by the sound of a pistol shot. I ran ahead to find the corporal prone on the ground, pistol in hand, along the left side of the building. I flopped down beside him.

"What's going on, corporal?"

"I just shot a Kraut, Lieutenant!"

"Great! Where is he?"

"Right out there! I'll finish him off with this grenade!"

Before I could react, he pulled the pin of a grenade held in his left hand, accidentally firing another round from the gun still held in the right one. The slug buried itself in the ground a few inches from my nose as he pooped the hissing grenade about ten yards ahead. I was pushing my face firmly into the dirt as it went off, fragments ricocheting off the wall beside us.

"That got him good!" The corporal was on his feet staring into the yard. I stood up beside him, scanning the moon-bathed area. The grass was hardly an inch high. There was no cover of any kind and certainly no body in evidence. I needed some time to think.

"Hold up right here a minute, corporal. He may be only wounded. I'll go around to that little outbuilding on the right there and we'll come at him from two directions."

I dashed around the house to a small edifice which may have been used to smoke meat. The corporal hadn't waited. He was walking slowly into the yard, pointing the pistol at the ground ahead and yelling over and over, "Get up! Get up ya sonavabitch!"

By the time I could reach him, the gun was pointed virtually at his own feet. His shouts had died to whispers. There was absolutely nothing there! I took the pistol from his unresisting grasp. By now I had finished thinking.

"Glad you're here, corporal! Captain Gregg just called and asked me to send an experienced non-com back to help guard some new equipment for the rest of the night. If you'll just follow that path to the company CP, I'll let him know you're coming." He left with no more than a dazed nod of acquiescence.

I scrambled to a field phone and filled Gregg in on the details. "The guy has had the course, Frank. Evacuate him back to where he can get the help he needs."

So far as I know, the corporal never returned for duty with the regiment. He was one more of those unbloodied casualties whose combat wounds could not be patched or sutured.

A night or two later, I started my stint of line-walking on the left flank where a young replacement from the mortar squad was standing sentry duty next to the road separating Heaton's platoon from mine. We chatted a few minutes, and I went on down the line past the house before turning off to check an outpost. Just as I reached it, a rifle shot rang out from the flank I'd left. I took off running.

A couple of the machine-gunners were standing on the road in front of the house. I skidded to a stop and asked if they knew what had happened. "Dunno, Lieutenant. We heard somebody speakin' German down there, then there was that shot. We're just waitin' by the gun to see what goes on!" I ran on toward the flank.

Precisely where I had chatted with the sentry, a figure lay face-up on the ground, breathing in gasps and gurgles. At the same moment, the frantic sentry came running back from the mortar position, accompanied by his squad leader. The labored breathing stopped shortly thereafter.

It seemed the young trooper had been standing at his post when a figure approached from up the road, apparently having strolled right past Heaton's sleeping outpost. The sentry challenged, "Halt!" only to be answered by a conversational stream of German as the figure kept walking toward him. The sentry fired at a range of about two feet and ran for his squad leader.

The dead German was very young. His pale face had a two-day stubble of wispy growth. His combat uniform pockets contained several apples and a harmonica. He reminded me of my brother who had turned 18 in January and was now training in a new infantry division back in the States.

As nearly as we could reconstruct events, the German had gotten himself lost and thought he was approaching friendly lines. Apparently neither he nor the sentry realized the command, "Halt!" sounds just about the same in English as in German. He may well have been telling our sentry how glad he was to find him.

His death was just another minor entry in the total loss called warfare.

Meanwhile, the liberation of Holland was moving north. The 82nd Airborne Division had captured the highway bridge across the Waal River at Nijmegen after long, hard fighting. The British had captured Antwerp, but their Airborne Division was being butchered across the Neder Rhine at Arnhem.

We wondered how soon we'd go back to England and start preparing for our next operation. Instead, we learned we were to remain attached to Montgomery's battered army and join the move north on October 4.

Chapter 24

Life on the "Island"

On September 17, our battalion had jumped with 608 officers and enlisted men. On October 4, we boarded trucks with 452, having lost more than one out of four. We convoyed north to Nijmegen where the bridge over the Waal River had been captured by the 82nd Airborne. It was still under German artillery fire. The British had festooned its railings with straw mats to deny the enemy as much observation as possible. Signs advised crossing drivers to "Get mobile!"

The bridge took us onto the "Island," the very low, very flat land between the Waal and the Neder (Lower) Rhine, currently occupied by both British and German troop units. The mission of the 101st Airborne Division was to relieve the British and clear out the Germans.

The only high ground was on the far side of the Rhine, giving the German artillery observers there a clear view of the entire area during daylight hours. The British units we were to relieve were spread thinly with intervals between positions often infiltrated by enemy forces. We left the trucks and marched the last five miles to arrive at the main dike on the south side of the Rhine at dark.

The 1st Battalion, moving up on our right, encountered Germans in the darkness and were engaged in heavy fighting throughout the next day before gaining their positions on the dike. Our battalion lucked out, reaching our assigned area with no opposition beyond harassing artillery fire. To our left, the 506th Parachute and 327th Glider Regiments fought off aggressive attacks for ten days before convincing the German command the 101st Airborne was there to stay.

At dawn the next morning, we found ourselves in rather strange circum-

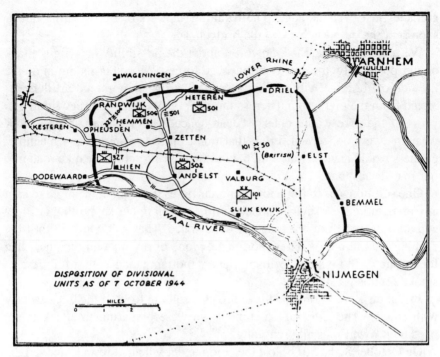

The "Island." (From *Rendezvous with Destiny, The History of the 101st Airborne Division*, enlarged edition (Sweetwater, TN: 101st Airborne Division Assoc., 1948), 391.

stances. The British we had relieved at dark were dug into the near shoulder of the main dike, some 400 yards from the river. The dike was about 30 feet high with sloping sides and a two-lane paved road along the top. There were Germans dug in on the opposite shoulder, less than 20 yards away! They were the outpost line of an enemy bridgehead located in a brick factory by the riverside to our immediate front.

British infantry had launched several attacks against that bridgehead prior to our arrival. We could tell how far each assault had gotten across the pool-table terrain intervening by the rows of dead Tommies still out there.

It being suicidal to raise one's head above road level, the only weapons we could employ against the Germans just across the dike were hand grenades. Unfortunately, if a grenade did not land right in one of their fox-holes, it would just roll on down the sloping side to explode harmlessly at the bottom. If it should enter a foxhole, it was quite apt to come sailing right back. That area of such close contact became known as "Grenade Court" among the troops involved.

That situation came to an end when some ingenious trooper tied enough bootlaces together to reach across the dike and dangle white phosphorous grenades just over the edge. The resulting showers of flesh-searing horror soon sent the outposts back to the bridgehead.

We remained concerned, however, about the possibility of a night attack on our position by the enemy bridgehead forces. We could not dig in on the far side of the dike without being shellacked by mortars and artillery directed from the high ground across the river. Any enemy getting within 150 yards of the dike would enter a "dead space" so far as our flat trajectory weapons were concerned. From that point on, our riflemen and machine-gunners would have to wait until they came pouring across the dike road into our lines to respond.

One solution was to fire enough mortar flares throughout the night to spot any preparations for such an attack in time to call in our supporting artillery and stop them before reaching the dead space. That worked well until the evening we ran out of flares. Fortunately, one of my platoon members had found one of those small British infantry mortars along with a full case of smoke rounds for it.

Just at dusk we "stonked" the entire area right in front of the brick factory with smoke. The Germans, assuming we were preparing to attack them, fired their own flares all night long.

On October 8, the 501st lost the commander who had formed and led the regiment since November 1942. Colonel Howard "Jumpy" Johnson was struck by fragments of a German artillery shell and died while being evacuated. His last words were addressed to Lieutenant Colonel Ewell, who was to succeed him: "Take care of my boys."

Within the next few days, we had shelled and sniped the brick-factory bridgehead forces into withdrawing across the river. I took a patrol down there to make certain they'd left and to establish outposts along the river dike in front of E Company's sector. The battle simmered down to ducking "incoming mail," as enemy shellfire was called, and making ourselves comfortable.

The British had evacuated all civilians from the area before our arrival there, so we were making use of their houses and buildings as well as much of the edible livestock left behind. Unfortunately, this freedom of access inspired boyish pranks such as looting and opening wall safes with bazooka rounds. It was a court-martial offense to remove any civilian item from any building. When these misdeeds came to light at division headquarters, a great furor ensued. A number of officers were relieved of command, and the area swarmed with investigators grilling any and all troopers remotely suspected of participation in the transgressions.

Enough suspicion was cast upon F Company men to mandate relief of Captain Bill Morgan, one of the staunchest combat leaders in the regiment.

Lieutenant Colonel Julian J. Ewell assumed command of the regiment when Colonel Johnson was killed in Holland. Wounded at Bastogne, he ended his military career as a lieutenant general. (Photo, courtesy of Mark Bando, 501st PIR Historian)

He was replaced by a senior lieutenant from outside our battalion who initially displayed no convincing evidence of Morgan's capabilities. Colonel Ballard informed me that I was being transferred to F Company to help bridge the change.

I took over the third platoon, the one I had trained and led at Toccoa. Several of the original members had survived. It was like coming home again. The platoon command post was in the basement of a fire-damaged house just behind the dike. The concrete walls still retained some heat from the conflagration, but the sturdy ceiling and remains of upper floors made it impervious to weather and mortar fire. The adjacent barn had lost much of its roof to artillery rounds.

Division command's reaction to the looting incidents was still very much being felt. Men were pleading for outpost duty assignments to avoid further interrogations. One of the "Toccoa originals" in the platoon was Corporal Eugene Terleki. A born maverick and free spirit, he was often a disciplinary problem in garrison but usually a solid asset in combat situations.

Shortly after taking over the platoon, I had spent a long night walking the line and checking our outposts. I was still asleep in the CP when I was awakened with the news that Colonel Ballard was headed our way on an inspection tour and would arrive in about five minutes. I rushed out to make my own quick check of our area.

Terleki's position was right in front of the CP. He had a covered dugout in the sloping side of the dike a few feet down from the top and foxhole firing position on the edge of the road above it. A grandfather clock protruded three feet out of the foxhole!

I bellowed "TERLEKI-I-I-I!" and his shaggy head emerged from the dugout.

"WHAT THE HELL IS THAT CLOCK DOING THERE?" His reply was truculent but classic.

"Lieutenant, there's not a watch in my squad. Last night the guy who was supposed to relieve me left me on guard for four hours and that will NEVER happen again!"

Ballard not yet being in sight, I helped him ease the clock out of the hole and lay it flat on the edge of the roadbed where it could not be seen from below. The CO arrived, and after a short exchange of pleasantries, he continued down the line, remaining behind the dike. That night, under sincere threat of physical violence, Terleki returned the clock to the home from whence it had come.

Another division reaction was to order that no livestock in the area could be eaten, even if killed by German artillery. That dictum was particularly onerous in that our rations were still being supplied by the British army. Our troops considered the fare semi-palatable and totally boring. The frequency of oxtail stew and hardtack on the menu was the subject of continuous grousing. Now we could no longer vary the diet by so much as a chicken struck by an enemy mortar fragment, and most certainly not by one shot while attacking a sentry!

One morning a week or so after the Terleki incident, one of our battalion surgeons visited the lines on a field sanitation inspection. As he was leaving our platoon area, he mentioned a change in division policy. It was now permissible to butcher any livestock killed by enemy artillery. Hallelujah!

Just outside our basement CP, a 200-pound sow was rooting in the garden, clearly observable from the ground-level window. I called the platoon sergeant over to help me evaluate its state of health.

"Wouldn't you say that pig has been struck by German artillery, Sergeant?"

"Oh, yes, Sir! I'd say it hasn't long to live."

"Well, then, why don't you round up a small detail and do the humane thing?"

It took several men some 20 minutes to chivvy the animal into another barn nearby where I joined them to provide any leadership required thenceforth. One lad who had been raised on a farm assumed the role of technical advisor.

"The first thing we gotta do is shoot her in the head."

"Just where in the head do I shoot her, trooper?"

"Right between the eyes, Sir."

I placed a carbine round precisely as directed. The disgruntled pig made a dash for the barn door where the technical advisor kicked her in the snout to turn her back. I placed a second shot right beside the first. This time she bowled the advisor over in departing the premises.

The detail chased her into an air-raid shelter that had been improvised by the evacuated civilians. They had covered a section of roadside ditch with logs and provided narrow entrances at each end. The pig evinced no desire to come out.

"I'll poke her with a stick from this end, Sergeant. You get her when she comes out the other."

The ploy worked. The sergeant grabbed her by the ear as she emerged and emptied his pistol into the top of her head where the advisor should have told me to shoot her. The troopers started dragging her back to the barn for butchering, and I returned to the platoon CP. Fifteen minutes later, one of the troopers in the detail came running in, breathless and ashen-faced.

"Sir, there's a Lieutenant Colonel at the barn who wants to see the officer in charge of the men who killed the pig!"

Hoo, boy! If it was Ewell, my military career was over. Instead, it was Lieutenant Colonel Griswold, commander of the 3rd Battalion. He was standing in front of the troopers, all veterans of the previous grillings. I got the impression they weren't even admitting there was a pig, despite the carcass on the floor of the barn. The colonel turned to face me and came right to the point.

"Sefton, who killed this pig?"

"Why, I killed it, Sir. It had been hit by German artillery."

Since the colonel's back was now turned to the troops, the platoon sergeant whipped out his trench knife and slashed the animal's flank, returning the blade to its sheath before joining the conversation.

"You can see the wound right here, Sir."

I doubt that the colonel was taken in, but he recognized a united front when he saw one. Besides, he had a little problem of his own.

"Tell you what, Sefton. My jeep is mired in the mud over there. You have your men get it out and we'll forget about this pig." The troops all but picked the vehicle up in getting it, along with my military career, back on firm ground.

Our part of the war had now simmered down to a stalemate with the enemy on one side of the Neder Rhine and us on the other. Exchanges of artillery and mortar fire continued, as did very limited patrolling across the river. Division badly wanted a prisoner from the other side to interrogate, but none of our patrols had succeeded in returning with one. Colonel Ballard asked me if I would have a try at it, but he was transferred to regiment as Ewell's executive officer before the project materialized. Meanwhile, Lieutenant Hugo Sims, the regimental S-2, decided to handle matters himself.

In a masterpiece of planning and execution, he took five men six miles beyond enemy lines at night to a house on the highway from Arnhem to Utrecht, capturing two Germans sleeping there. The patrol remained in the house throughout the next day, capturing three more Germans who came there and temporarily holding a number of civilian visitors, including a Dutch Underground member.

Sims had a radio set up in the attic and used it to relay all information from prisoners interrogated by Master Sergeant Peter Frank, who spoke fluent German, as well as that provided by the Underground man. At dark he decided to capture a vehicle on the highway and ride back to the river on an unimproved road shown on his map of the area. The truck he stopped had 14 fully armed SS troops in the back, all of whom were too surprised to resist. A bit later they captured the SS captain who came looking for his truck, along with the driver of his jeep.

The truck bogged down as Sims was trying to find the unimproved road, and the SS captain tried unsuccessfully to escape in the darkness. Sims thereupon decided to march his captives in column down a paved road to the dike with Frank counting cadence in German. They passed numerous houses full of Germans en route and marched right through the village of Renkum, the clatter of hobnail boots allaying the suspicions of enemy troops observing their progress.

On reaching the dike, they surprised several outposts, increasing their bag by another ten. They were ferried across the river by our troops awaiting their flashlight signals, returning safely with 32 prisoners. Sims was rewarded by having dinner with General Taylor, receiving the Distinguished Service Cross, and being promoted to captain. His feat was featured in the January 15, 1945, issue of *Life* magazine as "The Incredible Patrol."

Meanwhile, something akin to boredom was setting in on the battalion front. The Germans would relieve it occasionally by firing their "Screaming Meemie" rockets at us. They made a horrendous noise coming in but were not nearly as accurate as regular artillery. Otherwise, we were left to provide our own diversions.

Dale Smith, my former E Company platoon sergeant, was one of the world's most avid fishermen. He had liberated some hooks, lines, and sinkers somewhere and invited me to go fishing with him on the Rhine. We would go down at night, having arranged for a mortar squad to fire flares every 15 minutes so we could see to bait our hooks and scan the river for any evidence of enemy patrol activity. We never did get so much as a bite.

Private First Class Jim Nadeau had found an abandoned .50-caliber machine gun and several belts of ammunition. We mounted it in the attic of a house so we could fire across the dike and into German positions on the other side of the river. It was placed on a table near an open window and stabilized by sandbags on the legs of the tripod. The table proved to be a tad low so far as clearance of the windowsill was concerned.

Our first short burst from the weapon solved that particular problem. The window sill dissolved, spraying chips and splinters on a very disconcerted Lieutenant Mertz who happened to be passing by on the walk below. His outraged comments were louder than the echo of the shots still reverberating in the attic. From that day on, he decided to make my CP the command post for his machine-gun platoon as well. Possibly he felt safer knowing where I was and what I was doing than becoming an unwitting participant in the results of any future attempts to alleviate our boredom.

Having been a cook and a mess sergeant during prewar Regular Army service, Mertz soon organized a "perpetual stewpot" in the barn adjoining the CP. It functioned 24 hours a day with anything edible being tossed in as soon as it became available. The trick was to pick out items that had been stewing long enough to eat. It became a bit of a social center for anyone not on duty and the setting for long philosophical discussions with Mertz, which ripened into our lifelong friendship.

Chapter 25

Other Memories of the "Island"

Since we spent the better part of two months on the dikes, there are a number of memorable incidents I find hard to place in chronological context. But then I've always prefaced my war stories to family and friends by explaining, "If I've told you this one before, don't stop me — I'd like to hear it again myself." So here we go.

Our outposts on the river bank were few and far between. Sentinels spending the nights there were subject to flights of nervous imagination as well as to the tricks human eyesight can play in the dark. Some troopers leavened their outpost duty with a sense of humor, as did the one I contacted by the sound-powered field phone on a particularly dark night.

"Anything goin' on down there?"

"Naw, Lieutenant, except the Krauts are crossin' the river by regiments and one fence post in front of me here just walked over and relieved the other."

The commo wires laid from the CP to each outpost phone were often cut by artillery fire. When this happened one night as it was nearing my turn to walk the line, I decided to find the break and splice it myself, then go on to visit the outpost. The wire was laid along a faint path leading to the river with marshy growth on each side. The moon was evading the clouds often enough to make it easy going.

About midway there, I heard a shell coming in that was going to land very close to me on the right. It inspired a flat dive into the marshy growth left of the path. The shell burst, the moon cleared a cloud, and I was lying nose to nose with the remains of a Polish paratrooper. He obviously had been there since the Polish Airborne Brigade had jumped into that area toward the end of September in their ill-fated attempt to cross the Rhine and reinforce the British Airborne Division being decimated at Arnhem. It may or may not have been Halloween night, but it was a very spooky experience.

One does not parachute into combat with a wardrobe exceeding extra socks and underwear. We had been fighting in the same clothes for seven or eight weeks before a quartermaster unit established a shower facility in the regimental rear area. It was a very long, narrow tent, floored with duckboard and featuring perhaps 50 open shower stalls.

Troops arriving at the site would strip off all clothing at the entrance and toss it on a pile, never to be seen again. Then they would proceed along the duckboard aisle in the tent until the first man in line reached the furthermost shower head. The following trooper would stop at the one immediately adjacent, with that process being repeated down the line until there was a man poised at each stall. The drill from that point was simple.

The quartermaster sergeant would blow his whistle and the shower would go on for precisely five minutes, during which the next line would enter and stand in front of the stalls awaiting their turns when the whistle blew again five minutes later. I was in one of those following lines.

I did not know the name or rank of the man in the shower before me, but I can still vividly recall the waves of irrational, raging resentment permeating my psyche throughout those interminable five minutes. He was delaying MY shower, the first one I was to enjoy since D-Day! When the whistle finally blew, I spent the next five minutes resenting the man now awaiting the signal that would terminate my own brief allotment of luxury. This was a minor but memorable example of the effect prolonged combat can have on human emotional responses.

Upon exiting the shower tent, we were issued complete sets of new clothing, and life seemed downright tolerable again. By mid-November, however, cold, driving rains started dominating the weather. On one such morning, the platoon sergeant was peering morosely out the ground-level window of our basement CP at the straddle trench latrine, which had been dug in the garden beyond. He was clutching a small roll of toilet paper and contemplating the growing necessity of baring his buttocks to the inclement downpour. The radio operator, viewing his superior with unconcealed amusement, offered some sage advice.

"Just eat some more cheese, Sergeant, and pray for clear weather tomorrow!"

Then there was the time the battalion went into reserve a couple of miles behind the dike and was alerted for an inspection by the division commander, Major General Maxwell Taylor. The alert was in the form of a full page of precise instructions as to how the troops would be garbed, groomed, and formed in a hollow square for the occasion. The fact that we would still be well within German light artillery range was not mentioned.

In making the inspection, General Taylor passed by the front squad of each platoon. He was followed by the regimental commander, the battalion commander, and the pertinent company commander and platoon leader, in that order. When he reached my platoon, I hooked onto the tail of the entourage as prescribed.

One member of my platoon's first squad was a proverbial Sad Sack, but the squad leader had done everything possible to make the man semi-presentable, short of straightening his posture on a rack and having him bronzed. The general gave our Sack a cursory glance and was about to move on when he stopped short and barked a question.

"Soldier, where's your bayonet?"

Hoo, boy! A number of acceptable replies were flitting through my mind, ranging from "I broke it off in a Kraut" to "Somebody stole it last night." The Sack, however, was not blessed with such creativity nor burdened by awe of high-ranking officers. His reply has remained forever seared in my memory.

"It got too heavy, General."

Taylor turned to glare at the regimental commander, who glared at the battalion commander, who glared at the company commander, who glared at me. It was to be some time before I began to appreciate the GI humor of that particular experience.

Sometime thereafter an infected molar required a trip to a dentist in the regimental rear area. Arriving near noon, I decided to join the chow line forming in the rain outside the mess tent. The cooks were carrying out large covered containers, which pervaded the area with the presence of their contents. It could only be the British army's haricot oxtail concoction.

As a cook removed the cover from the first container, the trooper at the head of the line looked in and clapped his hands. He then turned to face the rest of the line and shouted in pseudo ecstasy, "STEW!"

The monotony of British rations was still affecting troop morale as Thanksgiving Day approached. The division policy regarding livestock hit by German artillery had been stiffened to the extent that any such incident had to be verified by a company commander before his troops could butcher the casualty.

F Company was holding a different section of the dike, and there was a hefty young steer in the area. On learning that we could expect no change in rations for our Thanksgiving meal, the platoon corralled it in a nearby barn the day before the holiday. The company CP was more than 500 yards away,

A trooper and his friend prepare to leave "the Island" in late November 1944. (Photo, National Archives, 111-SC-329000)

so I waited until it was raining very hard before calling the company commander.

"Lieutenant, we have a cow hit by artillery here and would like to butcher it. C'mon down and verify it for us."

"Well, Sefton, I'll try to get down there later this afternoon."

"That'll be too late, Lieutenant. If we wanna use the meat, we've gotta finish bleeding it right now!"

"Well, in that case, go ahead. But save a front quarter for company headquarters, huh?"

Every man in the platoon enjoyed as much Thanksgiving steak as he could handle, and we disdained British rations for days thereafter. Meanwhile, the heavy rains continued, causing the river and the water table in the terrain to rise accordingly. The Germans still held the dikes that protected the Island to the east. Once the rivers were high enough, they could blow those dikes and flood the entire area. Rumors of such impending disaster merged with word the division might be pulling out of the area soon.

Very late in November, we were relieved by Scottish troops as the division started withdrawing unit by unit. By the time F Company left the dike, we had been in combat for 72 days. Now we were going to someplace called Camp Mourmelon in France. The Germans did, indeed, blow the dikes shortly thereafter, completely flooding the Island.

My most compelling recollection of the trip to Mourmelon is that of riding in the back of a truck as our convoy wound through Brussels. We had run short of water purification tablets during our last days on the dike, and several of the men were suffering attacks of dysentery. When their cramps reached the critical stage, they had no recourse but to hang their bared tails over the tailgate and let nature take its course. Anyone doing so would, perforce, "moon" the cab occupants of the following truck as well as any civilians watching the convoy pass.

One of the afflicted troopers kept asking me to stop the truck, becoming more and more insistent as his cramps increased. I told him that I was not in charge of the truck, which could not leave the convoy regardless, and that he could follow the example of his fellow-sufferers if he were so inclined. His reaction was verging on outrage when the convoy suddenly pulled to the side of the boulevard we were traveling on and stopped.

The trooper leaped over the tailgate, landing a few feet from a roadside slit trench presumably dug by Germans during their retreat across Belgium. He jumped into the shelter, clawing at his belt buckle. Directly across the sidewalk from the trench was a much wider walk coming from a soccer stadium some 50 yards beyond. And a well-attended match had just ended!

Soccer fans came down the wider walk 10 or 12 abreast. Those in the first wave spotted the helmet of the trooper in the trench and stepped over to see what he was doing. Enough of those following joined them until the site was completely surrounded by giggling gawkers. The occupant, thoroughly outraged, was starring in what may well have been the most publicly witnessed defecation in the annals of warfare.

Somehow it seemed a fitting conclusion to our service under Monty.

Chapter 26

Brief Respite at Mourmelon

Camp Mourmelon was an old French artillery post, less than 20 miles south of Reims and 80 miles north of Paris. The brick buildings were sound but dilapidated. The landscape was dreary and still scarred by World War I's stalemate along the Meuse River. During a night training exercise, I gashed a leg on barbed wire remaining from that war and still have the scar to prove it.

Shortly after arriving there, I was transferred to D Company as executive officer. The company commander had been a platoon leader from Toccoa until Normandy, where CO Captain Bill Osborne's chute was shot apart on the jump, resulting in a severely broken leg, and the plane carrying executive officer Lieutenant Ian Nicholson was shot down short of the DZ. As senior platoon leader, he had taken command of the company.

D Company went into Holland with replacement platoon leaders who had not served in Normandy. There were rumors, reportedly emanating from the CO, that they had lacked bold leadership qualities. I was to learn that those rumors were grossly unfounded. For this and other reasons that would become apparent, I will refer to the D Company commander henceforth only as "the CO."

Having received virtually no replacements while in Holland, a primary job was to assign and train those now pouring in as well as to requisition new armament and equipment for that which had been lost, damaged, or destroyed in combat. While there was a lot to be done, we did not expect another mission for several months.

Meanwhile, there were passes to Reims and Paris. Unfortunately, SHAEF (Supreme Headquarters of the Allied Expeditionary Force) headquarters was in Reims, and the exuberance of paratroopers just returning from 70+ days of combat soon palled on the galaxy of high brass stationed there. Pass allocations to Reims became highly restricted, but then Paris was much the preferred destination so far as our troops were concerned. Naturally, of course, they attracted attention there, as well. Consequently, Colonel Ewell called all regimental officers together to discuss the problem of troop conduct in Paris. His comments are still engraved in my memory.

"Now I know the story. Our lad says, 'the MPs are picking on us because we're paratroopers.' The truth is he was staggering down the street drunk. The MP said, 'Hey, soldier, your fly is open,' and our boy said, 'F—- you, Jocko!' " Ewell always understood the enlisted man's point of view, despite being a West Point graduate.

For company grade officers not on pass, our quarters became our social center. Champagne was cheap, and even cognac was downright reasonable. I bought a case of the latter for which I had developed a sincere appreciation. The bottles of cognac were corked, and we were a bit short of corkscrews, but we developed the technique of placing a folded towel on a table and banging the bottom of the bottle sharply upon it. The cork would then ooze slowly upward, freeing the contents for consumption.

Early on the morning of December 17, Lieutenant Joe McGregor awakened me to request a personal favor.

"Bill, the pass convoy for Paris left an hour ago. Somebody got sick and couldn't go. I'm the next name on the list and a jeep driver will take me to catch the convoy, but it's gonna be a hard, cold ride. How about a good slug of your cognac for insulation?"

"Sure, Joe, let me open a bottle for you." With that I placed a folded towel on a table as he stood across from me, resplendent in his Class A pinks and greens. With assurance verging on bravado, I raised the bottle on high and brought its bottom down on the towel with flourish and force. It shattered, dousing Joe's uniform from the waist down. He left for Paris smelling like a distillery. I was not to see him again until the morning of the day he was killed.

That evening there was the usual booze 'n bull session in our quarters, ending somewhat short of midnight. I was sleeping soundly when the CO shook me awake, saying "Get up — we're goin' in again!" I made several uncomplimentary remarks regarding his sense of humor before realizing he was serious. According to him, the division had been alerted to move out in 12 hours to "exploit a breakthrough." It was to be a very busy 12 hours.

In being transferred to D Company, I had relieved Lieutenant Denver Bennet who became battalion mess officer. The CO asked that he be returned to his old job and that I take over a platoon for the new mission. I was not a bit unhappy with such news, having already discovered the job of executive officer was quite reminiscent of staff service.

We spent a chaotic morning getting ready to go. Many critical items of equipment, including weapons, had gone in for repair or exchange. There were virtually no overcoats available. According to our regimental history, *Four Stars of Hell,* ten percent of the men boarding the trucks that afternoon were unarmed!

The trucks were simply cabs with long trailers resembling box cars with sides four feet high and no tops. We clambered aboard two hours after noon and were on our way to becoming the "Battered Bastards of Bastogne."

Chapter 27

Butting Heads at Bastogne

The trucks jammed with our troops rolled north for some 12 hours. It was a long, cold, miserable trip with no room to lie down except on top of each other. I was fortunate enough to be riding in a cab where I reflected on the fact that I hadn't yet had time to learn the names of key NCOs in my new platoon. Nor had I received further enlightenment from the CO regarding our mission since the "exploit a breakthrough" bit when he had awakened me the night before.

Sometime near midnight, the convoy pulled over along a tree-lined road, and travel-weary troops stumbled from the trucks to flop on the ground wherever they found room. I fell asleep in a muddy ditch. Recalling my father's descriptions of countries from his World War I experience, I thought we might be in Luxembourg.

In the first foggy light of dawn, the 2nd Battalion lined up on the road and marched past a sign that read "Bastogne," which meant nothing to most of us. It had, however, meant a lot to Colonel Ewell, who had arrived the day before. Our regimental commander had taken a short leave while we were on the dike in Holland and had visited that focal road net in the Ardennes, the historic German invasion route into France. The fact that the 501st Regiment was the first major unit of the 101st Airborne Division to arrive on the scene also proved fortuitous in the course of events to follow.

A short, potbellied sergeant wearing a 28th Division patch was standing on the roadside as we entered the town. Weaponless and traumatized, he kept repeating, "Go back! Go Back! There's a million of 'em out there!" His regiment had been assaulted and routed by two German divisions.

From *Rendezvous with Destiny, The History of the 101st Airborne Division,* enlarged edition
(Sweetwater, TN: 101st Airborne Division Assoc., 1948), 443.

Meanwhile, vehicles crammed with VIII Corps staff personnel, MPs, and
other rear echelon types were streaming south out of town. The breakthrough we were to "exploit" wasn't ours.

Our column halted on the sidewalk in midtown. A window in the building beside me opened a few inches, and a hand offered a cup of coffee. I
accepted it gratefully as the window closed without a word having been spo-
ken. Just ahead an American flag had been painted on the side of a building
beyond an alleyway. A civilian was hastily covering it with black paint. A
few minutes later, two artillery shells landed somewhere nearby.

Major General Troy Middleton commanded VIII Corps headquartered in
Bastogne. His thinly spread divisions had been severely punished by the
German surprise offensive, and communications with them had been badly
disrupted. He had been ordered to withdraw his headquarters farther south.

From *Rendezvous with Destiny, The History of the 101st Airborne Division,* enlarged edition (Sweetwater, TN: 101st Airborne Division Assoc., 1948), 475.

All he could tell the 101st advance party was that the enemy was approaching in great force and could be expected to attack very soon.

Colonel Ewell was assigned the 501st mission of proceeding to the village of Longvilly, 6½ miles east-northeast of Bastogne, where an element of the green 9th Armored Division had reportedly established a roadblock. Specifically, he was to "Move out on this road at 0600, make contact, attack, and clean up the situation." The 1st Battalion left town in the heavy fog at precisely that moment. Less than halfway there, near the small village of Neffe, the battalion found the enemy in sufficient strength to stop their progress. Their CO, Major Ray Bottomly, radioed Ewell that he had hit a German roadblock estimated to be comprised of "two infantry platoons and two tanks." In fact, he had butted heads with the point of General Bayerlein's Panzer Lehr Division, leading the 47th Panzer Corps to Bastogne. Ironically, the Germans assumed they had encountered an American roadblock.

By 10:00, it was obvious that the 1st Battalion could not advance against the increasing strength of the "roadblock," so Ewell ordered our battalion to move up on the left and seize the hamlet of Bizory, a mile north of Neffe. We moved out in a column of companies with D following E and F.

The leading companies entered Bizory without opposition and deployed on the high ground just beyond, while D Company halted on the road awaiting orders. Lieutenant Bennet came along to bum a chew of tobacco, which I didn't have.

"Sorry, Ben, all I've got is some cigars."

"Well, how about one of them?"

The cigars had arrived from my nurse friend, now stationed in Paris, the day before we left Mourmelon. There were 14 big black ones, wrapped in gauze and protected with tongue depressors. I had tossed the packet in my musette bag and now unwrapped them to hand one to Bennet. He promptly bit it in two, tucking the bitten part into his cheek and putting the rest in a pocket.

"That's a helluva way to treat a good cigar, Ben!"

"Well, Bill, a man's gotta have something to chew," with which he went on his way along the column. Shortly thereafter, D Company moved ahead to the near edge of Bizory, which nestled in a gentle little valley with higher ground fore and aft. Bennet and the CO went ahead, leaving me as senior officer with the company.

The road at that point was in a slight defile, cluttered with some 15 armored unit vehicles that had exfiltrated from their roadblock at Longvilly where they had been trapped and pounded by the advancing Germans. A bird colonel who resembled movie star Frank Morgan was indecisively in charge, but it was no time for me to be daunted by four grades difference in rank.

"Sir, all these vehicles are gonna draw fire pretty soon. You've gotta move 'em out of our area."

"What do you suggest, Lieutenant?"

"Well, Sir, Bastogne is just three miles back on this road. That's where I'd take 'em."

Five minutes later the little column started up the slight grade to where the road leveled off toward Bastogne. At that point a single anti-tank gun started pecking away at the vehicles from the direction of Neffe a mile away. Our troopers watched their progress with spirited interest, making bets as to which vehicle would be the first to get hit. None did while still within our sight.

Word finally came back from the CO that D Company was being held in reserve and that I was to put my platoon in a barn just across the road entering Bizory from the north. We were just getting nicely settled in when a runner arrived with a message for me.

"Lieutenant Bennet's been hit, so you're executive officer again! I'll take you up to company headquarters."

The CO had selected a small house on the edge of the high ground beyond the hamlet where E and F Companies were already engaging enemy units attempting to advance on Bizory. Lieutenant Bennet lay on the floor of that CP, his chest matted with blood and his face the gray-green color we had long since recognized as the portent of imminent demise. But he spoke in a surprisingly strong voice.

"Well, Bill, they got me." It was an occasion for the usual comforting lies.

"Don't worry, old buddy. We'll getcha outta here and the docs will patch you up!" Then I got busy checking with the 1st Sergeant, the message center, and other elements of company headquarters important to the executive officer function. Ben was still alive when the medic's jeep arrived to evacuate him. Two days later, we heard the entire Medical Company of the division had been captured by the Germans as they encircled Bastogne, but we figured Ben hadn't lasted that long anyway.

Some two months later, while fighting in Alsace-Lorraine, we received a letter from Ben enclosing a snapshot of him surf casting in Florida. It seemed he had been standing on the porch of the CP house when an artillery shell struck an eaves trough and a piece of shrapnel had sliced off an inch or so of pectoral muscle, causing severe bleeding. It also caused him to swallow the half of my cigar still tucked in his mouth, which, in turn, had resulted in the gray-green color. Apparently, the as yet uncaptured division medics had him evacuated further for intensive treatment in view of his symptoms. He never was returned for combat duty as I recall the incident!

By dark, the advancing Germans had been repulsed by E and F Companies backed by division artillery fire, but renewed assaults were expected at dawn. D Company was alerted to provide a platoon to lay anti-tank mines well beyond the battalion lines after dark. The CO recognized a good mission for his executive officer when he saw one.

It was 4:00 before the truckload of mines arrived in the area. In addition to strings of the mines, the troops also were burdened with engineer picks and shovels as well as their shoulder weapons. With the clanking of those accouterments, we sounded like a hardware store on the move.

Less than 200 yards on our way, an uncommonly heavy artillery piece started lobbing shells into our vicinity. They made a horrendous noise coming in and shook the ground when they hit. We heard one we knew would be closer yet, and the whole platoon went flat in a crescendo of clanking. Clods of dirt were still falling on us when someone in the darkness behind me yelled, "Lieutenant, I've been hit!"

"Can you make it back by yourself?"

"I think so."

Peering back into the darkness I could see a stocky figure hopping to the rear on one leg. He was making a good two yards per hop. We got underway again, following the guide who led us through the outpost line.

A bit later a fire fight started somewhere ahead. I'd heard a combat patrol had gone out earlier and assumed they were now probing the enemy outpost line. Our guide had disappeared, but I decided we should veer away from the fighting and get on with our mission. I called out for the platoon sergeant to advise that decision, but he didn't answer. Another voice explained why.

"He got hit, Lieutenant, and you sent him back." So much for operating in the dark with unfamiliar troops.

The level terrain was featureless, and visibility was virtually nil. The whole blessed area seemed a good avenue of approach for enemy armor. And it was getting on toward dawn. I halted the platoon, indicated an extent of ground that would provide for a reasonable density of mines and ordered, "Dig 'em in here."

By the time we'd finished, the eastern horizon was noticeably lighter. It was high time to hightail it, but the chances of hitting our outpost line precisely where we'd come through it ranged from slim to none. Looking back at the platoon, I realized they were already silhouetted against the skyline, so I preceded them by 50 yards, calling out loudly enough to be heard by trigger-happy troopers, "Five-oh-one! Five-oh-one!" My compass assured me we were heading back to Bizory, but where th'hell was our battalion line?

The question was answered by a machine-gunner some 70 yards ahead who opened fire without bothering to challenge. The platoon hit the ground behind me, but my own outraged reaction was to stand there as tracers streamed by my head and scream obscenities at the gunner. It was idiotic but effective. He stopped firing before I quit swearing, and we passed through the line unscathed.

The enemy did, indeed, attack across that terrain early that morning only to be repulsed by heavy losses from E and F Companies backed by a coordinated artillery barrage and tank destroyer support. If the mines we'd planted played any role in the action, I never heard about it.

D Company remained in reserve, digging in on the forward slope just short of Bizory. Our fresh foxholes were readily visible to enemy artillery observers as evidenced by incoming rounds. The attitude of the troops, however, was summarized by one Geronimo who noted the increasing number of shell holes among us.

"Throw in a few more, you bastards," he yelled in the Germans' direction, "and you won't be able to tell which holes are ours!"

By midmorning it was snowing steadily as temperatures dropped. Meanwhile, Colonel Ewell had committed the 3rd Battalion to the right of the 1st. I Company was sent into the village of Wardin on the extreme right flank where it was trapped by an armor/infantry assault, losing 45 men and 4 officers, including the company commander. After dark, both battalions were hit in aggressive two-pronged attacks, which also were repulsed with very heavy enemy losses.

The day before, the 506th Regiment had moved up to reinforce an armor roadblock at the village of Noville well to the left of our battalion of the 501st, leaving a considerable gap between the two regiments. Our A Company, in 1st Battalion Reserve, had been attached to 2nd Battalion to fill that gap, but as yet had only patrol contact with the 506th. They were positioned in pine woods just beyond a railroad track which ran straight into Bastogne.

On the night of that second day, A Company was hit with an attack that drove it out of position. Our battalion commander, Major Sammie Homan, thereupon issued an order I found very hard to believe. D Company was to pull back well over a mile, hook up with A Company and attack, two companies abreast, through the woods, with a rolling artillery barrage 200 yards ahead. Then we were to assault and restore the position! Helluva plan, Sammie!

All we had to do was barge a mile or more through unreconnoitered woods in the Stygian night, dodging tree bursts from unobserved artillery support, until we could stumble upon an awaiting enemy force of unknown strength. Provided, of course, we could maintain any semblance of a two-company front until we got that far.

No military terrain maps of the area were available at company level, but we did have a civilian road map with woods indicated in green. It showed a solid expanse of green from immediately left of D Company's position to the railroad track where A Company had been attacked. So I approached the CO.

"Look, our left flank platoon is right up against the edge of this woods now. Why not ask Sammie if we can't send a recon patrol to see if the enemy is still on the other side of the railroad, then move out at dawn to hit 'em with a flank attack?" He did, and the order to move out was deferred accordingly.

I picked an assistant platoon leader for the patrol. "Take five men and ease through the edge of this woods until you've reached the railroad track or found any enemy this side of it, whichever happens first. Then get back here and report." He returned in a couple of hours to say the mission was accomplished — there was no enemy this side of the track. The change in orders was confirmed.

It had been a good mission for us, so far. Since breaking through with their massive surprise assault on December 16, the German forces approaching Bastogne had been rolling over retreating elements of demoralized American units. Now they were encountering spirited and effective resistance at a very key objective, and their progress was thrown off stride.

During a postwar debriefing with American intelligence officers, General Bayerlein of the Panzer Lehr Division said, "The movement of the infantry regiment which had come out of Bastogne to attack me had reacted decisively on my thinking. Their fire superiority at Neffe was something I had witnessed with my own eyes. I thought and said that we should attack Bastogne with the whole XXXXVII Corps."

He was speaking, of course, of the 501st. Jumpy Johnson would have been very proud of us.

Chapter 28

Becoming "The Hole in a Doughnut"

While D Company fitfully spent the cold night awaiting dawn, German forces cut the road running south from Bastogne to Neufchateau, the last paved route out of town. In describing the situation of the 101st Division to VIII Corps headquarters by radio in the clear, G-3 Lieutenant Colonel Harry Kinnard explained: "You know what a doughnut looks like? Well, we're the hole in the doughnut."

When a tanker, now besieged along with us, heard the news, he yelled in alarm, "We're surrounded! We're surrounded!"

A paratrooper standing nearby was comparatively unconcerned. "Hell!" he remarked. "We always start out that way."

The most apt remark, reportedly by an unidentified trooper, was this: "They've got us surrounded, the poor bastards!"

When dawn arrived, it was accompanied by heavy fog and convincing evidence that the road map was wrong. The woods on our immediate left was not the one from which A Company had been driven the night before. There was a gap of several hundred yards between the two.

The patrol I'd sent had gone to the far edge of the near woods, thought they were looking at the railroad track, and returned to report the mission accomplished.

The CO, in near panic, issued what may well have been the shortest attack order on record. "Sefton, take two platoons and go that way. I'll take the other one and go this way!"

The "that way" bit was indicated by a wave of his arm at the road to our front, which ran northward from Bizory to Foy, intersecting the railroad at

From *Rendezvous with Destiny, The History of the 101st Airborne Division,* enlarged edition (Sweetwater, TN: 101st Airborne Division Assoc., 1948), 506.

the Halt station, some 200 yards beyond the woods where A Company had been attacked. He did not feel constrained to mention that four patrols sent up that road the day before had withdrawn under fire. Meanwhile, he took the remaining platoon and disappeared into the woods on our immediate left. So much for coordinating plans for a dawn attack.

Visibility in the murky half-light was hardly a hundred yards. We moved up the road in a column of twos, at tactical interval, with scouts out in front. I had no radio nor any idea where the CO might be with the other platoon. Great way to start a new day!

We had gone about 500 yards in silence broken only by the shuffling of our boots on the roadway. Visibility was improving steadily. I could make out the railroad crossing our road on somewhat higher ground ahead. On our left, the open ground sloped 150 yards up to a woods just short of where the railroad entered it. That had to be our objective. If any enemy were there,

From *Rendezvous with Destiny, The History of the 101st Airborne Division,* enlarged edition
(Sweetwater, TN: 101st Airborne Division Assoc., 1948), 507.

they should have been shooting at us already.

Just then the scouts returned to report unidentified troops moving about in the woods alongside the road ahead where the Halt station had to be. It was decision time in the valley! I told the leader of the lead platoon to head for the trees at the left in tactical formation, ready to fight if required. I would follow with the other platoon 50 yards behind. The troops left briskly.

The lead elements had reached the edge of the woods unopposed, and I was halfway there, myself, when a ragged volley of rifle fire broke out behind me. I looked back to see a German soldier going down as he had attempted to run up the slope toward the Halt station. He was less than 30 yards from the troopers at the tail end of our column. They had shot him as they were preparing to leave the road en route to the woods we were entering.

Concerned with the attention this brought to our presence, I pumped my right arm as the signal for double time and yelled for the troops ahead who had not yet reached the woods to hustle on up there. Twenty yards later I heard another volley of shots behind us and saw the same German going down a second time!

We all got into the woods without further incident. I deployed one platoon to dig in facing the way we had come and the other to turn our left flank by facing the railroad track. Meanwhile, a sergeant who had been at the tail of the column enlightened me concerning the twice-downed German.

The sergeant and his squad were just ready to leave the road when two figures came strolling down the slope from the Halt station area. One trooper, not knowing our scouts had already returned, remarked, "Here come our scouts back. Gee, in this fog they look just like Krauts!" Which, of course they were, coming to welcome what they assumed to be another German unit.

They walked right up to the squad, rifles still slung on their shoulders. A trooper grabbed the nearest one and jerked his weapon away. The other, who had stopped a few feet short, turned around and started walking, then running, back from whence he'd come. Several troopers opened fire and he went down, only to get up a few seconds later, inviting a repeat of the process.

"I think he's still alive," the sergeant noted, "and I'd like to take a coupla guys and bring him in." I told him to go ahead, but to hurry before it got much lighter. They were back in less than ten minutes.

The German had been shot several times through the back of each leg. The exit wounds were gory. When an aid man had stanched the bleeding, I tried to interrogate him without benefit of an interpreter. He knew enough English to keep mumbling, "I am not a soldat. I am a student." He couldn't have been more than seventeen, and the glasses he wore had very thick lenses. Hitler had, indeed, scraped the bottom of the barrel to launch his surprise offensive. That particular victim of *Der Fuhrer's* lunacy lived to be evacuated later in the day.

Meanwhile, the CO arrived with the remainder of the platoon, having delayed progress on the shorter and more covered route until we'd reached the objective. I was to learn that the wait-and-see-what-happens ploy was characteristic of his combat philosophy. He positioned the platoon to extend our right flank and moved deeper into the woods with his company headquarters group to get the CP dugout established.

By the time front-line positions were half completed, visibility had improved enough to reveal a lone German soldier digging a foxhole on the shoulder of the road we had left so shortly before!

Guarding the road to Bastogne with a bazooka. (Photo, National Archives, 111-SC-246723, by Al Krochka, December 25, 1944)

One of the men offered me his M-1 rifle. "You wanna shoot him, Lieutenant?" I took the prone position and sighted the weapon. It would not be a tough shot, less than 200 yards, slightly downhill.

The German obviously was an outpost, digging forlornly alone in the muddy ground. He looked old, small, and tired with a coal scuttle helmet too large for his head. I handed the rifle back with a reasonable explanation: "Let's not reveal our position until we're fully dug in." Then I resumed walking the line to encourage faster emplacement progress. The only sound we were making was the clinking of entrenching tools in the somewhat flinty earth.

Halfway toward the right flank, a machine-gun team was completing its V-shaped emplacement, each man almost three feet down in his side of the V. I paused in front of them, with my back to the road, to comment on their field of fire and moved on. I had taken two steps when a burst of machine-gun fire from the fog in the direction of Halt station got them both. One, struck in the chest, died instantly. The other, hit in the head, kept jerking spasmodically.

There was no enemy follow-up to that one random burst. The gunner could not have known he cost us two casualties. If not for the two steps I'd taken, it would have been three. Half-an-hour later, all positions were completed, so I went to find the CP and dig my own slit trench.

The CO had chosen a spot some 100 yards back in the woods near a small, shallow stone quarry. The aid men had put the trooper who had been shot through the head on a stretcher and placed it in the quarry. He was lying on his back, plumes of his breath in alternating lengths were visible in the cold air. His spasmodic jerking continued, causing him to bounce slightly on the stretcher. Company headquarters troopers, digging in nearby, would stop to rest momentarily, glance at the man on the stretcher and go right back to digging more briskly.

As his plumes of breath became yet more irregular, I started wondering if he had ever been baptized. A check of his dog tags showed the RC for Roman Catholic. I went back to digging my slit trench as the plumes slowed and then stopped.

Later that morning, units of the 506th attacked along the other side of the railroad track. The sounds of the fire fight were like those of a giant popcorn machine as the crescendo built. Some of the enemy fled across the track into the guns of the platoon I had flanked in that direction. Their bodies remained there for days.

Some time thereafter, Lieutenant Mertz brought Battalion Headquarters Company up into the next woods behind us. He was commanding the unit in lieu of Captain Rhett, who had been on leave in Paris when we left

Mourmelon. The entire regiment was to remain in the positions now held for the better part of three rather quiet weeks.

The Germans had learned they would not enter Bastogne through the 501st. Meanwhile, the snow grew deeper, and the temperature continued to fall.

Chapter 29

"Aw, Nuts!"

At 11:30 on December 22, a German major accompanied by an English-speaking captain and two enlisted men approached the lines of the 327th Glider Regiment under a white flag. They carried a written demand for surrender of the American forces holding Bastogne. The two officers were blindfolded and taken to division headquarters where Brigadier General Anthony McAuliffe was commanding in lieu of Major General Maxwell Taylor, who had flown to the Pentagon while we were at Mourmelon.

The German captain translated the demand which warned that failure to surrender promptly would result in destruction of Bastogne by artillery barrages and that the blood of civilians killed would be on American hands. The general's reaction was to mutter, "Aw, nuts!" knowing we had been bashing the enemy wherever they'd attacked. Then he asked his staff for suggestions in wording a reply.

Colonel Kinnard said, "That first remark of yours would be hard to beat." The one-word reply, "Nuts!" was to be emblazoned in headlines at home and abroad as the press dramatized the bravado of the besieged. We became "The Battered Bastards of the Bastion of Bastogne" to alliteration-loving reporters.

The threat of massive artillery barrages failed to materialize, but the Germans continued to attack aggressively against other sectors of the perimeter which comprised a rough circle with a three-mile radius around Bastogne. Defense plans called for a ring of infantry strong points on key terrain features with armor task forces in reserve to repel enemy break-throughs. The 501st faced primarily east with the 506th on our left. The 327th Glider Regiment was on our right, holding nearly that half of the perimeter which featured less threatening avenues of approach for enemy armor. The 502nd completed the perimeter between them and the 506th. All three of the other regiments were to become fiercely engaged periodically over the next four days. The 501st, however, was subjected only to probing attacks despite the favorable terrain to our front.

Aside from the punishing weather, our greatest concern by December 22 was the rapidly diminishing stocks of food, ammunition, and medical supplies. Front-line troops were receiving two meals per day — a couple of flapjacks before dawn and half a canteen cup of stew after dark. Many artillery pieces and tank guns were down to ten rounds each, and small arms ammunition also was running low. In gallows humor, some troopers suggested gathering rocks to throw at the enemy.

On December 23, the weather finally cleared; and that afternoon a sky train of 241 C-47s dropped 1,446 bundles containing 144 tons of supplies into a mile-square Drop Zone within the perimeter. Another 100 tons was dropped by 160 planes the next day. The shortages were hardly corrected in full, but things were looking up.

The good flying weather also brought swarms of close support dive bombers to hammer and harass German armor, which the pilots could pinpoint by the tracks they made in the snow.

None of these welcome factors, however, could protect against the bitter cold. In that regard we fended for ourselves, lining the frozen bottoms of foxholes and slit trenches with small pine boughs and pulling ponchos over the tops when sleeping. Those lucky enough to have galoshes filled them with straw and wore them in lieu of their jump boots. Even so, D Company was losing more men to frozen feet than to enemy action.

There were numerous farmsteads within our sector of the perimeter occupied by Belgian families. Battalion headquarters arranged for use of some of their kitchens as warming rooms. We sent squads back one at a time during daylight hours to clean weapons, dry socks, and enjoy brief respites from the cold. Then it was back to the line for another miserable night.

Those nights were spent in sleeping bags when circumstances permitted. The bags, which replaced the blankets and shelter-halves previously issued, were simply "cocoons" made of Army blanket material with an outer layer of shelter-half cloth and a zipper running from the tapered bottom to the opening for the face near the top. In that weather, almost every man on the line got into his bag fully clothed. The trick was to open the zipper, stand in the bottom, pull the bag up over shoulders and head, then zip it up and wriggle into whatever degree of comfort might be feasible in the frozen bottom of slit trench or foxhole.

To rifle company men, division headquarters troops were strictly "rear

From *Rendezvous with Destiny, The History of the 101st Airborne Division,* enlarged edition (Sweetwater, TN: 101st Airborne Division Assoc., 1948), 523.

echelon," enjoying the comforts of billets in Bastogne. The fact that the town received almost continuous artillery fire did not generate much front-line sympathy, nor did the four consecutive nights of enemy bombing attacks which started December 22.

On the third such night, which happened to be Christmas eve, I was walking the line just as the Luftwaffe struck again. Bombs were crunching and anti-aircraft guns raging, filling the dark sky with streams of tracers.

I came up unnoticed behind two of our men standing guard in adjacent foxholes, both staring straight ahead at the snowfields between us and the distant woods from which the Germans would come if attacking. The air strike had been underway for five minutes before one of them slowly craned his neck to observe the fireworks in the sky behind him. Then he slowly returned his gaze to the front with a single remark to his buddy.

"They're bombin' hell out of Bastogne again."

From *Rendezvous with Destiny, The History of the 101st Airborne Division,* enlarged edition
(Sweetwater, TN: 101st Airborne Division Assoc., 1948), 547.

The other trooper took his own slow look and confirmed the observation.
"Yeah. They sure as shit are." So much for the hardships of rear echelon
types compared to our own.

Each day at dawn the Germans would plaster our D Company area with
mortars, apparently just in case we might be preparing to attack. In the
middle of one barrage, I was huddling in the bottom of my slit trench when
the field phone rang in the communications section position 20 yards away.
A muffled voice yelled, "Lieutenant Sefton, it's for you. Sounds like the battalion commander!"

I scrambled through the snow and shrapnel fragments from tree bursts
only to hear the familiar voice of Lieutenant Mertz. He had been listening to
the pounding from the sanctuary of the woods behind us and wanted to
know, "Are you okay?" I thanked him for his concern, noted that it could
damned well get me killed, and got th'hell back to my slit trench.

A medical emergency guard at Bastogne. (Photo, National Archives, by Al Krochka)

During the quiet daylight hours, I would go back to visit Mertz. Toward the rear of our woods, American bodies were stacked head to foot between two pine trees like so many layers of cordwood, waiting in frozen silence for eventual evacuation as the covering snow blended them into the landscape. All were casualties of the fighting along the railroad track.

From Mertz's Battalion Headquarters Company dugout, we would go on back to the cluster of farmsteads where one of the warming facilities had been arranged. An adjacent farmer had a very small auxiliary kitchen no longer used by his family, and he readily made it available to us. It became a two-member Officer's Club, quite likely the only such establishment within the Bastogne perimeter.

Mertz had a partial bottle of gin, and I had my dwindling supply of cigars. We would ration ourselves to one drink and one cigar per day while debating possible courses of action if the enemy should succeed in breaking through one of the other regiments. Surrender was not one of the options considered. Instead, we decided, we would take as many volunteers as we could handle and attack through the German units facing us. If successful, we could then hide out during the day and make our way toward American lines beyond Bastogne each night.

Our host farmer had a 12-year-old daughter whose curiosity concerning Americans would bring her popping into our kitchen on the pretense of seeing if there was anything we needed. Mertz decided he would like some milk and tried to request it via a small French/English dictionary. In the faltering attempt, he asked her to "Bring us the water of the cow." I managed to recall the word "lait" for "milk" by the time her hysterical giggling had ceased.

Just before we had jumped into Normandy, Mertz had dreamed things would be screwed up beyond recognition, which, of course, they were. Before the Holland jump, he had dreamed all would go well, as indeed it had. He became a believer in his prophetic dreams.

On our early hikes back to "The Club," Mertz would leave his carbine in the dugout, carrying only his pistol. On Christmas Day, however, he brought his carbine along as well. About halfway back to the farmsteads, the dirt road made a sharp right/left jog through an underpass beneath the railroad. As we reached that point, he dropped to one knee, saying, "My bootlace has come untied. Just keep going and I'll catch up."

I noted that we were in no hurry whatsoever, and I certainly didn't mind waiting for him. He fumbled with the lace a bit, then held his carbine at the ready as he accompanied me with uncharacteristic wariness through the underpass.

Only after we had downed our shots of gin and shared two of the last three cigars did he confess the significance of the bootlace incident. During the night he had dreamed he was captured by a German MP. He'd wanted me to navigate the jog under the railroad first just in case the Kraut was hiding there in ambush!

By the afternoon of December 26, we could hear the guns of Patton's 4th Armored Division battering the Germans south of Bastogne and could see their artillery observation planes overhead. Relief of the siege was at hand! Mertz and I headed for our sanctuary to celebrate. We ceremoniously killed what was left of the gin and devoured the K-ration fragments we'd been hoarding for emergency use. I had one cigar left for the two of us. Mertz said, "Hand it here."

He laid it on the table, whipped out his trench knife, and whacked it across the middle. It shattered from end to end. We might possibly have smoked it in pipes, had there been any available. The role of cigars in our relationship will reappear later.

By the time we'd returned to our units, the first 4th Armored tanks had entered the 101st Airborne lines on the south side of the perimeter.

The encirclement was broken.

Chapter 30

Bloody Bois Jacque

General Taylor accompanied advance elements of the 4th Armored Division into Bastogne on December 27 and radioed corps headquarters that the 101st was "ready for offensive operations." The prospect of wading into enemy fire through knee-deep snow was viewed with less than overwhelming enthusiasm by front-line troops.

The fighting that followed was the most bitter and costly to date for the 101st Airborne Division. Temperatures ranged from 0 to 20 above. The ground was frozen. Our green combat garb stood out like firing range targets against the snow. The Germans defended fanatically against the American drive to pinch off the "Bulge" before they could withdraw. And Bastogne was a wedge in that bulge, pressing on the nerve center of a main withdrawal route.

Things kicked off on or about January 1 with a tank/infantry attack through our D Company position to secure an assembly area in the heavy woods several hundred yards to our front. Le Bois Jacque (Jack's Woods) extended north from there some 1,000 yards, intersected by the railroad near its south end.

The tanks surged into the open field from our woods, festooned with clusters of infantry riders, and were promptly subjected to a barrage from the artillery unit supporting their attack! The shells fell right among the tanks, miraculously missing everyone. The only casualty I observed was the full colonel, apparently commanding the inept artillery unit, who had come up to observe the attack. He was screaming into his radio, "Check the elevation of those guns! You've dropped a load on our own people!" Then he keeled over from stroke or heart attack and was carried away on a stretcher.

I never did learn his identity or that of the attacking unit and their supporting artillery, but I suspected they were part of the new 6th Armored Division that had just arrived in Bastogne.

From our distance, we could not observe detailed progress of the attack which did succeed in securing the assembly area for our own assault initially scheduled for January 2. I do vividly recall one husky young rifleman returning to our lines on foot with a light bandage on the side of his head. He was striding right along as he passed me, explaining he was headed for a casualty evacuation point at the rear of our woods. I asked if he wanted any help, but he declined, continuing jauntily on his way.

A short time later I learned he had dropped dead when climbing into the medic's jeep. The significance of a seemingly light head wound is hard to determine accurately by aid men on the field of combat.

While my recollections of incidents has remained graphic over the years, getting the chronology straight has taken a bit of research, some of which has been more confusing than enlightening. Our regimental history, *Four Stars of Hell*, written by Larry Critchel, who was an officer in Regimental Headquarters Company, reports the attack I'm about to describe as occurring on January 4. The 101st Division history, *Rendezvous with Destiny*, says it took place on the 3rd. Whatever the date, it was my war and this is the way I remember what happened.

We moved into the assembly area in Bois Jacque just east of the railroad track, preparing to attack the next day with D Company abreast of F Company on our right. The 3rd Battalion would be attacking on our left. The CO selected a log-covered dugout, prepared by the prior German occupants, as the company CP and asked me to share it with him, the first such invitation since we'd arrived at Bastogne. Well after dark, he called the platoon leaders to join us and receive the attack order. I was not surprised to hear him conclude by saying, "Hold up jumping off long enough to let the others cross the tracks first."

When the platoon leaders left, the CO and I removed our boots and got into our sleeping bags. Lieutenants Willis Robinson and Don Beechinor were still standing outside the dugout accompanied by a runner. The Germans had provided a small ledge near the roof on one side of the dugout upon which we had placed some C-ration cans. A heavy shell came in right beside the position. In the millisecond flash of its explosion, I saw frost form on the cans from the heat of the burst.

There was moaning outside the dugout. The CO didn't move or speak, so I called out, "Is anyone hurt?"

Lieutenant Robinson replied, "My arm is broken, the runner's hit in the

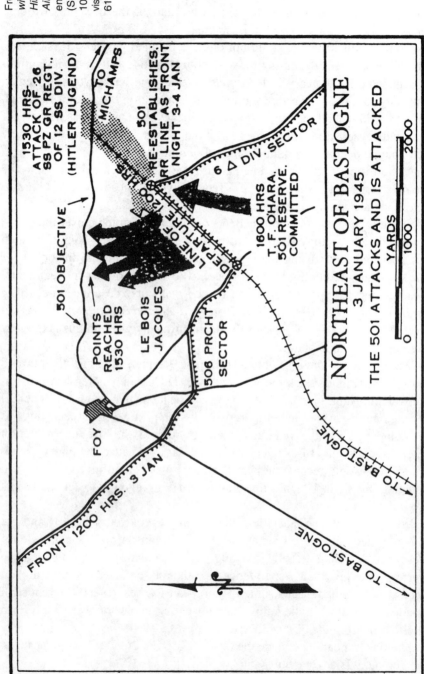

NORTHEAST OF BASTOGNE
3 JANUARY 1945
THE 501 ATTACKS AND IS ATTACKED

YARDS

0   1000   2000

1530 HRS- ATTACK OF 26 SS PZ GR REGT. OF 12 SS DIV. (HITLER JUGEND)

TO MICHAMPS

501 RE-ESTABLISHES RR LINE AS FRONT NIGHT 3-4 JAN

6 Δ DIV. SECTOR

1600 HRS T. F. O'HARA. 501 RESERVE. COMMITTED

501 OBJECTIVE

POINTS REACHED 1530 HRS

LE BOIS JACQUES

LINE OF DEPARTURE 1200 HRS

508 PRCHT SECTOR

FOY

FRONT 1200 HRS. 3 JAN

TO BASTOGNE

TO BASTOGNE

N

leg, and I think Beechinor's dead." I fumbled into my unlaced boots and left the dugout, shouting for the medics. The CO hadn't left his sack.

I could hear the medic's jeep coming in the darkness, but the tangent it was on would miss us by 40 yards. It took several minutes to chase it down and lead it back. In that interim, the CO came out of the dugout, shined a flashlight on Robinson's hand, which was dangling by a tendon, vomited, took Robbie's .45 pistol, and returned to his sleeping bag.

We got Robbie on a stretcher and were lifting it to the hood of the jeep when another shell came shrieking in. We dove for the ground. Fortunately, the deep snow cushioned the impact of the stretcher, and no one was hit by shrapnel. Once both Robbie and the wounded runner were aboard, the medic decided he would come back for Beechinor's body after dawn. The jeep started a slow, careful trip to the aid station, and I returned to the dugout.

The CO waited until I had wriggled back into my own sack, then asked if Beechinor was still out there and if he still had his .45 pistol. I said he was and did. The CO said, "Go get the .45 for me." I gave the time-honored, two-word reply involving a sex act, plus the option of getting it himself now or waiting until I got up in the morning. That concluded our conversation for the night, during which the medic returned to remove the body, pistol and all. The CO's subsequent unhappiness with that turn of events didn't really bother me much under the circumstances.

We crossed the railroad track at noon with D Company dutifully allowing the companies on our flanks a brief head start. The woods beyond were rather open at first, then became thick plantations of fir trees, some 35 feet high, so close together their lower branches often intertwined near the ground. Enemy resistance, initially rather light, intensified as we waded ahead in deep snow.

Mortar and artillery fire became increasingly heavy as I moved along with the right flank platoon. During one barrage, I jumped into a nearby foxhole to find it occupied by Sergeant Fletcher "Doc" Gainey of F Company, who had been my platoon runner during the basic training phase at Toccoa. Doc flashed his infectious grin and voiced his favorite expression, "I can't appreciate this, Sir!" An hour or so later a mortar round blew one of his legs off near the hip.

One warm spring day in Toccoa I had come across my platoon as it was supposedly engaged in a tactical exercise against another platoon of the company. The "front lines" had somehow gotten within ten yards of each other, and both sides were idly speculating as to what they might be fed during the upcoming noon chow call.

In high dudgeon and a burst of shavetail fervor, I had reminded them that failure to master the tactic involved could cost their lives in combat. The

174

only part of the lecture they obviously retained lay in my concluding remarks: "I _know_ we don't have blank ammunition. I _know_ we don't have artillery simulators. But you could at least yell '_Bang, Bang_' at each other."

The nickname "Bang Bang" was promptly affixed and long to survive. Two weeks after Doc was evacuated, I received a letter from my nurse friend in Paris with the salutation, "Dear Bang Bang," and I knew he was in her competent and compassionate care.

As our attack reached the thick fir plantation area, visibility became limited to the ten yards between one row of trees and the next. A trooper would part the intertwining branches of one row and find himself under pointblank fire from German positions in the one just ahead. The attack bogged down despite furious expenditures of ammunition sprayed to suppress defensive fire from the enemy so close but unseen.

The company mail orderly and I were floundering through the snow with more machine-gun ammo when fire suddenly came from the right flank as well as from the front we were approaching. F Company on our right had been guiding on the east edge of Bois Jacque as they paralleled our advance. An armored infantry battalion was supposedly attacking across the open ground on their right. But they weren't there. German tanks, half-tracks, and infantry were counterattacking that completely exposed flank, their fire reaching into D Company's sector, as well.

We were still short of the front when I heard the unmistakable whisper of incoming mortar rounds. There was a formerly German foxhole a few yards ahead. I yelled, "Mortars!" and jumped into it feet first.

The mail orderly, from a few feet behind, made a flat dive and landed across my lap just as a shell hit in the tree directly above us. He yelled, "I'm hit! I'm hit in the back! Stop the bleeding! Don't let me die!"

There was a hole the size of my hand in the back of his combat jacket. I cut away material with my trench knife. The hole got smaller in each successive layer of clothing beneath it. Eventually, I reached a jagged fragment of half-dollar circumference nestled on the unbroken skin just above his kidneys. There was no bleeding to stop, but the next day he sported a magnificent, multicolored bruise as wide as a cantaloupe.

In retrospect, there was a more sobering aspect of the incident. Had he not landed across my lap, I might never have fathered ten children after the war.

As we floundered up to the CO behind the front line, the company operations sergeant was telling him Sergeant Beale had been killed in a gap between the attacking platoons. The CO's only reaction was to turn to me and say, "Go get his dog tags and his .45." I asked the sergeant to show me the way.

I knew dog tags should stay with the body and intended to leave them there, suspecting the mission was assigned in pique for my failure to get Beechinor's weapon the night before. What I didn't yet know was that the CO was collecting .45s as personal mementos and that Beale's would become the fourth in his possession. In any event, I was damned if I would give him reason to accuse me of refusing to obey an order in combat.

The sergeant led me through the dense fir plantation to the gap between platoons, stopped to point at the next row of trees ahead, and said softly, "Right through there." I parted the intertwined branches to find Beale's body, shot through the face. Snow was still crumbling into the tracks of the departed German who had killed him from ten yards away. I took his .45 back to the CO, who accepted it without comment.

Meanwhile, the counterattack against the battalion right flank had reached the crisis stage. Mertz's machine-gun platoon had been moved over there to support F Company, and E Company had been committed from reserve. Bazooka teams and artillery fire had knocked out some of the German armor, but the tide did not turn until some tanks finally arrived to help repel the attack as it was reaching the edge of the woods.

Toward dusk we were ordered to give up the ground gained at such cost and withdraw across the railroad track. D Company had incurred 31 casualties, killed or wounded; 2nd Battalion losses totaled 86. The troops were exhausted, their mood somber. The CO had departed promptly on receipt of the order, leaving me to accompany the withdrawal.

We had two men seriously wounded in the final stages of the debacle. We laid them on large branches blown from trees by artillery rounds and dragged them through the snow. It was getting dark.

We finally stopped on a slope beyond the railroad. The CO had left word to wait there for orders. We waited. And waited and waited for some two hours while the temperature dropped and the two wounded men died.

Most of the men sat huddled in silent misery, but one young trooper kept pacing back and forth demanding, "When are we gonna move outta here?"

I could only reply, "We'll move when we get orders to move, soldier."

Finally he blurted, "Well, I'm leaving now!" and disappeared into the darkness. I don't know who he was or where he went.

The fighting in bloody Bois Jacque would continue, but our battalion would have no further role in it for seven days.

Chapter 31

Old Sector, New Fighting

Late the next afternoon, our battalion was ordered to replace the 2nd Battalion of the 506th just north across the railroad from the position we had held in the weeks before the Bois Jacque attack. We were to move out in a column of companies with a 200-yard interval between units, D Company bringing up the rear. The CO had gone ahead, so I was leading our company.

While we were waiting for the company ahead to gain the 200-yard interval, a 3rd Battalion trooper came along with a German prisoner. Obviously unhappy with his assignment, he asked me where the POW collecting point was. I could tell him only that it must be somewhere farther along. Disgruntled, he continued on.

The first part of the route was along the edge of a woods on our left with a firebreak cut through its center. The guard, plodding 50 yards ahead, suddenly turned his prisoner into the break. Sensing what was about to happen, I started running. Ten yards short of the break, I heard the shot.

The prisoner was dead in the snow. The trooper said, "He made a break for it!" Their respective tracks told a different story. The German had not changed pace. The guard had stepped aside, assumed an off-hand firing stance, and shot him in the back. It was a waste of potential intelligence via interrogation and the waste of another life in the total waste called war.

Dusk was coming on fast as the company ahead passed over a long, gentle hill. Two artillery shells landed in rapid succession just behind them. My "hunch organs" working overtime that day said, "Those could be registering rounds. Do you really want to take this company over that hill?"

Detouring around the lee side would mean losing sight of the battalion column in the rapidly encompassing darkness, and no one had told me exactly where we were headed. But my hunch said, "Do it!" I designated two men to follow the company ahead as file closers and angled D Company left to keep the high ground between us and the direction from which the shells had come.

German artillery chased the two troopers all the way across, nicking one of them with a small shell fragment, but never found the rest of us. We reached our assigned positions in the dark and gratefully took to the fox-holes and slit trenches left by the 506th.

Early the next morning the CO told me to accompany the supply sergeant into Bastogne to scrounge some equipment he wanted. As we were starting off in the jeep, there were some scattered shots in the near distance behind us. We stopped long enough to hear a commo man listening on his phone announce that the troops were just "shooting at a German patrol." So we continued on our way.

When we returned several hours later, a full-fledged fire fight was in progress. The CO was deep in his dugout, yelling into the phone for more artillery support. His order to me was, "Take the reserve platoon and fill in the foxholes of the casualties!"

Having arrived in the dark and without time to check out our new posi-tions, I decided to see which foxholes he meant before moving the reserve platoon. There was a lull in the firing as I spotted the protruding helmets of some troopers in the general direction from which the shooting had seemed to start.

They were dug in along the near side of a farm road which continued east to intersect the Foy-Bizory Road, the direction from which I'd assumed the attack was coming. A thick stand of trees and brush some 150 yards wide came right up to the far edge of the narrow road they faced. They told me their platoon leader was on up the line, so I trotted alongside the road, annoyed but undeterred by the occasional snap of a rifle round from my left.

Lieutenant Anderson was in the farthest foxhole. An anti-tank gun had been knocked out a few feet away, and he was still somewhat dazed from the concussion. I flopped down to ask how things were going. That's when I learned a full company of Volksgrenadiers, supported by artillery and mor-tars, had tried to overrun his platoon from the thick woods across the road!

Fortunately, they could not bring aimed fire on his troops until emerging from the brush lines 20 yards away, which made them very, very easy tar-gets. My apparent bravado in jogging along the front line had been due to sheer ignorance of the situation.

The German attack was bogged down, but they still held the woods in considerable force. I had the reserve platoon dig in 50 yards behind Anderson's line for defense in depth, then took a machine-gun team and a

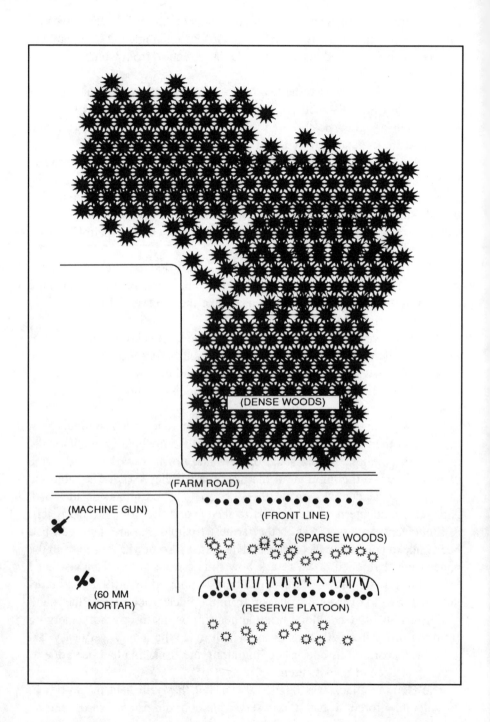

(DENSE WOODS)

(FARM ROAD)

(MACHINE GUN)

(FRONT LINE)

(SPARSE WOODS)

(60 MM MORTAR)

(RESERVE PLATOON)

60mm mortar squad over to where they had a clear view of the south edge of the woods. The machine-gunners hosed away while the mortar men launched rounds in such rapid succession as to make the bottom third of their tube glow red.

Meanwhile, artillery support fire increased. Within an hour, the surviving Germans were gone. They had taken a terrible beating as evidenced by the number of bodies and bloody trails of departing wounded. One body was on a stretcher with a tree blown down across it, particularly eloquent testimony to the futility of their attack. D Company had suffered only ten casualties, all wounded.

Four days later, January 9, our battalion was ordered to capture the village of Recogne as the right flank unit of a division attack. F Company would make the assault with E following in support and D trailing in reserve. The CO being elsewhere, I was leading the company as the column stopped while F Company prepared to cross the line of departure.

Lieutenant Joe McGregor was standing at the tail of E Company just ahead, so we stepped aside to chat for a moment. As we stood there, a shell hit in a tree nearby, and shrapnel kicked snow on the toes of our boots. Joe looked up with a peculiar expression and remarked, "Y'know, Bill, a man can get killed in a war like this."

In a little over an hour, F Company had gained the center of Recogne, and E was committed to help finish the job. That's when Joe McGregor was killed.

That same day, our regimental commander, Colonel Julian Ewell, was wounded by shellfire and evacuated. Lieutenant Colonel Ballard assumed command and would lead the 501st through the rest of the war.

Chapter 32

Back to Bois Jacque

The 3rd Battalion had relieved us at Recogne after dark, and we had returned to our previous position, alerted to attack again the next day. Our mission was to cross the Foy-Bizory Road and clear Bois Jacque of the stubborn enemy. Our first phase line was the road running southeasterly from Foy to Mageret, 1,000 yards from our line of departure. We jumped off at 9:50, January 10.

We were the right flank battalion of the division and were guiding on the railroad track. Once again, a battalion of another division was to coordinate by paralleling our attack along the other side of the track on our right. Once again, they weren't there.

My memories of those next two days are blurred and fragmented. I recall going into the attack carrying an engineer's pick for use in digging new positions in the solidly frozen ground. Enemy infantry resistance was not as intense as on January 3, but artillery and mortar shelling was heavy, and we kept receiving small arms fire from the unprotected right flank.

Bodies from previous fighting were still scattered in the snow. A husky 506th officer with a blond mustache had been killed while wearing the brown leather flight jacket normally worn only in training. I could have used the extra garment in the bitter cold, but his arms were locked across his chest in rigor mortis.

A lieutenant admittedly squeamish about bodies was eating a K ration while seated on what he assumed to be a snow-covered log. When someone asked, "Why are you sitting on that dead Kraut?" he lost his appetite.

We reached the phase line of our battalion's attack by mid-afternoon, despite the open right flank. Then things came to a halt as the division's offensive was stopped on orders from higher headquarters. The 501st was ordered to outpost the Foy-Mageret Road and to pull back to our jump-off positions on the Foy-Bizory Road.

Our outpost line pressed a tender spot of German withdrawal plans, being only a 100 yards short of critical defensive position. Late in the day the enemy made a determined attack from across the railroad and forced the outposts back 150 yards. On January 12, E and F Companies attacked to restore that line in preparation for an assault by the 327th Glider Regiment the next day. Our regiment, less the 3rd Battalion which was temporarily attached to the 506th, reverted to Division Reserve where we were to remain for the rest of our stay in the Bastogne arena.

In that interim, we received some superb replacements. They were from the 1st Special Service Force, an elite assault regiment composed of Yanks and Canadians, which had been fighting with valor in Italy. Their insignia featured crossed arrows instead of rifles. When the Canadians could no longer maintain their flow of replacements, the unit was deactivated, and all qualified parachutists were assigned to the 101st.

By this time, due to D Company officer casualties, I was in the dual role of executive officer and platoon leader, the latter of which I enjoyed.

I drew a platoon sergeant from the Special Forces replacements. As nearly as I can recall, his name was Sanderson, but he became "Sandy" so quickly I no longer remember. In any event, he was one fine non-com.

By January 16, the rest of the division accomplished all remaining objectives. My last vivid memory of Bastogne is that of the dugout Sandy and I had prepared on our last day in Division Reserve. We had moved to a new position and were determined to make ourselves comfortable at last. We spent the entire night digging a 6'x 6'x 6' hole and covering it with logs. At dawn we made repeated trips to a haystack until we had floored it with a good two feet of the lovely stuff. With sighs of total exhaustion, we took off our boots, resolving to sleep through the day.

Just then a runner arrived to announce we were moving out! The division had been ordered to move to Alsace-Lorraine.

The 501st had lost 865 killed, wounded or injured, captured or missing in action — well over 40 percent of our strength at the start and the highest casualty count in the 101st Airborne Division.

As usual, the rifle companies had suffered the most. Of the 35-member platoon I had led on December 19, only 14 were left, including the mortar squad.

Chapter 33

On to Fight in Alsace

As we prepared to leave Bastogne, General Taylor received a Memorandum Receipt from General Troy Middleton, VIII Corps Commander. It read: "Received of the 101st Airborne Division, The Town Of BASTOGNE, Luxembourg Province, Belgium. Condition: Used But Serviceable, Kraut Disinfected."

For two days the division was quartered in small villages southwest of Bastogne. On January 20, we entrucked for a very miserable trip of 36 hours' duration. Most of the vehicles were topless ten-ton trucks into which troops were crammed like so many sardines. It was bitter cold, the roads were slippery, and apparently meaningless halts were frequent. Troopers stamped on the steel floors to restore circulation in numbed feet. There was no room to stretch out. Any sleep accomplished was in the form of mild comas from exhaustion.

In the late afternoon of January 22, the trucks hauling our 2nd Battalion stopped in a small village. I was told, "Put your platoon in that barn." The mow was several feet thick in soft, curly, fragrant hay. I got the men bedded down, zipped into my sleeping bag, and wriggled until sure I was a foot below the surface of the lovely, fluffy stuff. My last conscious thought before blissfully sleeping the clock around was, "NOW let the bastards try to find me!"

Alsace was in the sector of the Seventh Army, which, with the French First Army, comprised the Southern Group of Armies. When Patton's Third Army headed north for the Bulge, the Seventh extended its lines left to fill part of the gap created, leaving them rather thinly spread.

Hitler had ordered an offensive, Operation Nordwind, to be launched in Alsace on January 1 under the personal direction of Heinrich Himmler. Its objective was to split the Southern Armies and defeat them in detail. They probed aggressively from point to point along the Seventh's sector. Their gains, while limited, were of sufficient concern to warrant attachment of the 101st as reinforcement.

We were to take over a sector held by the 222nd Regiment of the 42nd (Rainbow) Division of World War I fame, with which my father had fought some 28 years before. The regiment was fighting as a combat team, and this was their first real taste of World War II. On the night of January 24-25, the Germans crossed the Moder River in force at two points and cut up one of their companies. The Rainbows counterattacked and restored the river bank by the time we relieved them two nights later.

The 101st took over a four-mile front with the 327th Glider Regiment on the right and our 501st on the left. The 502nd and 506th Regiments were billeted in reserve. There were villages, farms, and various buildings throughout the area. Every unit headquarters staff, from company through division, operated inside a solid and usually heated structure of one kind or another. The division never "had it so good!"

The luxury was hardly shared by troopers on front-line duty, however. Much of our battalion's sector was along open high ground facing the Moder River, in full view of Germans in the heavily forested area on the other side. The snow was deep, the nights miserably cold. Rifle platoons would spend six days on the line before enjoying three days of sheltered comfort in reserve.

The day before D Company was to go on line, we heard that one of the Rainbow units just down the street was issuing snowpacks, boots with rubber bottom sections, insulated and waterproof. The CO was nowhere around, but this was no time to wait for a decision. I called "fall out" and hooked onto the tail of the Rainbow line.

We had been ordered to remove our Screaming Eagle shoulder patches for security reasons before leaving Bastogne. When I led our column up to the harassed supply officer with his big pile of the new footgear he simply asked, "What company?" and accepted my "D Company" reply. The only further question was the one he asked each man, "What size?" We returned with each trooper clutching his prize, leaving the supply officer to wonder later about any shortage detected.

After our first six days on the line, we returned at night to the village where the battalion was billeted. A Headquarters Company cook who saw us arrive called out to me, "Hey, Lieutenant Sefton, you'd better get down to Lieutenant Mertz's quarters right away. He's got two cigars!" Bemused at how closely the men kept track of relationships between officers, I broke into a run.

Mertz was sitting in an easy chair in the living room of a house, his stocking feet on a hassock. There was a stub of a cigar in his mouth, and the room was wreathed in layers of smoke. When his face turned beet red, I knew he was finishing the second stogie. Having no desire to complicate his embarrassment, I said merely, "I know you had two," and left.

Shortly thereafter Mertz was sent back to Mourmelon to bring the battalion kitchen equipment to Alsace. I was back on the line with my platoon the night he returned, crawled in the door of my dugout, and hurled a full box of king-sized cigars into my lap. His apology was stated in terms only a close comrade-in-arms could appreciate. "THERE, YOU SONAVABITCH! NOW STOP LOOKING AT ME THAT WAY!"

One morning in mid-February, spring arrived full force in Alsace. The heavy snow cover melted dramatically, disclosing bodies long concealed and filling ditches with water. We were scheduled to go back on the line that night.

The position we were to occupy was along the face of a large, bare hill. A farm track came down the hill, making a slight jog as it continued toward the river. Another farm track, running left along the face of the hill, intersected it at the jog, which created a slight defilade. The foxholes we were to take over had been dug in the ditch along the intersecting track.

Every foxhole was full of running ice water! The troopers being relieved had been lying in the melting snow alongside the holes for hours, trying miserably to avoid the water coursing along in the ditch. In short, we had no holes to occupy.

We had now been in the sector long enough to know that the Germans were not about to conduct any offensive operations. On February 1, two companies of our 501st 1st Battalion and one company of glidermen had crossed the river at night as reconnaissance in force, returning with some 35 prisoners — more than the rest of the entire Seventh Army took in the period we were with them. As a result of intelligence gained, we knew the likelihood of being attacked was zilch.

In view of that circumstance, I used the field phone to call the CO in his village billet and asked him to request battalion's permission for us to establish a reverse slope defensive position on the other side of the hill. I never knew how hard — or even if — he tried. We were ordered to dig new holes as feasible along the existing line.

The sloping ground under the melting snow was frozen solid for the first two feet and heavy going thereafter. The platoon front extended left about 500 yards from the jog where the farm tracks intersected. I had some 20 men to cover it with new positions.

I placed a machine-gun team and the platoon medic in the defilade provided by the jog, then selected a knoll halfway along the line as the site for platoon headquarters consisting of Platoon Sergeant Sandy, the communications corporal, and me. The rest of the troopers I divided into two-man fire teams spaced roughly 50 yards apart and told everyone to start digging briskly. The night was wearing on, and we would be under direct observation by the enemy at dawn.

The names of the two men placed nearest the platoon CP on the left indicated Italian and Polish lineage, respectively. They argued that the position I'd assigned them was too exposed. I noted that it was no more exposed than any other on the line, including mine, so they should commence digging. It was one of those "Shut up, I explained" situations so often occurring when time is short.

That seemed like the longest night of my life. We would hit the frozen soil with a full swing of an engineer's pick, to be rewarded with an icy chip the size of a silver dollar. When finally through the frost line, we had the slope of the hill to contend with. By the time our dugout was six feet deep on the back side, it was only two feet deep in front. Within four hours, the blisters on our hands were broken and bleeding.

Periodically I floundered along the line to check the progress of the others. An hour and a half before dawn, I told everyone to stop digging and start camouflaging. There were some boards in and about the flooded positions. We found enough to roof the CP dugout, then shoveled on a thick layer of dirt from the excavation. We covered the raw dirt with fragments of frozen sod in the optimistic hope of fooling enemy observers.

The eastern horizon was paling as I made my last inspection of the line. One exhausted fire team had given up on digging in the past hour and had moved 20 yards down the slope to a huge pile of rutabagas, nearly 8 feet high and 20 feet wide at the base. They had climbed to the top and tossed enough of the large vegetables down the back side to create a roomy firing position. It was too late to do anything other than tacitly admire their GI enterprise.

I was more perturbed by the two who had bitched about their exposed location. When finished digging, they had climbed up the hill to an orchard and carried back armloads of prunings to stack in front of their shelter. All I could do was express my fervent hope that no German observer would think Americans could be dumb enough to make such a clumsy attempt at camouflaging.

Dawn was coming on fast by the time I rejoined Sandy and the corporal in the Command Post dugout. We speculated as to how long it would take the enemy to spot our new positions along the snow-covered slope and what they'd do about us when they did. Knowing we'd done all we could, we succumbed to exhausted but fitful sleep.

Nothing happened that morning, but early in the afternoon a single artillery piece started pecking away at our line. It was not direct fire, and each round shrieked for several seconds coming in. One of the first few fired cut our field phone line. No one at company headquarters responded to our radio calls for counterfire.

The gun probed almost leisurely up and down the line as we sweated out each round, knowing our flimsily contrived dugout roof would merely increase the effectiveness of a direct hit. Later we counted 12 shell holes within ten yards of our own position.

The firing went on for seemingly interminable hours, each succeeding round ratcheting our nerves another wracking notch. We lay there in silence, each locked in his own prayerful thoughts. Then Sandy, lying nearest the dugout's side entrance, pulled back the burlap curtain and looked out at the sky. "If they don't hit us pretty soon," he noted, "it'll be too dark for their observer to see!"

Almost as he spoke, a shell came in to our left, and someone in that direction started screaming. I had removed my boots, but Sandy was still wearing his. He bolted out the entrance while I groped for mine. Meanwhile, the screamer was approaching our position.

By the time I located my boots, pulled them on unlaced, and exited the dugout, the trooper of Italian descent was crawling alongside, still screaming. A bloody trail in the snow marked his progress from the prunings-camouflaged position where Sandy was attempting to crawl while straddling the Polish lad face up beneath him with arms wrapped around his neck. I yelled at the screamer to keep crawling to the medic in the jog defilade and ran to help Sandy.

By the time I got there, the other casualty had lost his grip on Sandy's neck and was slumped in the snow. We each grabbed an arm and started dragging him at an encumbered run toward the jog at the end of the track. It seemed to take us forever, each expecting the enemy observer to be frantically calling for another round on a highly visible target. It never came.

That last round had scored a direct hit on the pile of prunings, spraying both occupants of the shelter behind it with shrapnel in the lower parts of their bodies. The Italian was hit only in the legs, but the Polish lad took several in his abdomen as well. He was dead before we could reach the medic.

His body lay there in the snow, his mangled legs a parody of someone doing a jig. It reminded me of his last letter that I had censored. It was to a girlfriend in the states, saying how much he looked forward to dancing with her again. Meanwhile the Italian had quit screaming and lay beside him, glaring at me in mute accusation.

It had been a particularly miserable day on the line.

Chapter 34

Robbie's .45

When Lieutenant Willis Robinson had lost a hand to a German artillery shell hitting just outside the D Company CP dugout the night before we were to attack, the CO had left the dugout only long enough to relieve him of his .45-caliber automatic pistol. Sergeant Stanley Koss, also of D Company, had lived only 50 miles from Robbie's home in the States, and the two had developed a close mutual regard. Koss had received a letter from Robinson after he had been evacuated. Dictated to a Red Cross girl, it read in part: "If you find my hand, give it a Christian burial. If you should find my .45, I'd love to have it as a souvenir."

While we were still in Alsace, a few enlisted men and one officer were selected from the regiment to return to the States and go on tour urging the purchase of war bonds. Koss was one of those tapped for such odious duty, but soldier that he was, he accepted. Knowing he would have some time at home and could look up Robinson, he asked the CO if he could take the weapon to him. The CO refused to surrender it on the grounds that Koss "could never get it through customs inspection."

Lieutenant Richard Brown was one of the platoon leaders the CO had rumored to "lack aggressive troop leadership traits" in Holland. I had found him to be an uncommonly courageous officer, ever-considerate of his men who would follow him anywhere. Koss had come to him concerning the problem of Robbie's pistol, and Dick had come to me for counsel.

As any reader may have surmised, by now my regard for the CO was probably less than that for anyone else in the world. Stanley Koss and Dick Brown shared my sentiment. Our determined goal became to get Robbie's .45 back to him.

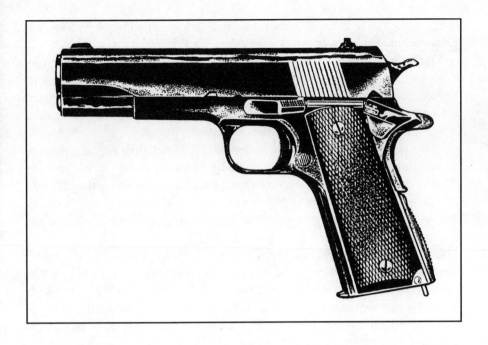

After weighty conferences, Koss returned to the CO to advise that he had constructed a false bottom in his footlocker and was more than willing to take the chance of smuggling the gun through customs.

Again the CO refused to accommodate the request. It was time for more direct action.

The CO had a large office with a big desk in a building with very thick walls. Dick Brown and I walked in on him unannounced, each with a .45 pistol dangling in our hands. Dick walked to the left side of the desk and I to the right. We eared the hammers of the guns back and laid them on the desk with our fingers still on the triggers. The muzzle of each weapon was directed at his navel as he sat in his chair.

He scooted the chair back three feet and stammered, "Whadda ya want, fellas?"

We each adjusted the angle of potential rounds to remain concentrated on his navel. I said, "We want Robbie's .45."

He blurted, "Why, sure! I've got it right here!" opening a drawer in the desk that contained four of the weapons. We took it and left without another word of conversation.

I've often wondered what would have happened had he refused our demand. If only one of us had fired, we could have sworn convincingly concerning the tragic accident. Two rounds through his brisket might have been difficult to explain. But then, knowing him as well as we did, we never really expected him to react any other way. All such speculation aside, Sergeant Koss did, indeed, deliver the .45 to Lieutenant Robinson at his home.

Shortly after that incident, I was transferred to Regimental Headquarters Company as assistant operations officer in the S-3 section. Colonel Ballard welcomed me without the slightest reference to my relationship with the D Company CO, then or ever after. My sentiments regarding staff duty aside, it was nice to be in a cordial atmosphere again.

The Alsatian campaign had been less costly, by far, than any of our operations to date. The 501st Regiment had only 51 casualties, six of whom were killed. Four of those deaths occurred during the two-company-strength night raid across the river by 1st Battalion troops. One of the remaining two was that of the man in my platoon. Now the division was being relieved for return to Mourmelon.

On the last day of February, the regiment boarded a train of "40-and-8" box cars, the type used in World War I to transport 40 men and 8 horses. No mounts accompanied us on the ride, but the floors were thickly covered with straw for our comfort. It proved a very pleasant way to make the 18-hour trip. The 502nd had preceded us, and music by their regimental band welcomed us as we detrained at Mourmelon-le-Petite.

It was time to start getting ready for the next operation, wherever it might be.

Chapter 35

Oddball Interlude

The new mission assigned to the 101st Airborne Division was to prepare for Operation Eclipse. Two American divisions and one British airborne would make a daylight landing on Berlin to help the Russians capture the city and wrap up the war. We had six weeks in which to get ready. On March 5, which happened to be my 23rd birthday, we started training the replacements who had been flooding into the units.

One of my S-3 section jobs was that of range officer. In that capacity I attended the demonstration of a new type of hand grenade on March 7. It was called the Beano grenade, as I remember. The size and shape of a baseball, it had a smooth, black metal surface and no handle. A leaden weight shaped like a pair of butterfly wings was embedded flush in the surface, secured there by a pin on a ring. A demonstrator explained how the grenade was to be used.

The technique was to keep two fingertips on the butterfly wings while pulling the pin and hurling the grenade. The weight of the lead would free the "wings" in flight, along with the arming device attached to them. The grenade would then explode immediately upon impact with anything solid. No more seven-second delay. Helluva concept!

The demonstration site was right behind a concrete pit some 20 feet wide and 6 feet deep. About 25 yards beyond the pit were several silhouette targets mounted on stakes. Approximately 30 observers, including several high-ranking officers, were standing short of the pit to watch. I was in the very front row.

The officer in charge provided step-by-step commentary as a sergeant threw several grenades with devastating effect on the targets, making a favorable impression on the audience. When the demonstration was completed, there was a goodly number of grenades left, so the officer asked if anyone there would like to try one.

Several of us in the front row promptly reached into the open case of the weapons to take advantage of the offer. The officer in charge yelled, "Wait a minute! One at a time! You, there, throw first." He was pointing at a lieutenant standing to my immediate right.

The designated thrower took one step forward. He must have been a baseball pitcher, because he turned the grenade in his hand as though groping for the seam on a ball. I saw the butterfly wings fall to the ground near his right heel. He may have put a centrifugal hop on the throw, as well. The grenade exploded in the air over the cement pit, no more than 20 feet away!

My face stung from the concussion, and I turned away momentarily in reflex. When I turned back, the thrower was laying on the ground with fluid running out of his ears. The face of the man who had been standing on my left was bleeding. An enlisted man who, for some reason, had been down in the pit, emerged with the flesh of one cheek hanging like a dewlap. Colonel Kinnard, farther back in the group, was sitting on the ground with his shirt pulled up, watching blood bubble from a wound a few inches below the center of his rib cage. Brigadier General Higgins, our assistant division commander, sported a gaudy gash across his prematurely balding scalp. As nearly as I can recall, 18 of the 30-some observers were wounded to some extent or other. We never saw or heard of the Beano grenade again.

Various units of the 101st Airborne Division, including all three parachute infantry regiments, had been awarded the U.S. Distinguished Unit Citation after Normandy. The entire division and our attached 501st Regiment had been awarded the French Croix de Guerre with Palm by the French government for that operation. The Belgian government had awarded us the Belgian Croix de Guerre for Normandy and again for Bastogne. For Holland we had received the Netherlands Orange Lanyard unit decoration.

Now, on March 15, we were awarded another Distinguished Unit Citation for Bastogne. It was the first time in U.S. military history that an entire division with all attachments was so honored. General Dwight D. Eisenhower reviewed the troops and read the proclamation from a platform crowded with high brass and national government notables. It was an uncommonly memorable ceremony.

Operation Eclipse, for which we had been preparing, was canceled. Eisenhower had decided to let the Russians take Berlin unassisted. Instead, the 101st, less our 501st Regiment, was alerted on March 30 to help mop up the Ruhr Pocket where Hitler had ordered his forces to hold that industrial heartland at all cost.

Our regiment was to prepare to jump on any of several Prisoner of War camps to assure the safety of the occupants as Allied or Russian Armies approached. Meanwhile, we were living in tents a few miles from the post, the buildings of which had been taken over by a hospital unit.

The Mourmelon interlude was oddball for me because of the varied assignments involved in my staff job. One, for instance, was to take a platoon and make a demonstration jump from the new C-46 troop carrier planes, which featured exit doors on both sides of the fuselage. The regiment would be drawn up on the parade ground in retreat formation to witness the event.

There were three planeloads of us. I would jumpmaster those in the lead ship and try the new, right-hand door for my own exit. All were well-experienced jumpers, and our mood verged on the festive. When the green light came on, I sent troopers out both doors and followed the last man leaving through the right one.

We had been trained, of course, to count "One thousand, two thousand, three thousand!" while awaiting the opening shock. I had done so on that first jump at Fort Benning but had never bothered to count since. For some reason, I found myself counting this time and getting to "seven thousand" before looking up to behold my very first "streamer," the full length of the unopened chute following me briskly earthward!

Parachute School doctrine called for me to pull the ripcord of the reserve chute. Instead, I grabbed two of the four risers in each hand and flipped them apart. The canopy popped open beautifully. I was still admiring it when I realized someone was walking across the top, his feet sinking impressively with each step until he was grinning down at me through the puckered vent at the apex! My delayed opening had occurred directly below a trooper floating down from one of the other planes.

If he stayed there, my canopy would steal the air from his, causing it to collapse. When I hit the ground, collapsing my own, his size 12 boots could plummet into the back of my neck. I engaged him in short conversation: "GET THE HELL OFFA THERE! NOW!"

His chute was already losing air as he walked off the edge of my canopy, so he ended up right beside me as it refilled. He was still grinning. I pulled on my right risers to glide away from the risk of entanglement and suggested he take the opposite direction. Then I looked down to discover I was about to land in the 2nd Battalion formation. There was just enough altitude left to glide away from that mishap, as well. It had been an unusually interesting jump!

There was a major advantage in having a hospital unit nearby. It was well-staffed with nurses, and we were planning an Officer's Club dance. Three of us went over to seek dates for the affair, both of the others being more social-ly accomplished than I. As we started up the main entrance, a stunning brunette emerged. While my compatriots were deciding which proven approach to use, I blurted, "Would you come to our dance with me?" She smiled, advising that she had gotten married the week before and wasn't dat-ing. Emboldened by having struck first, I followed up hopefully. "Is there anyone else here like you?"

"Well, there's this girl they call my 'little sister' who's on duty right now, but she'll be off this evening. Her name's Beth Huie. Give me your name, and I'll tell her you're coming over."

Ed Allworth was with me on the return trip to ask for Lieutenant Beth Huie, who was, indeed, raven-haired and almond-eyed. All petite five feet one inch of her was strikingly attractive in my highly gratified opinion. She also was somewhat confused in that the brunette had failed to tell her to expect us. A convoluted conversation ensued during which she punched a goodly number of verbal holes in my paratrooper ego. In reviewing it later, Ed observed, "Boy! Does she ever bat it back fast!"

When the purpose of our visit, including our need for three dates for our dance, was finally made clear, Beth called a caucus with two other nurses during which she voiced her decision: "I'll go if I can have the harmless looking one."

We dated for nine nights straight before her unit was moved to Marseilles to stage for the Philippines. On May 4, 1946, we were married in her home town, Sioux City, Iowa. The first of our ten children was born a year and a day thereafter.

Meanwhile, the war with Germany had ended. V-E Day (Victory in Europe) caused a mere ripple of excitement among the troops on May 8, 1945. The prospect of jumping in Japan still loomed ahead.

The 501st Regiment had been activated on November 15, 1942, at Camp Toccoa, Georgia. A second birthday celebration had been planned for that date in 1944, but we were still in Holland then, so it was decided to hold it six months later. The First Annual Geronimo Field Day was to be a very grand affair.

Intra-unit competitions in softball, volleyball, track, and platoon drill were scheduled for the morning hours, using a 400-meter oval track sur-rounded by a high wooden fence and featuring a small, roofed grandstand. A noon meal of fried chicken, baked beans, and assorted goodies would be served following the events. In the afternoon the entire cast of singers and dancers from the famed Bal Tabarin in Paris would perform for the regiment at the post theater.

Two days prior to the gala, Colonel Ballard summoned me to his office

George William Sefton.

and assigned a single mission: "Your job is to get things started off with a bang!" I didn't ask any questions, just rounded up a small detail, solicited Ed Allworth's help, and got started.

We got colored chutes from salvage and cut them into pennants to be strung throughout the festival area, then got serious about the "started-off-with-a-bang" bit. In the center of the oval we dug a circular mini-trench about 4 inches deep and 3 inches wide in a 12-foot diameter, then placed explosive Primacord along the bottom and filled it in with flour from the kitchen and fine dust from the edge of the road.

Next we planted half-pound charges of C-2 plastic explosive well beyond the circle in four directions, hiding the connecting wires in the grass. In the center of the circle we built a small yellow pyramid of empty C-2 cartons over a single dynamite cap with a foot-long fuse.

On the morning of the event, those who had survived all three major missions were seated in the small grandstand, barely filling it. Everyone else sat three deep against the surrounding fence.

The emcee at the PA mike announced that the regiment had been carefully surveyed to find the trooper who most typified the epitome of young American manhood comprising the 501st. "Kid Geronimo" would now start the festivities by detonating the C-2 charges in the center of the arena.

A trooper clad in fatigues and a blue-painted helmet liner worn backward emerged from beside the grandstand juggling three lemons as he trotted out and bowed to the cheering crowd. With a flourish, he lighted the fuse to the dynamite cap, yelled, "Fire in the hole!" and ran toward the low stand occupied by the emcee and the regimental band 50 yards away in the oval.

The crowd watched the smoke from the fuse with bated breath, only to hear the muted bang of the cap and see the pyramid of C-2 cartons tumble. Meanwhile, the Geronimo Kid had hit the ground beside a big wooden maul used for driving in large tent stakes. He picked it up, brandishing it above his head and charged back at the C-2 cartons. The emcee was yelling into the mike, "No, Kid! Don't do it!"

In a well-rehearsed move, the Kid went prone as he smashed the maul into the empty cartons, shielding his face and ears with his extended arms. At the precise moment of impact, demolition men triggered electrical detonators to the Primacord and the outlying C-2 charges. The results were rather sensational.

The front of the grandstand roof rose a foot in the air like the hinged lid of cigar box and fell neatly back into place. The flour and dust mixture from the mini-trench around the Kid became a giant shower curtain which hung in the breezeless air, completely hiding him from view. The crowd was utterly silent, stunned by the obvious tragedy. One man of our preparation detail yelled, "Medic!" on cue, and two others rushed out with a stretcher, completely disappearing into the curtain of flour and dust. Lieutenant Colonel Dick Allen screamed at me from the bandstand: "SEFTON, YOU'VE KILLED A MAN!"

We had slit every seam of the Kid's fatigues with a razor blade, and he was industriously ripping them apart while sitting there, out of sight. The two "medics" emerged, carrying only the maul on their stretcher as the dust started settling. Then the Kid appeared, his garment in tatters, juggling his lemons and bowing to the tumultuous cheers of the audience.

At the same moment, the band struck up a stirring march, and demolition men around the circumference of the oval started shooting flares into the air from ground dischargers. One of them landed on the bandstand, setting crepe paper decorations afire. Dick Allen was busily stamping them out.

An oddball mission had been eminently accomplished, and our festivities had started with a bang!

Chapter 36

Ruffling the Russians

As May ended, our regiment rejoined the 101st Airborne Division at Berchtesgaden in that idyllic finger of Germany sticking into the Tyrolean Alps. It had been captured by the 506th as hostilities were ending and was virtually untouched by the war.

We arrived at night to be billeted in the barracks formerly occupied by the SS troops guarding Hitler's Eagle's Nest on the mountain above. I woke up early and was going along a walk next to the building to survey the surroundings. At the corner I all but ran my nose into the chest of a 6-foot 6-inch German mountain troop officer in dress uniform coming from my right. In a flood of conflicting emotions, I couldn't decide whether to shoot or salute!

Life was downright enjoyable in the new surroundings. The Berchtesgaden Hof (Hotel), where Hitler had conned Chamberlain and other European heads of state, became a rest center for division officers. There were deer to be hunted in the hills. Souvenir seekers were having a heyday, with confiscated weapons and cameras abounding.

Also, there were many German army vehicles available. For one glorious week, I had an open-top command car with six wheels, three rows of seats and a German soldier in dress uniform who was delighted to serve as a chauffeur in return for rations. After someone reportedly siphoned gas from General Taylor's jeep to fuel such private enterprise, a division order terminated that particular luxury. Having played no part in the petrol piracy myself, I can only relate the story as I heard it at the time.

A few weeks later, the 501st was moved south into Austria to occupy an area directly across a river from the Russian zone. A road sign there read

"Vienna — 240 kilometers." Mertz was intrigued, figuring it was a once-in-a-lifetime opportunity to visit that fabled city.

The British were escorting a convoy of German POWs through the village where Mertz was billeted and had halted there for a rest. He commandeered a small military Volkswagen by the simple expedient of ordering the lone occupant to get out, getting in himself, and driving away. The German chased him down in a block or so, not to argue about the vehicle, but to retrieve his lunch sack from the seat. Mertz was now motorized and dangerous to my future.

He showed up at my billet accompanied by Lieutenant Vince Carrol and seven five-gallon jerry cans, two full of gasoline and the rest filled with cognac. After some libation-accompanied discussion, an excursion to Vienna began to seem manifestly reasonable.

Late in the afternoon, we drove down to the bridge crossing the river. The MPs manning a post on our side made no attempt to stop us. The Russian guards on the other side spoke no English, but we kept repeating the word, "Commandant," until one of them led us to a platoon headquarters in a nearby house. Despite the seemingly unbreachable language barrier, we were welcomed with open arms and liberal glasses of vodka.

Communication was restricted to gestures and pantomiming, but the vodka made us all quite eloquent in that regard. The Russians marveled at our wristwatches. We learned that their felt boots had been made by their mothers or wives. After two hours of lubricated conviviality, we had managed to explain our desire to drive to Vienna. They invited us to return at 9:00 the next morning to be taken to someone who could authorize the trip. Damned nice guys, these hard-drinking Allies!

Ever since arriving in the area, I had wanted to go deer hunting, so I proposed a dawn try for a buck as a prerequisite of the trip to Vienna. Mertz was unenthusiastic but finally agreed. Carrol demurred entirely, opting to await our return. At first light the two of us started up the mountainside, Mertz carrying a canteen of cognac for sustenance. Halfway to the spot I had perceived from below to be a meadow where deer might graze, he flopped down on a mossy spot beneath a tree and told me that he would still be there when and if I got back.

The "meadow" turned out to be an area of brush four feet high with no signs of grazing deer, and it had taken longer to reach than anticipated. By the time I located Mertz and we got back to Carrol, it was well after ten when we drove to the bridge. Since Mertz had been making considerable progress on the contents of his canteen, I was the designated driver.

Our MPs stopped us only long enough to ask if we knew anything about "some officers from the 11th Armored Division," but we didn't. We stopped at the Russian guard post across the river and tried the "Commandant" bit again. To our pleasant surprise, a soldier came running out, jumped on the back end of the Volkswagen and pointed ahead. Mertz was sitting beside me, Carrol was in the back seat, and the Russian was hanging on behind.

We proceeded some six miles along the empty mountain road, swerving around an occasional burned-out tank as our guide pointed ahead. Mertz kept admonishing me about the brakes not working too well, but I didn't feel we were going fast enough to be concerned.

Suddenly we were going down a long incline with a railroad crossing ahead. There was a Russian guard post there with a barrier lowered across the road. I hit the brakes. Mertz was right, we didn't lose enough speed. The sloped nose of the vehicle banged the hinged barrier high enough in the air to clear Mertz and me and come down right in front of Carrol, only to bounce over his head as well, then sweep the guide into the road.

He was yelling, "Nyet! Nyet!" at the two guards who were raising their weapons as I finally managed a stop 100 yards away. He came limping up to us with a hurt look, climbed aboard, and once more pointed ahead.

Shortly thereafter, he indicated we should take a side road to the left. It led to a massive stone edifice, something between a multi-story chateau and a small castle. We rattled to a stop in the courtyard where an officer barked some commands to a platoon-sized detail that presented arms smartly; we saluted in return.

Mertz was favorably impressed. "Pretty sharp reveille formation!" Just then another officer wearing a Sam Browne belt and carrying a briefcase came running from the building shouting, "American Offiseers?" We assured him we were, and he hastily led us inside where we proceeded at a near trot through a maze of corridors. At every corner there was an armed Russian guard, looking about 15 years of age, in rumpled brown uniform and burr haircut. Each saluted and attempted to shake hands with the nearest of us as we rushed past.

Eventually we arrived at the large office of a Russian full colonel sporting a black spade beard and at least eight rows of medals on his dress uniform. His entire staff seemed to be in attendance. Our escort announced "American Offiseers" with obvious relief, and the colonel led all of us into an adjoining room with a long conference table, indicating we should be seated at it. Oh, how often I've longed for a film of those next 20 minutes!

At first we sat there looking expectantly at each other. Then the colonel asked a one-word question in barely understandable English. "Interpreter?"

At our negative reply, he stroked his beard in puzzlement, at which point Mertz took command of the conversation despite the stub of cigar in his mouth. "We want pass to Vienna. Got own transportation." He elaborated by making motor sounds around the cigar and steering motions with his hands. The Russians jabbered among themselves in confusion.

The colonel sent for a sergeant who knew perhaps 50 words of English, and Mertz tried harder, to no avail. The Russians muttered among themselves, and the sergeant asked a question. "How old you?"

We answered by finger count; Mertz was 26, I was 23, and Carrol 22. Confusion was now reigning supreme.

The three of us were not uniformly dressed. One wore fatigues, another ODs, and the third sported a jump suit. Suddenly the colonel realized we all had Screaming Eagle shoulder patches and asked in a somewhat incredulous tone, "Parashooteests?"

We proudly confirmed his observation, and Mertz made another arduous effort to explain our mission to the sergeant who finally reached the stage of stunned enlightenment. He leaned toward us from across the table and asked in near amazement, "You mean you only want go to Vienna?"

At that precise moment, the officer in the Sam Browne belt burst through the door yelling almost hysterically, "AMERICAN OFFISEERS!" The colonel stood up, looking at us as though we had kicked his dog, and pointed emphatically to the door through which we had entered the conference room. As we went through it, a colonel from the 11th Armored Division was entering the office with his staff entourage in tow. He also glared at us as they swept by us into the conference room, pulling the door firmly closed behind them, leaving us alone.

Two of us recognized the moment as high time to get th'hell outta there, but Mertz was adamant. "Stick around. We're gonna get that pass to Vienna!" Carrol and I each seized an upper arm and propelled him back through the corridors, saluting and shaking hands with the page-boy guards as we briskly departed the premises.

The honor guard Mertz had regarded as a "sharp reveille formation" had long since returned to its barracks, leaving the 11th Armored group's arrival unacknowledged. The group had gotten lost on its way to the bridge and was two hours late for the meeting to coordinate boundary lines with the Russians. The fact that we had unwittingly usurped their guide at the river guard post probably hadn't helped the situation.

The venerable Volkswagen got us back to the American side without mishap or unwelcome notice. Two days later, Colonel Ballard summoned me to ask if I had heard anything about some of our officers being over in the Russian zone. I dutifully promised a thorough investigation.

I did, indeed, render a full report on the incident, omitting not a single detail. It was while we were having dinner in Miami in 1961.

Chapter 37

Beth

General Taylor had returned from the Pentagon with "the Word." The 101st would go back to France for training. Our 501st Regiment would be filled by those who had accrued enough points, based on months of service, time overseas, and wounds suffered. Eighty-five such points warranted return to the U.S. for demobilization, if desired. The 501st would take them home and then be deactivated. Members of the regiment with insufficient points, or the desire to remain with the division, would be transferred to other units.

Mertz and I opted to stay with the division since the war with Japan remained unfinished. We were both reassigned to the 506th Parachute Infantry Regiment.

During our stay in Mourmelon before the 101st had been sent to the Ruhr Pocket, a division-wide track meet had been staged. My sole participation had been to prepare and sign all memos organizing the 501st teams, which proceeded to win a preponderance of awards. Colonel Robert Sink, commander of the 506th, was an avid sportsman who backed his regiment's entrants with any and all bets available. He reportedly lost a bundle in the process.

It requires a considerable stretch of the imagination to feel that he or his staff had attributed any part of the 501st's performance to my minor administrative talents, but I was assigned to the 506th as regimental athletic officer and Officer's Club manager. Shortly after reporting in, I was sent to a one-week Athletic Officer School in Paris. I accepted that hazardous duty without complaint.

The school was a bit of a farce. Big league baseball pros explained the

Beth and Bill Sefton, December 1945. The best thing to come out of my war and the start of a lifelong partnership.

intricacies of playing various positions, but no one taught us how to set up a regimental athletic program. When classes ended, attendees from the 101st faced a four-day jeep ride to Munich where transportation from their respective units would meet them. Lieutenant Ed Allworth, who had been transferred to the 502nd, had just returned to Paris from a leave in London and looked me up at the school. He had a much better idea.

"Why don't we hitch a C-47 ride to that airfield near Marseilles and visit the girls for a coupla days? Then we'll catch one back here and another on to Munich in plenty of time." It sounded very good to me.

We caught the first flight with no problem, and the Air Corps gave us a command car ride to the military hospital complex serving as a staging point for shipment to the Philippines. It was on the coast of the Mediterranean in an isolated area a good number of miles from Marseilles and featured a prominent sign at the entrance: "All visiting officers must be off the post by midnight."

We solved that problem by locating the sergeant major of the complex. For a bottle of Ed's scotch, he agreed to put a couple of stretchers on the floor of the commandant's office after hours, which we were to vacate at reveille. Now all we had to do was avoid the MPs after midnight. Ed was to have some trouble in that regard.

Beth and I strolled the spacious grounds well into the night. The chemistry originating in Mourmelon had not waned a whit in the interim. The intensity of the attraction took us both somewhat by surprise.

My plans for the future had been limited to surviving the war, going back to college, and becoming a world-class novelist. Beth had been weighing a proposal by a hometown boyfriend, currently serving as a Navy officer, as well as the ardent attentions of a medical administration officer in her unit. I still refer to each of them as "one of the two guys she was engaged to when I met her."

Sometime after midnight, we ducked into the shrubbery to avoid an exasperated MP escorting Ed toward the exit gate for the third time. Ed, obviously in high spirits, was giggling, "Go ahead, throw me out again!"

The MP was demanding, "How the hell do you keep getting back in here, Lieutenant?" The undiscovered answer was the limb of a tree overhanging the high brick wall just beyond sight of the guard post. Ed was back with his nurse friend ten minutes later.

Beth was off duty the next day. We went to sea in a paddle boat, swam, and picnicked, luxuriating in the Riviera summer. That afternoon Ed and his friend joined us in the Officer's Club on a cliff overlooking the water. We had the place to ourselves.

Ed had brought along a bottle of particularly potent liqueur, Cointreau as

I recall, which soon had him and his friend in a state of giddy jocularity. Beth's personal code of conduct was uncommonly high by any standard, and in true feminine logic, their overindulgence somehow became my fault. She left the place in tears, taking one of several footpaths trailing along the chalky cliff from the building. In a case of love conquering all, her pique dissolved as soon as I found her, sitting on a log.

More than a year later, as newlyweds, we were reminiscing about that day. Beth was still marveling at my tracking technique, which had allowed me to select the exact path she had taken and follow the faint signs of her progress on that hard surface. Missing a once-in-a-lifetime opportunity to keep my mouth shut, I admitted knowing precisely which path she'd taken since I had stood on a balcony and watched her depart. She has yet to fully forgive me for destroying her romantic illusion.

Ed and his friend left shortly after we returned to the Club. No one else came in the rest of the evening. We danced and talked for hours until the weight of my jump boots was dissipating my airborne energy. It was well after midnight when Beth sat down on a sofa saying, "Put your head in my lap and rest a bit." Romantic devil that I was, I fell soundly asleep in moments. She sat patiently until dawn and time to get back to her quarters.

Her fellow nurses, well aware that we had spent the night together, were sure Lieutenant Huie had finally "been had," which, of course, she had not. The fervor of our farewell kiss did nothing to dispel their convictions, so they offered her the cot with the best cross-ventilation to sleep for the rest of the morning.

Our romance would progress via letters crossing two oceans as Beth's unit sailed for the Philippines and I returned to the 506th. We would arrive in the States on opposite coasts in late November, meet at her Sioux City home the following month, and become engaged to marry in May.

She was by far and away the best thing to come out of my war.

Chapter 38

Wrapping It Up with the 506th

As July ended, the 506th Regiment was moved by train from Austria to the French town of Joigny on the Yonne River, population about 7,000. Within days of our arrival, atomic bombs had been dropped on Japan, and Russia had attacked through Manchuria. On August 14, terms of surrender were accepted and the war in the Pacific theater all but ended, awaiting only the signing of official documents on September 2 aboard the battleship *Missouri.*

The public clamor to "bring the boys home immediately" was heartily endorsed by a vast majority of 506th troopers, but the logistics involved were preclusive. With the absorbing intensity of training for combat no longer a factor, morale problems became a major concern for unit commanders. Mertz overheard a conversation between two men, which illustrated this point.

"Hey, didja hear Joe got court-martialed for sleeping on guard duty?"

"Sleeping on guard duty? That's an easy rap to beat! Just swear ya saw 'em comin' but didn't bother to challenge 'cause ya knew who they were."

"Yeah, but they had a pretty tough case against Joe. He had his clothes off and was in the sack."

The need for a good athletic program was obvious, but there was no equipment available through supply channels. Hearing an Air Corps Wing in Chartres was packing to go home, I made an impromptu trip there with a small detail in a 2½-ton truck. We found the Wing headquarters in a turmoil of last-minute packing but were told where to find the athletic officer in an outlying area of the city.

The facility to which we'd been directed was an isolated one-story building directly behind the billets of an MP battalion. The front entrance was open, but there was no one inside. A very large interior room was securely locked. Peering through the keyhole, we could see shelves stacked with equipment from floor to ceiling. Since it was nearing noon, we assumed the officer had probably gone back to the headquarters mess hall and set out to track him down. Being hungry ourselves, we stopped at a restaurant en route.

As we were finishing our meal, the sergeant of the detail posed an interesting question: "Lieutenant, what if we find this guy and he says we can't have any of that equipment?" At that point I recalled seeing a crowbar in one of the rooms of the building.

We returned to the facility, backed the truck up to an entrance on the side away from the MP billets, pried open the locked door of the storage room, and started loading the vehicle, briskly. We had it more than three-quarters full when a guard suddenly appeared in the doorway!

There was an envelope with a letter in it from Beth in my hip pocket. I pulled it out, scanned it as though it were a requisition list, and kept on directing the detail. "Three more cases of those softballs, two more cases of bats, four cases of footballs. . . ."

Turning back to the young, uncertain guard I asked, "Do you mind holding that door open for us, soldier?" Relieved that nothing must be amiss, he dutifully complied while I continued to specify "requirements" until the truck was loaded to capacity.

We drove out through the MP billets, where I cheerfully returned the snappy salutes of those on duty, and gave Wing headquarters wide berth on our way out of Chartres for the 80-mile return trip to Joigny.

Colonel Sink, the 506th regimental commander, had been hounding conventional supply channels for athletic equipment to no avail. He walked into my storage area the next morning just as the detail had completed unpacking the impressive inventory of loot. For a moment he stood stock still, then voiced one of his well-known expressions.

"Great gawd from Georgia, Sefton! Where did you get all this stuff?"

"If you really hafta know, Sir, I took a truck to Chartres and stole it from the Air Corps."

"Great gawd from Georgia! Did anybody get the number of the truck?"

I assured him that all unit identification on the vehicle had been well-smeared with mud and that I had not divulged my name or unit during the brief stop at Wing headquarters. He left in high good humor. When we completed inventorying the haul, we found that we had enough to share with the other regiments of the division. The trip to Chartres had capped my career as a scrounger.

With an effective athletic program soon underway, my duties as Officer's

Club manager became my primary concern. The Club was a somewhat ram-shackle, two-story frame hotel in the center of town. The ground floor fea-tured a fairly spacious barroom with floor suitable for dancing and a kitchen beyond. There were ten or twelve guest rooms upstairs entered from a cen-tral corridor.

It had been established as an Officer's Club by a regiment of an Airborne Division which had jumped in the August 1944 invasion of southern France, ending up in Joigny. They had left the Club to us when we came there behind them.

They also left us one George Ferrand, a French underground member who had escaped into Spain two jumps ahead of the Gestapo. When the invasion occurred, George volunteered to serve the regiment as an unpaid interpreter and accompanied them to Joigny where he worked in the Club for billet, rations, and the GI uniform he'd been issued. He was willing to continue with us on that basis as well.

As my unauthorized assistant Club manager, George was a gem! He would accompany me to Brussels to buy liquor, negotiating discounts from distillers and finding black market sources for items not otherwise available. He interviewed and hired local help for the evening trade and worked the bar himself whenever required. On the personal side, he arranged pheasant-hunting privileges on nearby estates and was elated to be taught the basic techniques of wing shooting in return for such favors.

On our first trip to Brussels, I had planned to stay in the hotel designated for American servicemen. As I recall, it was managed by the Red Cross. George objected, "Mais, non! Zey charge too much!"

He led me to a small, clean hotel where, sure enough, the room rates were half the amount of the other. Once our room was assigned to his satisfaction, he said, "Come, now I show you zee town!"

As we left the building, I noticed that there were iron rings embedded in the sidewalk across its front and idly asked George why they were there. He pointed to a roll of metal mesh positioned well above and explained that it was lowered at night and locked to the rings, "For security of zee guests." When I asked what time they performed this service, he said, "Hah! I better go check!"

I followed him back inside where his query to the clerk evolved into a furious argument in rapid-fire French. It climaxed when George pointed dra-matically to me with a final burst of Gallic verbiage that left the clerk thor-oughly cowed. George said, "Come, we go now."

Once outside I asked why all the contention, and George explained. "I ask heem what time do zey lock zee curtain to zee sidewalk. He say 'midnight.' I tell heem we may not be back by midnight. He say zey will lock it down at midnight anyway! I tell heem your are zee Azzletic Officer for zee entire regiment! If zey lock it down before we come back, you will tear it up with zee bare hands!" It was still up there when we returned after 2:00.

Thanks in large part to George, the Club was now running smoothly. Some of the upstairs rooms featured poker and craps tables. We had a regular evening barmaid, a big, buxom young lady whose only drawback was her very limited command of English. She would go up to a poker room to take orders and nod intelligently as each of seven players specified his favorite mixed drink. Then she would return with a tray of seven beers every time.

George was an avid fisherman, and also a professional chef. He caught a two-pound trout from the Yonne River, prepared it with a special recipe, and served it cold, leaving the word "delicious" a totally inadequate accolade. His overriding ambition was to emigrate to the United States. Several field grade officers in the regiment had promised to help him in that regard.

The most glaring deficiency in the Club operation was the dismal lack of female companionship. There were just two types of women in Joigny. In one category, their parents wouldn't allow them near our Club. In the other, I wouldn't permit their access from the streets.

As September wore on into October, I knew my orders for departure were getting close, and I wanted to leave on a high note. "George, we should throw a Club party. BIG party with lotsa girls. Nice girls. Whadda we hafta do to pull it off?"

"Well, first I must have zee jeep for three days. Zen we must go to Paree and buy zee oysters. Zen, on zee day of the party, I must have ten trucks." Go for it, George!

He took the jeep for three days, disappearing into the hinterlands each morning and returning late in the evenings. Then he announced we were ready to buy oysters in Paris, six bushels of them to be precise.

We were driving down the Champs Élysées when I noticed a line of French civilians, four abreast and at least 200 yards long. The head of the line was at the entrance of an impressively large building. It stretched from there to the end of the block in the distance and disappeared around the corner. I asked George what the building was and why the line.

"Oh, zat is zee American Embassee and zey all want to go to zee United States. Zey are applying for zee visas."

"I see. And won't you have to get a visa so you can get to the United States?"

"Oh, mais oui!" I told him to stop the jeep.

A burly MP sergeant was controlling the line near the door. I approached him and asked brusquely where I might find "Lieutenant Smith." He didn't know a Lieutenant Smith. "Never mind, Sergeant, we'll find him." With that we passed quickly into the building.

The barely moving line ended at a large desk beneath a rotunda. We strode by purposefully and headed down a main corridor. There were closed double doors at its end. I knocked briskly, and a muffled voice said, "Come in."

We entered a very large office featuring a massive desk with a row of at least 12 buttons on the surface. A distinguished looking gentleman in a cutaway coat and striped pants was standing beside it. He smiled cordially and asked if he could help us.

I explained that George was a French civilian who had been serving the Army without pay for more than a year and that he would like to emigrate to the United States. The man nodded and pressed one of the buttons on his desk. Within maybe 20 seconds an aide hurriedly entered and stopped short with a How-the-hell-did-you-two-get-in-here expression on his face. The realization that we had invaded the office of the American Ambassador was beginning to dawn on me.

The Ambassador grinned and addressed the aide. "Take care of my friends here, please." We were led promptly to a much smaller office where the aide listened to my story, called a secretary in to type up a form, and handed it to me. "When you get home, sign on this line as his sponsor and turn it in at your local immigration office."

For the day of the party, I had a large hospital tent erected in the Club courtyard and filled with tables and chairs. Late that afternoon, George dispatched ten trucks with detailed instructions as to routes and stops to be made. They started returning early in the evening bringing girls. Lotsa girls. They also brought their parents and quite a few aunts and uncles!

For the adults, it was the greatest social event since the German occupation of France. They gathered in the tent where the oysters were served as a prelude to continuing courses, each a testimony to George's culinary talent. Beverages of choice never stopped flowing as candles on the tables were lighted at dusk. The decibels of chatter and laughter built steadily into the night.

The young ladies were inside the Club where provender and libations fueled dancing and romancing to levels unlikely precedented in their provincial experience. By the time the trucks returned for their passengers at midnight, it had been one hell of a party for all concerned.

The next day I was visited by a delegation of Joigny city fathers who had one request to make. Should I ever schedule a repeat of the event, would I please provide "rooms in zee Club for zee lovers."

It seemed flower beds for blocks around had been flattened in the course of the evening!

Chapter 39

Getting Home

My orders arrived late in October, and I left the 506th for one of the "Cigarette Camps," assembly centers for troops headed homeward. Each camp was named for a brand of smokes. As nearly as I can recall, I was sent to Chesterfield, or maybe Camel. Whatever. My clearest memory involves getting paid in U.S. currency instead of French francs. Stakes in the poker games dropped dramatically when we suddenly found ourselves playing for "real money."

In November I boarded a ship with elements of the 75th Infantry Division. The PA system played "Sentimental Journey" as we left port. My feelings were subdued and mixed.

The Army had been my adult world, the 501st Parachute Regiment my home. There had been a single, engrossing objective — to wage and win a just war. The cost of accomplishing it had been sobering.

So many close comrades were now buried in Europe, so many others maimed for life. I had no sensation of returning triumphant, only one of gratitude for having survived unharmed and of sorrow for those who hadn't. There also was the realization that a profoundly dramatic chapter of my life was coming to a close.

We landed in Newport News, Virginia. A troop train jammed with Midwesterners headed for Camp Atterbury in Indiana, 70 miles from Anderson. Unable to sleep in the cramped quarters, I was standing in a vestibule as we were somewhere in Ohio at dawn. I saw a big red barn beyond a cornfield, and suddenly I felt like I was home.

We pulled into Atterbury late that afternoon. It was the day before Thanksgiving, and mother had driven down to meet me. A personnel clerk advised that out-processing was suspended until after the holiday, and that I should remain in camp until Friday morning. Su-u-u-u-re I would!

We left immediately for a family Thanksgiving at home. I drove back, unmissed, the morning after. The out-processing involved promotion to captain warranted by time overseas in grade, plus notification that I had compiled six weeks of terminal leave. It also provided an invitation to join the Army Reserve, which I accepted.

My father, Pete, was still on duty with the Air Corps in Grand Island, Nebraska. In a telephone conversation, he suggested that I visit him for some pheasant hunting, which was fantastic there. Because Beth had now returned from the Philippines and was at her home in Sioux City, I had double reason to go. It proved a great two weeks of unwinding!

The pheasant population, lightly hunted during the war years, was at an all-time high. Literally hundreds of birds could be seen in the fields when there was snow on the ground. Getting close enough to be in good range required some technique, but we seldom failed to bag our limit while hunting during the weekdays.

On Friday evenings, I took the 50-mile bus ride to Sioux City and spent the weekend at Beth's home. On the second trip, I brought along a ring purchased at the Base Exchange, and we became officially engaged.

The day before Christmas Eve, Pete located a bomber crew scheduled for flight-training time and picked us up in Sioux City for a trip to the Indianapolis air base and the chance for Beth to meet my family. She won everyone over handily and was welcomed into the clan.

With the holidays over, I decided to escort her back to Sioux City. Both still on terminal leave and in uniform, we should have no trouble catching an Air Corps ride from Indianapolis. It didn't turn out quite that way.

There were no flights going to Sioux City, but we could catch a ride to Memphis where there were sure to be such connections. The crew was jovial, friendly, and helpful. When we arrived in Memphis and found still no desired flights available, they invited us to accompany them the next day to Dallas where they knew for certain we could catch the ride we needed. It seemed the best choice under the circumstances.

Unfortunately, storms and icy conditions developed in the Dallas area, and we ended up in El Paso, also flightless with regard to Sioux City. Our new friends urged us to ride on with them to their base in Bakersfield, California, and try from there. We thanked them and declined. Our phone calls reporting our whereabouts already had Beth's parents thoroughly confused, so we bought Greyhound bus tickets instead.

The bus route went through Colorado Springs, where Captain Bill Osborne was still hospitalized with the leg so severely broken on the jump into Normandy. We stopped off to visit. It had been six months since his latest, and hopefully last, corrective surgery. He was in a cast up to his hip. His wife, Fran, and their two-year-old daughter were living in town, but he had not been at home with them since that operation. Obviously, there was a good deed waiting to be done.

When the attendants had served Bill's evening meal, I scrounged a pair of crutches from a supply room and helped him into his uniform. The pants zipper wouldn't close over the cast, but no one noticed as we departed casually through a side entrance. Fran was delighted to have him home. We spent the night with them, and I smuggled him back into the hospital early the next morning.

By the time I finally got Beth to Sioux City and myself back to Anderson, my terminal leave was expiring. On its very last morning, I was emptying my footlocker and discovered the form from the American Embassy in Paris. I grabbed the phone book, found that there was an immigration office in Anderson, and hustled down to present the paperwork. I was asked only one question, "Are you employed?"

I gave them an honest answer. "I'm a captain in the United States Army." I could see no relevance in adding that I would become an unemployed civilian at midnight.

In April the following year, George appeared at the Chicago office of the McCann-Erickson advertising agency where I worked in the production department. He had two Frenchmen in tow who were trying to interest American marketers in a new printing process they had developed. After meeting them on the ship from France, George had volunteered to serve as their interpreter for calls on prospective clients between New York and Chicago in return for expenses. We enjoyed two evenings of reminiscing before he returned to New York and started to work as assistant to the executive chef of the Waldorf Astoria.

George became an American citizen, acquired an exceptionally personable wife, and was executive chef for a number of fine hotels before crowning his career in that capacity at the famed Broadmoor in Colorado Springs. Even the hotel owner there addressed him respectfully as "Chef Ferrand."

Under the pressures of our respective careers, opportunities to be together as the years flitted by were few and far between, but they were always most enjoyable and memorable. The last occasion was in the mid-1980s when Beth and I had attended a conference in Aspen and extended the trip to visit the Ferrands in their home. George and I went duck hunting so he could show off his well-trained retrievers. Every Christmas since his arrival from France I had received a Christmas present from him. That year it was the shotgun I used to double on mallards.

George retired from the hotel the following year, anticipating full-time devotion to outdoor activities. All too shortly thereafter, a particularly virulent form of cancer took him from all who had known, admired, and loved him.

He was one of those characters who keep so many aspects of my war aglow in my recollections.

Chapter 40

The Lessons Learned

Those four years in the Army were the most formative of my life. Learning experiences were continuous, compressed, and frequently critical to survival. It has been interesting to find how many of them applied to civilian life, as well.

As enlisted men in the training phase, we lived in a barracks with identical cots, wore the same clothes, ate the same food. We shared the same doubts, fears, and uncertainties, the same simple pleasures and occasional joys. In short, we were stripped to a common denominator with all of our barracksmates and were taking a crash course in basic traits of human nature.

Morale and *esprit de corps* in a unit wax or wane in relation to the nature of experiences shared. If training is rigorous and challenging, troops feel good about their accomplishments. If it is undemanding and haphazardly conducted, they lose confidence in leaders, commanders, and themselves.

As a combat arms officer, your job is to train men to fight as a team and to survive as individuals. This cannot be accomplished in the lecture hall. It must be taught in the field under conditions simulating combat as closely as possible. Troops are most receptive to such training when they understand the importance of mastering it if they are to succeed and survive in battle.

I learned never to underestimate the intelligence of my men. They will see through bluff and bluster, perceive and resent any cavalier attitude. They will respond favorably to discipline they consider consistent, fair, and pertinent. They will respect you in direct ratio to the consideration you exercise on their behalf.

The first time in combat is a traumatic experience. People you've never met are trying earnestly to kill you. The human tendency is to hug any cover available rather than expose yourself by returning fire. Only the intensity and effectiveness of previous training will modify that impulse.

When attacking enemy positions, audacity may well reduce your casualties. Hesitancy inevitably will increase them. The unit that moves up briskly, directly behind its artillery and mortar suppressing fires, may catch the enemy emerging from their holes. The one that muffs that opportunity and gets pinned down short of the objective will be chopped up in the process.

When your attack starts to falter and momentum hangs on your next decision, the only order to give is "Follow me!"

There are always casualties in combat, but they are incurred more predominantly by green replacements than by battle-wise veterans. The experienced soldier has learned to make optimum use of cover and concealment, to anticipate likely enemy actions, and to be ever alert for the sound of incoming shells. He has not become immune to the hazards of combat, but he has minimized the risks.

There is just one effective shield against the mental and emotional stresses of combat. It is the firm conviction that there is a Supreme Being who decides the extent of your survival. So you do your job to the best of your ability and let Him call the shots.

The lessons I had learned were directly applicable throughout postwar service in the National Guard and Army Reserve. I was promoted to major as a regimental S-3 in the Guard and to lieutenant colonel as a battalion commander in the Reserves. I completed my military career as colonel, teaching Command & General Staff College courses in the Army Reserve school program. It has been an absorbing 30 years.

Most military principles of leadership applied in business enterprises as well. Maintain a positive attitude, assign attainable objectives and communicate the importance of accomplishing them, specify individual responsibilities and timing of reports on progress, praise successes in public and critique failures in private.

Those principles served me well during my 5½ years at the Chicago office of McCann-Erickson, where I had started in 1946 as a free-lance copywriter and ended up as director of sales promotion and merchandising. Looking back on that period, I must admit lacing the principles with liberal dashes of audacity in violating office protocols to bypass burcaucratic roadblocks.

But then I learned to do that in the Army, too.

In 1951 Beth and I agreed that the metropolitan rat race was not the most desirable atmosphere in which to raise our growing family. I resigned from McCann-Erickson and went to work for a local ad agency in Grand Rapids,

Michigan. By 1954 I was a partner in a new agency, which evolved over the next decade into Sefton Associates, Inc.

That agency developed a forte for off-beat promotions and an avid interest in tackling unconventional client assignments. The staff had grown to more than 50 members, each posing interesting leadership challenges, by the time I sold it to key employees in 1988 and retired in 1991. Since then, I've chaired two small companies, one with an awesome potential for international success.

When asked how I'm enjoying retirement, my stock reply is, "Great! I'm down to half-days — twelve hours."

My sentiments in that regard reflect the two most important lessons learned in combat. One is to thank God for every new day and to squeeze all possible juice out of it. The other is to keep forging ahead. It's harder to hit a moving target.

My prayer is that not even encroaching senility will cause me to forget them.

Index

by Lori L. Daniel